WILDFLOWERS
of the Rocky Mountains

A Field Guide to Wildflowers of

Banff National Park

Glacier National Park, British Columbia

Glacier National Park, Montana

Grand Teton National Park

Jasper National Park

Kootenay National Park

Mount Revelstoke National Park

Rocky Mountain National Park

Waterton Lakes National Park

Yellowstone National Park

Yoho National Park

*and numerous provincial and state parks,
national recreational areas, national monuments,
national forests, and wildlife management areas.*

WILDFLOWERS
of the Rocky Mountains

**George W. Scotter
& Hälle Flygare**

whitecap

Edited by Mark Macdonald
Proofread by Joan Tetrault
Design by Janine Vangool
Maps by Eric Leinberger
Jacket design by Five Seventeen

Printed in Canada

Library and Archives Canada Cataloguing in Publication

Scotter, G. W. (George Wilby)
    Wildflowers of the Rocky Mountains / George Scotter ; Hälle Flygare,
photographer. — Rev. and expanded ed.

Previously published under title Wildflowers of the Canadian Rockies, 1986.
Includes bibliographical references and index.
ISBN-13: 978-1-55285-848-6
ISBN-10: 1-55285-848-0

    1. Wild flowers—Rocky Mountains, Canadian (B.C. and Alta.)—Identification.
I. Flygare, Hälle   II. Title.

QK203.R63S36 2007   582.1309711   C2006-905003-1

The publisher acknowledges the financial support of the Government of Canada through
the Book Publishing Industry Development Program (BPIDP) and the Province of British
Columbia through the Book Publishing Tax Credit.

**Do not use plants for food or medicine based on the information in this book. The infor-
mation included here is for education and entertainment only. Using misidentified plants
could cause sickness or death.**

Dedicated to Etta and Linda,
who share our love and enjoyment
of nature

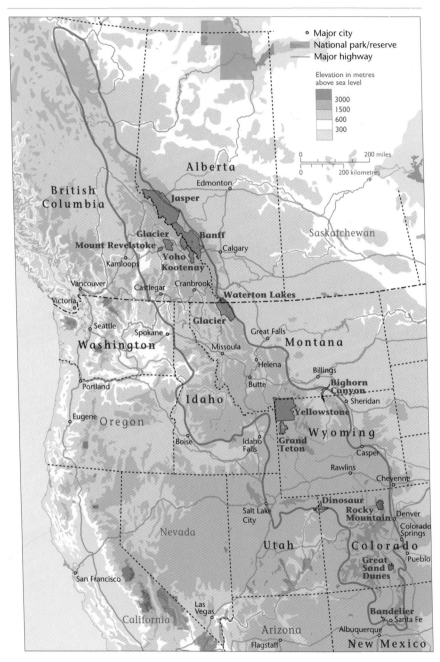

FIGURE 1. Map of the Rocky Mountains showing provincial and state boundaries, cities, national parks, and major highways as modified from Cannings (2005).

Contents

Acknowledgements

I owe a debt of gratitude to a number of colleagues and friends who contributed to this field guide. Derek Johnson verified identifications of some plants illustrated in the photographs. Ben Gadd offered useful suggestions on the geology section. Particular appreciation goes to my wife, Etta, who accompanied me on numerous outings, although the trails were often steep and the sun did not always shine, while searching for wildflowers over a period of more than 40 years. She also allowed me to escape from many other duties while I penned this updated edition. Our son, Troy Scotter, provided computer assistance while the manuscript was in preparation. Mary Fabris and Etta Scotter read the manuscript, correcting errors and made many useful suggestions. Mark Macdonald at Whitecap Books was patient with this slow writer and made several suggestions for improving the book. Thanks also go to friends, Ernie McNaughton and Malcolm Martin, who shared their knowledge of plants in southeastern British Columbia with me since my retirement. Hälle Flygare's wonderful photographs were complemented by contributions from Katherine Darrow (pp. 142, 155, 194, 199, 218), Barry Gordichuk (pp. 96, 98, 153, 215), Bill Hitz (p. 209), and George Scotter (pp. 50, 114, 122, 154, 178).

Introduction

During the summer months, the Rocky Mountains come alive with color. The great variety of elevations, climates, soil types, slopes, directional aspects, and rock formations provide an abundance of habitats for a wondrous variety of wildflowers to grow and flourish. The opportunity to become acquainted with new wildflowers is nearly endless in this spectacular mountain setting.

This book is a revision and major expansion of the previous edition, entitled *Wildflowers of the Canadian Rockies*, first published in 1986. The original book was written for several reasons. Laypeople who had attended my wildflower classes over the years found that most field guides assumed a level of botanical expertise they did not have, and wanted a wildflower book they could use and understand. I also wanted to commemorate the centennial of Banff National Park since the treasures there and throughout the Rockies have done so much to enrich my life. The principal reason, however, was to educate the curious-minded about the incredible natural wonders to be found there. I believed then, as I do now, that an informed public is paramount in ensuring the wise management of these areas at the present and in the future.

The first edition received flattering reviews. More importantly, over the 20 years the book has been available, many readers have commented that being able to identify and learn about wildflowers has enriched their experience of the Rocky Mountains and given them great pleasure. The goal of this edition is to greatly expand the coverage, to update the information provided, and to add new features such as distribution maps and standardized common plant names. Most of the plants included here are the more prevalent ones that people will encounter in the Rockies. A few less common ones are included to challenge the users of this book to search for and enjoy some of our rarer plants.

Millions of people visit or live near the many national parks, provincial and state parks, national recreational areas, national monuments, national forests, and wildlife management areas within the Rocky Mountains (Figure 1). This field guide was written to assist everyone in recognizing some of the wildflowers they may encounter along the highways and hiking trails or near campgrounds and in the towns. My goal has been to make this book user friendly, simple, enjoyable to read, and accurate in detail. Being able to recognize the plants encountered and to call them by name is an indispensable and exciting first step in a deeper understanding and appreciation of the natural world. Be forewarned that a flower-finding hobby can become addictive and develop into a lifelong voyage of discovery!

The level of detail provided in this field guide is likely adequate for most users. For those who are inspired to learn more, and I hope there will be many, a few selected references are included at the end of this book.

Accurate identification of wildflowers requires an examination of each plant and its component parts. Here are some tips for using this field guide. Look carefully at the characteristics of the flowers, leaves, stems, fruits and berries, or seeds of the plant in question.

Flowers

- Are the petals in 3's, 4's, 5's or more?
- What shape are the flowers – urn-like, tubular, 2-lipped, or other?
- Are the flowers symmetrical or irregular?
- Are the flowers arranged in spikes, racemes, panicles, umbels, corymbs, or cymes?
- Do the flowers have special features like hoods, spurs, glands, or markings such as dots or stripes?

Leaves

- Are the leaves at the base of the plant or all along the stem?
- Are the leaves arranged alternately or opposite one another along the stem?
- Do the leaves have petioles or do they clasp the stem?
- Are the leaf margins smooth, toothed, or double-toothed?
- What shape are the leaves?
- Are the leaves simple or divided?
- Are the leaves smooth or hairy?

Stems

- What color is the stem?
- How tall is the stem?
- Is the stem smooth, hairy, or bumpy?
- Are there spines, thorns, shedding bark, or other markings?

Fruits and berries

- What color are the fruits or berries?
- What shape are the fruits and berries?
- Are they shiny, powdery, or hairy?
- Are the fruits simple like strawberries or aggregate like raspberries?

Seeds

- What color are the seeds?
- What shape are the seeds?
- Are the seeds single, few, or many?
- Are there special mechanisms for dispersal such as burs or feathery attachments?

Habitat

- Is the plant growing in a forested or non-forested area?
- If the plant is growing in a forest, is it a broadleaf deciduous forest or a coniferous forest?
- If the plant is growing in a non-forested habitat, is it in a grassland, wetland, meadow, or disturbed site?
- Is the plant in the foothills, montane, subalpine, or alpine zone?
- Is the plant growing in full sun, partial sun, or full shade?
- Is the soil wet, moist, dry, rocky, peaty, sandy, or otherwise?

While my goal has been to keep technical terminology to a minimum, there is a need for readers to understand the basic structure of a plant and the parts that form a flower. Diagrams of a few flower structures (Figures 4 and 5), flower arrangements (Figure 6), leaf arrangements, leaf margins, and leaf shapes (Figure 7), and a glossary of terms have been included to assist the reader.

Start by going to the relevant color section. The wildflowers are arranged by plant families into six color groups: (1) white; (2) yellow to cream; (3) green; (4) pink; (5) red, orange, and brown; and (6) purple to blue. Arbitrary decisions had to be made because some flowers are intermediate in color or show a range of variation at different stages of maturation or even on the same inflorescence. No one section is so large that determination is difficult, though it is advisable to check more than one section if color deviation is suspected. Identification is based entirely on comparison with a photograph and brief description. Identification from a color photograph has its limitations, but in most cases each photograph will lead the reader directly to the exact species or in those instances where a large number of species is involved, to the genus.

In the past, confusion resulted because a multiplicity of common names was used for the same plant, often varying from region to region and country to country. Recently, the United States Department of Agriculture standardized common names for plants and those names have been used throughout this field guide. Since all users may not accept some of these names, some of the old common names have been added to help in the transition to the standardized ones.

For each plant, the scientific name has also been given. These names are more consistent and precise than the common names and are used by botanists all over the world. Each botanical name consists of two parts, comparable to the way in which we give names to people belonging to different families. In plant names, however, the first part tells the genus (group) to which the plant belongs; for example, *Rosa*, which refers to members of the rose genus. This is the same as a surname or family name, such as Jones. The second part of the botanical name indicates the species (particular member of the group); for example, *acicularis*, which means "with needle-like prickles." This is comparable to the given name of an individual, such as Tom in Tom Jones. The Latin names used here follow those suggested by the United States Department of Agriculture. Several examples of how scientific names were derived are included among the plant descriptions.

For all of the species described and illustrated, I have added observations about their distribution within the Rocky Mountains. Each description gives information about the vegetation zone or zones in which the plant occurs. In addition, a map accompanies each description showing where the plant may be found among the two provinces and eight states within the limits of the Rocky Mountains.

The term "throughout the Rockies" does not imply that a wildflower or shrub is distributed from the northern to the southern limits of the Rockies. It implies only that the plant is found in each of the provinces and states where the Rockies occur, as shown on the small maps. A plant may be limited to a small portion only of any province or state.

As flowering times vary so much according to altitude, latitude, and other ecological conditions, and because the growing season is so short in the Rocky Mountains, no attempt has been made to include this information for all species. The Rocky Mountain region is a vertical land where spring and summer ascend the slopes and a flower that blooms in May in the river valleys might not flower until July, or even later, at higher altitudes.

I have not discriminated between native plants and introduced plants, many of the latter being among today's common species. Only herbaceous plants and shrubs have been included; trees, ferns, horsetails, grasses, sedges, rushes, lichens, and mosses have been excluded.

To add interest to the field guide, I have added supplemental notes on use of the plants by wildlife and humans past and present, as well as some of the rich folklore surrounding the origins and powers of various plants.

Wild plants should not be collected or used unless they are abundant and grow outside protected areas. **Extreme caution should be taken before eating, *or even handling*, certain plants. Misidentification and improper use of plants can cause sickness or even death.** Children should be educated about wild plants, but always with an awareness of their sometimes toxic nature.

Remember that wildflowers within our parks and wilderness areas are protected by law and should not be picked or removed. However, this does not prevent the enthusiast from looking at them, photographing them, enjoying them as they are, and leaving them to give similar pleasure to those who follow. There is a challenge in looking for different kinds of wildflowers in their native habitat without depriving the next passerby of similar enjoyment. Wildflowers are for all to enjoy today and for future generations to enjoy tomorrow.

With this book, I have attempted to cultivate an appreciation of the beauty and fragility of the wildflowers of the Rockies and the urgent need to protect and preserve them. Wildflowers in the Rockies have survived avalanches, wildfires, floods, windstorms, and other natural disturbances for many centuries. But there are new threats. Collection of plants from the wild for medicinal herb markets, for home gardens, and for so-called "wildcrafting" is putting pressure on some wildflowers. A plethora of alien weeds that have been accidentally or purposely introduced are crowding out native wildflowers, particularly at lower elevations. Habitat loss from agriculture—including livestock grazing, roads, suburbs, and other development—is the greatest threat to the existence of many wildflowers.

Perhaps the greatest future challenge for wildflowers in the Rockies will be the impact of global warming. Some studies warn that parts of North America may be 2 degrees warmer sometime between 2026 and 2060. How will native plants that evolved over thousands of years adapt to such changes over an extremely short time period? Predicting those changes accurately is impossible.

In the words of Baba Doppi, spokesman for the International Union for the Conservation of Nature and Natural Resources (IUCN):

In the end we will conserve only what we love.
We love only what we understand.
We understand only what we are taught.

I hope that I have been a good teacher and that you have been an even better student so that the great diversity of life in the majestic Rockies may be protected and continue to inspire this and future generations.

Geology of the Rocky Mountains

The Rocky Mountains are a chain of rugged mountain ranges in western North America, extending from northern British Columbia to northern New Mexico (Figure 2), a distance of about 1,700 miles (2,800 km). The Rockies cover a portion of two Canadian provinces: western Alberta and eastern British Columbia, and eight states: northeastern Washington, the northeastern corner of Oregon, western Montana, north-central Idaho, western Wyoming, northeastern Utah, western Colorado, and north-central New Mexico. The Rocky Mountains in the United States are bordered on the east by the Interior Plains or Great Plains, and on the west by the Great Basin. In Canada, the eastern slopes border on mixed grasslands and the boreal forest to the north and by the dry interior plateau on the western side. The Rockies are the crown of the continent and the source of most of the major rivers. The Continental Divide separates rivers flowing to the Pacific Ocean from those draining into the Arctic and Atlantic oceans. For example, water from the Columbia Icefields in the Canadian Rockies flows to the Arctic Ocean via the Athabasca and Mackenzie rivers, to the Pacific Ocean via the Columbia River, and to the Hudson Bay via the North Saskatchewan River. Similarly, water from Triple Divide Peak in Glacier National Park, Montana, flows to the Columbia, Missouri, and Saskatchewan rivers. Water from the mighty Colorado River is used for irrigation and other purposes and disappears in the arid southwest before it reaches the ocean. These and other rivers with their headwaters in the Rockies are the major sources of water in North America.

The Rocky Mountains can be divided into four major sections: Canadian, Northern, Central, and Southern. The Canadian Rocky Mountains, the northern segment of the Rocky Mountain system, are made mostly of layered sedimentary rock. Widely known for their rugged vistas, the Canadian Rockies extend nearly 870 miles (1,450 km) from the Liard River in northern British Columbia across the United States border for about 75 miles (125 km) into northern Montana. The composition of the mountains in that portion of Montana, including Glacier National Park, has a close affinity with mountains in the Canadian section. The Canadian Rockies are aligned northwest-southeast and divisible into three strip-like physiographic regions: main ranges, front ranges, and foothills. The foothills lie along the eastern boundary, rising above the Interior Plains as linear ridges and hills of Mesozoic shale and sandstone. The rugged front ranges, made mostly of Paleozoic limestone and shale, form the middle strip. The main ranges are the western strip, the highest and most glaciated region, with the oldest rock: Precambrian gritstone and slate. The Rocky Mountain Trench, western boundary of the main ranges and thus the western boundary of the Canadian Rockies, is a major fault line distinctly visible on satellite photos.

Some of the named geographic ranges of the Canadian Rockies include the Muskwa Ranges of the far-northern Rocky Mountains, which are broadest and highest around Mount Sylvia, 9,646 feet (2,940 m) in elevation near Kwadacha

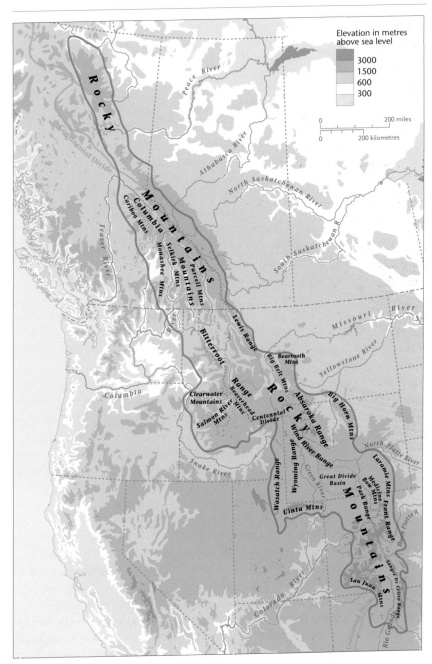

FIGURE 2. Map of the Rocky Mountains modified from Cannings (2005).

Wilderness Provincial Park. The terrain in that area is as rugged as any other part of the Rockies, having been carved by glaciations from great sections of stratified rock. A number of glaciers continue to carve the highest peaks. The Rockies narrow where crossed by the Peace River. To the south, the Hart Ranges rise gradually and form a relatively subdued terrain, with summits under 9,000 feet (2,750 m) in elevation. Farther south, the Continental Ranges are linear, with great cliffs and precipitous faces sculpted by glaciers. The Continental Ranges are broad, and their summit elevations increase to that of the highest peak, Mount Robson, 12,972 feet (3,954 m) in Mount Robson Provincial Park, British Columbia. A number of high peaks on the Continental Divide cluster around the Columbia Icefield, the largest of many glaciers in the Rockies. Farther south peaks up to 12,000 feet (3,600 m) in elevation occur at intervals or in groups along the mountain backbone through Banff National Park. Still farther south, around Waterton/Glacier International Peace Park, summit elevations are lower although the mountains are still very rugged. Gadd (1995) provides an excellent discussion on the geology and landforms of the Canadian Rockies for the interested reader.

The American Rockies look geologically and physically different from the Canadian Rockies, but they were both formed by movement northeastward along the continental plate thrusting rock upward. There are, however, two main differences. In the American Rockies the ancient gneiss and granite of the plate itself has been thrust up to the surface, while in the Canadian Rockies the plate rock remains deeply buried under sedimentary layers. In the Canadian Rockies glaciation has been heavier, producing deeper, wider valleys and steeper peaks. Individual ranges within the Canadian Rockies are long and continuous, while in the American Rockies there are often wide gaps and plains between ranges.

The Northern Rocky Mountains include western Montana (excluding the small portion included within the Canadian Rockies), Idaho, northeastern Washington, and a small portion of northeastern Oregon. The western part of the Northern Rockies merges northward into the Columbia Mountains of British Columbia, which include the Cariboo, Monashee, Purcell, and Selkirk mountains. These ranges, which run north-south or northwest-southwest, are composed of granitic and metamorphic rocks, like the western part of the Northern Rockies. The highest peak in the Northern Rockies section is Borah Peak at 12,662 feet (3,859 m) elevation in the Lost River Range of southern Idaho. Glacier National Park, Montana, is geologically and biologically part of the Canadian Rockies, but because it is located south of the international boundary it is often placed within the Northern Rockies.

The Central Rockies in northeastern Utah, western Wyoming, eastern Idaho, and southern Montana have an astounding geological diversity. This region is 90 miles (150 km) to more than 300 miles (500 km) wide, and includes the Beartooth, Bighorn, and Uinta mountains; and the Absaroka, Salt River, Snake River, Teton, Wasatch, and Wind River ranges, in addition to other minor ranges. These mountains and ranges are mostly made up of metamorphic and igneous rocks such as gneiss and granite, but lava flows and other volcanic rocks of various ages are found in the Yellowstone Plateau and Absaroka Range. The Uinta Mountains are unusual in that they trend east-west rather than north-south. There is often vertical relief between the valleys and summits of 5,000 feet (1,500 m). Some peaks, such as Gannett, Grand Teton, and Fremont, are more than 13,000 feet (4,000 m) high. Both Grand Teton and Yellowstone national parks are within the Central Rockies.

The Southern Rockies extend from southern Wyoming through Colorado to just northeast of Santa Fe, New Mexico. This is the southern end of the entire Rockies chain. The Southern Rockies are comprised of two north-south aligned belts of mountains, with basins between the belts. The eastern belt includes the Laramie Mountains south of Casper, the Front Range west of Denver, which includes Rocky Mountain National Park, and the Sangre de Cristo mountains of southern Colorado and northern New Mexico. These peaks are composed mainly of upthrust ancient Precambrian granite and gneiss. In the western belt, the major ranges are the San Juan Mountains made up mostly of much younger volcanic rock, and the Sawatch and Park ranges, which display a great variety of rock types. The Sawatch Range includes the Rocky Mountains' highest peak, Mount Elbert, 14,433 feet (4,399 m) elevation. More than 50 peaks in Colorado exceed 13,000 feet (4,000 m) whereas the Canadian Rockies have none over 13,000 feet (4,000 m). However, mountains in the Canadian Rockies are actually taller, meaning that they have greater elevation gain from bottom to top, because valleys in the Canadian Rockies are deeper than valleys in the American Rockies. For example, the topographic relief of Mount Robson in the Canadian Rockies is nearly 10,000 feet (3,000 m) while the greatest topographic relief in the American Rockies is about 6,500 feet (2,000 m) at Pikes Peak. Hunt (1973) provides a detailed discussion of the natural regions of the United States and Canada.

Ecoregions of the Rocky Mountains

The World Wildlife Fund has developed an ecosystem-mapping scheme that divides the Rocky Mountains into ten ecoregions (Ricketts *et al.* 1999 and Cannings 2005). An ecosystem is a geographically distinct area of land that is characterized by a distinctive climate, ecological features, and plant and animal communities, which interact ecologically in ways that are critical for their long-term persistence. A brief description of the vegetation and climate for each of those ecoregions follows with a map (Figure 3) to indicate the location of each ecoregion. Those readers wishing greater detail are referred to Ricketts *et al.* (1999).

Northern Cordillera Forests

The Northern Cordillera Forests Ecoregion represents a combination of alpine, subalpine, and boreal mid-Cordilleran habitats. Alpine communities, starting at about 5,500 feet (1700 m), include dwarf ericaceous shrubs, dwarf birch (*Betula* spp.), grasses, lichen, and bare bedrock above the tree line. Subalpine forests are characterized by Subalpine Fir (*Abies lasiocarpa*), Black Spruce (*Picea mariana*) in boggier areas, and White Spruce (*P. glauca*) together with deciduous shrubs. Closed boreal forests at lower elevations include White Spruce, Black Spruce, Lodgepole Pine (*Pinus contorta*), some Paper Birch (*Betula papyrifera*), and Quaking Aspen (*Populus tremuloides*).

The climate is characterized by long, hot summer days with mean summer temperatures of 50°F (10°C) and cold winter days with mean winter temperatures of 9° to −1°F (−13° to −18.5°C). Mean annual precipitation is about 14 to 24 inches (350 to 600 mm).

Central British Columbia Mountain Forests

The Central British Columbia Mountain Forests are warmer and wetter than the Northern Cordillera Forests. This ecoregion has a greater diversity of tree species than any other in the Rocky Mountains. Low-elevation forests include Western Red Cedar (*Thuja plicata*) and Western Hemlock (*Tsuga heterophylla*) in the northwestern area; and Lodgepole Pine, Quaking Aspen, White Spruce, and Black Spruce in the east. The subalpine section includes Engelmann Spruce (*Picea engelmannii*), Subalpine Fir, Lodgepole Pine, and White Spruce. Heathers (Ericaceae), Pink Mountainheath (*Phyllodoce empetriformis*), sedges (*Carex* spp.), and Hooker's Mountain-avens (*Dryas hookeriana*) occur in the alpine.

The mean summer temperature is 54°F (12°C) and the mean winter temperature is between 14° to 19°F (−7° to −10°C). Annual precipitation ranges from 20 to 28 inches (500 to 700 mm).

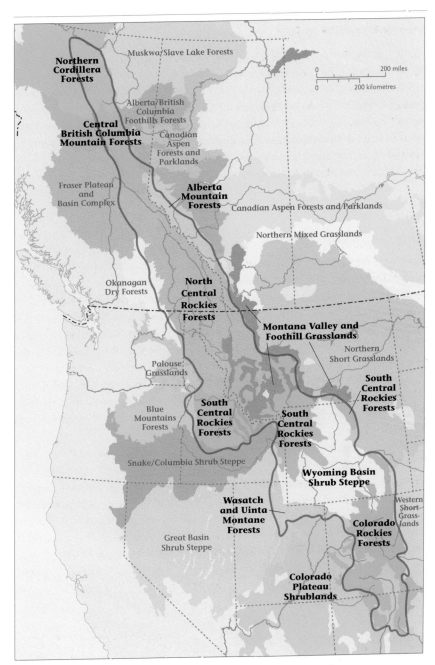

FIGURE 3. Ecoregions within the Rocky Mountains following Ricketts et al. (1999) and modified from Cannings (2005).

Alberta Mountain Forests

Occurring on the drier and cooler eastern side of the Continental Divide, the Alberta Mountain Forests support Quaking Aspen on lower slopes while Douglas-fir (*Pseudotsuga menziesii*) cloaks the southern portion. Mixed forests of Lodgepole Pine, Engelmann Spruce, and Subalpine Fir characterize the subalpine ecosystems. Alpine vegetation is characterized by heathers with sedges and Hooker's Mountain-avens. Subalpine Larch (*Larix lyallii*), a deciduous conifer, is a treeline specialist with a northern distribution limit near Lake Louise in Banff National Park.

Mean summer temperature is 54°F (12°C) and mean winter temperature is 19°F (−7.5°C). Precipitation is 24 to 31 inches (600 to 800 mm) per year, increasing from east to west.

North Central Rockies Forests

Mostly on the wet, western side of the Continental Divide, the North Central Rockies extend approximately 550 miles (950 km) from north to south. Coniferous forests, often with dramatic vertical zonation, are the dominant vegetation within the ecoregion. Montane forests include Western Hemlock and Western Red Cedar while White Spruce and Subalpine Fir forests are more prevalent in the southern portion. Lodgepole Pine, Douglas-fir, some Western White Pine (*Pinus monticola*), and also some Western Larch (*Larix occidentalis*) occur within the montane. Subalpine Fir and Engelmann Spruce are characteristic of subalpine forests. Other vegetation communities throughout the ecoregion include mountain meadows, foothill grasslands, riparian woodlands, and alpine tundra. The tree line is at about 7,000 feet (2,100 m).

Mean summer temperatures range from 55° to 58°F (12.5° to 14.5°C) and winter temperatures from 20° to 26°F (−3.5° to −6.5°C) with warmer temperatures in the west than the east. Annual precipitation in the valleys ranges from 20 to 31 inches (500 to 800 mm) to over 40 inches (1,000 mm) at higher elevations. Accumulated snow depths of over 65 feet (20 m) occur during some winters.

Montana Valley and Foothill Grasslands

Warmer and drier than the Alberta Mountain Forests, the Montana Valley and Foothill Grasslands, as suggested by the name, are dominated by grasslands at the lower elevations. The Canadian portion of this ecoregion is dominated by Rough Fescue (*Festuca campestris*), and lesser amounts of Wheatgrass (*Agropyron* spp,), Parry Oatgrass (*Danthonia parryi*), and Junegrass (*Koeleria* spp.). Drier sites support increased amounts of Needle and Thread Grass (*Hesperostipa comata*). Sticky Purple Geranium (*Geranium viscosissimum*), Bedstraw (*Galium* spp.), and Goldenbanner (*Thermopsis* spp.) are abundant members of the forb community. In the United States portion, Wheatgrass and fescue (*Festuca* spp.) are dominant members of the ecoregion. The southwestern part is predominantly a shrub steppe with Sagebrush (*Artemisia* spp.)

and Antelope Bitterbrush (*Purshia tridentata*) as the dominant shrubs.

This ecoregion is within the Chinook belt with dry, warm summers and mild winters. Mean summer temperature is 57°F (14°C) and mean winter temperature is 18°F (−8°C). With a pronounced rain-shadow effect in the ecoregion, the annual precipitation is limited to approximately 17 inches (425 mm).

South Central Rockies Forests

The dominant vegetation type in the South Central Rockies Forests is coniferous forest dominated by Engelmann Spruce, Subalpine Fir, and Douglas-fir. Because of prior disturbances such as fire, avalanches, and wind, large areas of the ecoregion are dominated by Lodgepole Pine. Whitebark Pine (*Pinus albicaulis*) is a dominant tree line species. A number of other vegetation communities such as mountain meadows, grasslands, and riparian woodlands are interspersed among the conifer forests with alpine tundra above the tree line. This ecoregion has marked vegetation zones because of steep gradients from the flatlands to the mountaintops.

This ecoregion has a continental climate with short summers and long, cold winters. Precipitation is variable depending on elevation, with snow typical at higher elevations.

Wyoming Basin Shrub Steppe

The Wyoming Basin Shrub Steppe is a high, open, and arid ecoregion. Dominant vegetation includes various sagebrushes, wheatgrasses, and fescues, with considerable variation in composition throughout the ecoregion. Desert shrublands, dunes, and barren areas are interspersed throughout the sagebrush steppe, with mixed-grass prairie near the eastern boundary of the ecoregion.

The Wyoming Basin Shrub Steppe is in the rain shadow of the Rocky Mountains and is generally arid to semiarid. Parts of this ecoregion are among the driest within the Rockies.

Wasatch and Uinta Montane Forests

The dominant vegetation of the Wasatch and Uinta Montane Forests are Ponderosa Pine, Douglas-fir, Subalpine Fir, and Engelmann Spruce forests in varying compositions. Limber Pine (*Pinus flexilis*) and Quaking Aspen have more limited distributions. At lower elevations the mountain brush community, dominated by Gambel Oak (*Quercus gambelii*) and Mountain Mahogany (*Cercocarpus* spp.), is a distinguishing feature.

Because of the extensive rainshadow effects of the Sierra Nevada Mountains to the west, this ecoregion is arid with large amounts of dry snow on the higher peaks.

Colorado Rockies Forests

Like the South Central Rockies Forests, marked vegetation zones characterize the Colorado Rockies Forests ecoregion. Changes in elevation are abrupt here in the highest mountains in the Rockies. The dominant vegetation type is coniferous forest with composition similar to that of the South Central Rockies with only a few exceptions. Both Ponderosa Pine and Quaking Aspen are common in the Colorado Rockies, with the former the dominant tree at lower elevations. However, Lodgepole Pine is much less common and Bristlecone Pine (*Pinus aristata*) is the dominant tree line species rather than Whitebark Pine. Mountain meadows, foothills grasslands, and riparian woodlands are interspersed among the coniferous forests. With the tree line at about 11,500 feet (3,500 m), alpine tundra communities are the most extensive within the Rockies.

Colorado Plateau Shrublands

Two major vegetation zones are found in the Colorado Plateau Shrublands. The largest is the Twoneedle Pinyon (*Pinus edulis*) and Juniper (*Juniperus* spp.) zone. Shrubs such as Big Sagebrush and Alderleaf Mountain Mahogany (*Cercocarpus montanus*), grasses, and various forbs provide sparse cover between the trees. In the mountain zone, Ponderosa Pine is more common in the south while Lodgepole Pine and Quaking Aspen are more abundant to the north.

Cold winters and summers with hot days and cool nights characterize the climate of this region. While the average annual precipitation is about 20 inches (510 mm), some parts receive only half that amount.

The Twoneedle Pinyon and Juniper community occurs in the foothills and montane zones and is common in the Colorado Plateau Shrublands ecoregion.

Vegetation Zones in the Rocky Mountains

Each of the ecosystems in the Rockies is part of one or more major zones (biomes) that form broad elevation bands across the mountainsides somewhat like the layers of a wedding cake. The primary vegetation zones covered in this field guide include the foothills, montane, subalpine, and alpine.

Foothills Zone

The foothills zone is not as well defined in Canada as those in the United States. In Canada the foothills zone is transitional from the plains and boreal forest in western Alberta and from the dry interior plateau of British Columbia to the coniferous forests of the montane zone. In parts of northwestern Alberta, the foothills zone is as wide as the other three zones combined. In the United States the foothills zone is a transition between the plains and the coniferous forests of the montane zone, but it is dominated by shrublands interspersed with grasses. West and Young (2000) and Cannings (2005) provide a detailed discussion of the intermountain valleys and lower mountain slopes.

Montane Zone

The montane zone is higher in elevation and generally has cooler temperatures and higher rainfall than the adjacent foothills. Coniferous forests, with fir, pine, and spruce trees, dominate the montane. Interested readers are referred to Peet (2000) and Cannings (2005) for detailed information on the forests and meadows of both the montane zone and subalpine zone.

Subalpine Zone

Temperatures cool, more moisture falls as snow during the winter, and growing seasons get shorter as elevations increase and the subalpine zone over takes the montane zone. In lower portions of the subalpine zone coniferous forest is common; in the upper portion the forest thins out, often giving way to meadows graced with wildflowers during summer months. The subalpine zone continues up the mountain slope to the tree line. Tree line is the upper limit for the growth of upright trees. The elevation of the tree line decreases at a rate of approximately 500 feet per 100 miles (150 m per 160 km) to the north. For example, the tree line in New Mexico extends to approximately 12,100 feet (3,700 m) while in northern British Columbia the tree line is at about 5,500 feet (1,700 m).

Alpine Zone

In the alpine zone between the tree line and the barren rocky peaks or glaciers of the mountains is a zone in which herbaceous plants exist but in which no trees of any significance can grow. If trees do exist, they grow no higher than a few feet (up to 1 m or more) and tend to sprawl across the ground. These stunted trees forms are called "elfin wood" or krummholz.

The alpine zone is fragmented on the tops of only the higher mountains. It is colder, more exposed to wind, and receives heavier precipitation than the other zones. Freezing temperature can be expected any day of the year. A combination of long, cold winters, short, cool summers, and high winds prevent tree growth. A mosaic of low shrub and herb communities characterizes the alpine zone. Lichens and xerophytic mosses, which are able to withstand extreme temperatures and desiccation, are found at the upper limits.

Adapted to make the most of what heat and moisture falls upon them, many of the plants take on special growth forms. Prostrate forms growing along the surface of the ground; cushion plants that wedge themselves in crevices; and leathery or hairy leafs and stems conserve water by reducing the desiccation by strong wind. Many alpine plants have bulbs or tap roots to store energy over the winter to fuel growth each spring even while still snow-covered. The shortness of the growing season and the severity of winter favor fast-growing perennials. In some alpine areas the growing season is as short as a month, allowing plants only a brief flurry of life in the austere conditions.

Despite the harsh conditions of the alpine zone, numerous plant species survive and thrive and offer a stunning display of flowers during the short summer. This great variation in vegetation over short distances is a feature of the alpine zone. Several distinct plant communities commonly occur together in a mosaic. Zwinger and Willard (1996), Billings (2000), and Cannings (2005) provide details on the environmental conditions, plant adaptations, and on individual plant species and plant communities in this land above the tree line.

Remember that elevation is the single most important factor in determining what plants you will see at any given site. As elevations increase temperatures cool. On average, the temperature drops 3°F (2.6°C) for every 1,000 feet (300 m) of elevation gained. Looking at it in a slightly different way, a gain of 1,000 feet (300 m) in elevation is similar to traveling about 600 miles (1,000 km) from south to north.

A wildflower or shrub species may be limited to one vegetation zone while others may be found in all four. Wildflowers found only in the plains or below the foothills elevation are not included in this field guide, but those that creep up into the mountains are included. Comments on the vegetation zone or zones where plants are found are provided for each description in the color sections that follow. There is much to discover in each of the ecoregions and vegetation zones.

Big Sagebrush communities occur in the foothills and montane zones and are particularly common in the Montana Valley and Foothills Grasslands and Wyoming Basin Shrub Steppe ecoregions.

Quaking Aspen communities range from the foothills zone throughout the subalpine zone as well as being found in all ten of the ecoregions within the Rocky Mountains.

Ponderosa Pine communities generally occur in the montane zone and in the Wasatch and Uinta Montane Forests, Colorado Rockies Forests, and Colorado Plateau Shrublands ecoregions.

Shrublands and White Spruce communities in the montane zone of the Northern Cordillera Forests ecoregion.

Lodgepole Pine is a seral species forming vast monocultures in fire-disturbed areas in the montane and lower subalpine zones in most of the ecoregions within the Rocky Mountains.

Engelmann Spruce community in the middle subalpine zone.

Mature Engelmann Spruce and Subalpine Fir communities dominate the upper subalpine zone from one end of the Rockies to the other.

Wildflowers in a meadow of the subalpine zone in the Alberta Mountain Forests ecoregion.

Engelmann Spruce communities and meadows in the subalpine zone in the Alberta Mountain Forests ecoregion.

Subalpine Larch, a deciduous conifer, community in the upper subalpine zone of the Alberta Mountain Forests ecoregion.

Krummholz or "elfinwood" near the tree line.

Heather community near the tree line in the low alpine zone.

Wildflowers and shrubs in the alpine zone of the Alberta Mountain Forests ecoregion.

*Nobody sees a flower, really.
It is so small it takes time.
We haven't time and to see
takes time, like to have a
friend takes time.*

— Georgia O'Keeffe

WHITE

Oxeye Daisy
Leucanthemum vulgare

ASTER FAMILY
Asteraceae

page 39

Western Poison Ivy
Toxicodendron rydbergii

SUMAC FAMILY
Anacardiaceae

Native only to North America, Western Poison Ivy is an erect to spreading shrub, up to 16 inches (40 cm) high, which spreads from a creeping rootstock to produce patches of the plant. The leaves consist of 3 large, shiny green leaflets. They are drooping, strongly veined, and pointed, with irregularly notched margins. In the autumn the leaves turn wine-red or orange-red. Numerous small, yellowish-green flowers are borne on erect stems. They develop into dull, yellowish, waxy fruits, less than ⅜ inch (1 cm) in diameter. This plant contains a mixture of chemicals called urushiol, which may cause intense skin irritation when touched. One writer reported that the amount of urushiol on a pinhead can raise rashes on 500 people and that 90 percent of North Americans are susceptible to it. Apparently, the substance itself is harmless, but the body's immune system reacts to its presence. Washing with soap and application of ointments may reduce these distressing effects. It is better to avoid the plant by remembering the saying, "Leaves of three, let them be." Western Poison Ivy may be locally abundant in shady woodlands and ravines.

Range: throughout the Rockies.

Western Water Hemlock
Cicuta douglasii

CARROT FAMILY
Apiaceae

Western Water Hemlock is one of the most poisonous plants on the continent and is fairly common along slough margins, lakeshores, and other wet areas. This stout-stemmed plant, from 20–80 inches (50–200 cm) tall, grows from a thick tuberous root that is divided horizontally into several chambers. Even a small piece of the root would contain enough poison, primarily the alkaloid coniine, to kill humans and livestock. The leaves are alternate and pinnately compound, with sharply toothed leaflets, and they vary in size up the stem. Rounded compound umbels, up to 4 inches (10 cm) wide, consisting of numerous small white flowers, rise from the tip of the stem. Secondary umbels grow from several narrow bracts. The oval-shaped seeds are yellow with dark brown ribs.

Range: Alberta, British Columbia, Washington, Oregon, Idaho, and Montana.

This very conspicuous perennial plant, up to 8 feet (2.5 m) tall, towers above its herbaceous neighbors. The prominently ribbed, green, rhubarb-like stems arise from a cluster of slender, parsnip-like roots. These stems bear large leaves up to 12 inches (30 cm) across, which are deeply lobed, sharply-toothed, 3-parted, and crinkly. They are capped by a myriad of cream-white flowers in large umbrella-like clusters. The fruits are flat and marked on the faces by narrow ribs and dark oil tubes, which extend from the top part-way to the base. Both the flowers and fruits have a pungent but not unpleasant aroma. Most parts of the plant are edible; however, positive identification is required because some similar plants are poisonous. Common Cowparsnip has been used for several medicinal purposes, including treatment of arthritis, rheumatism, and intestinal pains. The stems and leaves are palatable to deer, elk, and bears, especially after early autumn frosts. Several species of birds dine on the copious seeds, and bears sometimes eat the flowering heads. Common Cowparsnip is found in damp meadows, along stream banks, and in poplar woods.

Range: throughout the Rockies.

Common Cowparsnip
Heracleum maximum

CARROT FAMILY
Apiaceae

Porter's Licorice-root is a perennial growing to about 3 feet (1 m) with stout, hollow, branching, reddish stems. Basal leaves are parsley-like, up to 10 inches (25 cm) long, divided into triple lobes and again divided into smaller toothed or cleft segments; stem leaves are fewer and much smaller. Flowers are clustered into flat-topped compound umbels. Individual flowers are small with white to pinkish petals. Roots have an intensely spicy celery-like odor. Indigenous people traditionally used Porter's Licorice-root or Osha as a medicine and in rituals, and it is still widely used in herbal treatments for sore throats, colds, and other viral infections. Bears also relish it. A similar looking plant, Idaho Licorice-root (*L. tenuifolium*) is smaller with narrow leaflets and a slender stem. Porter's Licorice-root often grows in masses under Quaking Aspen and in meadows from the montane to the subalpine.

Range: Montana, Wyoming, Utah, Colorado, and New Mexico.

Porter's Licorice-root; Osha; Bear Root
Ligusticum porteri

CARROT FAMILY
Apiaceae

Indianhemp
Apocynum cannabinum
DOGBANE FAMILY
Apocynaceae

Indianhemp is a herbaceous perennial, reaching to 5 feet (1.5 m) tall but generally shorter, growing from long spreading roots that develop from an initial taproot. Stems are reddish and secrete a milky sap when bruised or broken. Leaves are entire, ovate to elliptic in shape, 3–6 inches (7–15 cm) long, 1¼–2 inches (3–5 cm) broad, smooth on the upper surface, and lighter with white hairs on the underside. Small, white to greenish-white flowers are produced in terminal clusters (cymes) at the end of stems and stem branches. The flowers are followed by 3–6 ½ inch (8–17 cm) long, narrow seedpods (follicles) that are produced in pairs. When mature the twin pods are reddish-brown and split open disseminating numerous seeds with tufts of silky white hairs at their tip. Indianhemp was a valuable plant at least as far as human technologies were concerned. Native Americans harvested the outer bark in the fall and wove it into twines, ropes, fishing lines, nets, and even bowstrings. It is a poisonous plant, which discourages browsing by animals. Look for this plant in riparian areas, partly shady sites in thickets, edges of tree groves, and roadside ditches from the plains to foothills.

Range: throughout the Rockies.

Wild Sarsaparilla
Aralia nudicaulis
GINSENG FAMILY
Araliaceae

Wild Sarsaparilla is a low-growing perennial shrub with a woody base. Its short stems scarcely break the soil surface. Both the flower stems and overshadowing leaves rise from that woody base. The single, long-stalked, compound leaves have 5 leaflets, each divided into 3 sections. The leaflets are elongated lance- to egg-shaped, with finely toothed margins. Hidden under the leaf, the small, greenish-white flowers appear in ball-like clusters on top of a naked stem. Usually 3 flower clusters, consisting of numerous very small individual flowers, are present on a stem but some plants may have from 2 to 7. This plant was used for several purposes. In earlier times, the aromatic roots were used in making sarsaparilla, a root beer-like drink. Young shoots were used as a culinary herb and the purplish-black berries were made into jelly. Wild Sarsaparilla occurs in dry to moist hardwood and mixed forests in the foothills and the montane.

Range: throughout the Rockies, excluding Oregon, Utah, and New Mexico.

Razor sharp spines, brilliant red berries, and enormous leaves make this shrub unmistakable. The stems of Devilsclub are upright to decumbent, usually 3–9 feet (1–3 m) tall but reaching up to 18 feet (6 m), and may form large sprawling clones. The maple-shaped leaves are large, 8–16 inches (20–40 cm) across. Alternately arranged, the leaves are dark green above and lighter green below, with at least 5 to 7 toothed main lobes. Stems, petioles, and leaf veins are covered with an armor of yellowish needle-like spines up to ¾ inch (2 cm) long. Greenish-white flowers grow in a dense spike, up to 10 inches (25 cm) long, at the end of the heavily armed stems. A cluster of inedible, waxy, flattened, bright red berries later replaces them. The stiff, irritating prickles can cause significant wounds. Devilsclub was widely employed by several Native American groups for its pain-relieving properties, as well as numerous other medicinal and spiritual purposes. This plant favors soft, moist to wet soils in shady sites from the foothills to the montane.

Devilsclub
Oplopanax horridus

GINSENG FAMILY
Araliaceae

Range: Alberta, British Columbia, Washington, Oregon, Idaho, and Montana.

This genus is named in honor of Achilles, the Greek warrior with the vulnerable heel, who was said to have made an ointment from Yarrow to heal the wounds of his soldiers during the siege of Troy. The stems of this aromatic perennial arise from a creeping rootstock and may be 8–28 inches (20–70 cm) tall. The flat-topped cluster of small blooms consists of two kinds of flowers. The white (rarely pink) ray flowers ringing each cluster have a 2-notched lip at the top of the tube, whereas the tube of the straw-colored disk florets is evenly notched with 5 short teeth. A leaf, or foil, may not be divided a thousand times as the scientific name (*millefolium*) implies, but it is very much dissected. Before flowering, Common Yarrow may be mistaken for a fern because of the lacy, much-divided leaves. These attractive plants are frequently used in dried arrangements. It is reported that Native Americans used the plant to treat cuts and open wounds, as a tonic, and as a cure for stomach disorders. Common Yarrow is equally at home anywhere from grasslands to mountain summits.

Common Yarrow
Achillea millefolium

ASTER FAMILY
Asteraceae

Range: throughout the Rockies.

Western Pearly Everlasting
Anaphalis margaritacea

ASTER FAMILY
Asteraceae

Western Pearly Everlasting is a perennial, 10–12 inches (25–30 cm) tall, growing from a rhizome. Its lance-shaped leaves are grayish-green on top and white and woolly underneath. At the tip of the stem there is a cluster of many pearly-white flower heads. The pearly effect is due to the whitened tips of paper-thin bracts, which surround the tiny yellow disk florets. These flowers retain their color, form, and fresh look for days after being picked, and are popular in dried arrangements, which makes the common name both appropriate and descriptive. Native Americans are reported to have placed dried, powdered flowers of this plant on horses' hooves and between their ears to make them long-winded, spirited, and enduring. This plant is fairly common in open woods at low to middle altitudes.

Range: throughout the Rockies.

Woolly Pussytoes
Antennaria lanata

ASTER FAMILY
Asteraceae

Several species of this genus grow in the Rocky Mountains and they are difficult to distinguish from one another. As suggested by the common name, Woolly Pussytoes has leaves and stems that are closely appressed with whitish, woolly hairs that give the plant a pale gray to grayish-green color. The rosettes of basal leaves arise from fibrous, creeping stems; the stem leaves, often with brown, nail-like tips, are quite small in size. This plant's 4 to 10 tiny flowers are arranged in heads at the tip of the stem. Each head forms a compact, rounded cluster and is surrounded by bracts, which are dark-colored below with pale tips. The long-lasting quality of the flowers makes them popular for dried arrangements. Woolly Pussytoes grows in moist alpine and subalpine meadows.

Range: throughout the Rockies, excluding Utah, Colorado, and New Mexico.

This stately thistle, 12–40 inches (30–100 cm) tall, is a biennial or short-lived perennial, which grows from a taproot. The alternate leaves, up to 8 inches (20 cm) long, are linear-oblong, lobed or merely toothed, and tipped with spines. They are white and woolly beneath and smooth above. The flower heads are 1¼–2 inches (3–5 cm) across and there may be a few or several on each plant. Each head has white or creamy white disk florets, sometimes tinged with purple, clustered at the top of the stem. The involucre is shaped like a cup, tipped with spines, and covered with loose, spreading, cobweb-like white hairs. The roots are very tasty and may be eaten raw or cooked with meat. Deer, elk, bears, and horses all favor this plant. Preferring moist sites in valley bottoms, White Thistle may be found in bloom during mid- to late summer.

Range: Alberta, British Columbia, Washington, Idaho, Montana, and Wyoming.

White Thistle; Hooker's Thistle
Cirsium hookerianum

ASTER FAMILY
Asteraceae

Tufted Fleabane has white flowers, sometimes blue or pinkish, with a yellow center. A single flower head is generally found atop each stem. The ray flowers, numbering from 30 to 100, are about ⅜ inch (1 cm) long. Each flower head has 3 to 4 rows of thickened bracts. Each plant has several stems, curved at the base and erect at the top, growing from 4–12 inches (10–30 cm) tall. Leaves of the plant are gray to olive green, smooth-margined, three-veined, usually downy white, and glandular underneath. Basal leaves are oblong and lance-like to narrowly spatulate; upper leaves lack petioles and are reduced in size. Tufted Fleabane prefers dry, open areas with rocky soils.

Range: throughout the Rockies, excluding Oregon.

Tufted Fleabane
Erigeron caespitosus

ASTER FAMILY
Asteraceae

Cutleaf Daisy
Erigeron compositus

ASTER FAMILY
Asteraceae

The pretty daisy-like blossoms of this fleabane usually have ray flowers that are white, pink, or mauve. The many disk florets are yellow. Several stems arise from the base, each crowned with a single flower head. Except for a few reduced bracts on the stem, the foliage is almost entirely comprised of deeply divided basal leaves. Both the leaves and stems are sparsely covered with short glandular hairs. The involucral bracts, as seen in the photograph, are also hairy and purplish, at least at the tips. Cutleaf Daisy grows in rocky soils from moderate elevations to the alpine zone.

Range: throughout the Rockies, excluding New Mexico.

Arctic Alpine Fleabane
Erigeron humilis

ASTER FAMILY
Asteraceae

Another charming little plant of moist alpine slopes, Arctic Alpine Fleabane is seldom more than 6 inches (15 cm) tall. The plant grows from a taproot and produces stems that are more or less erect. Each stem is crowned with a solitary flower head with 50 to 150 white ray flowers that age to a light purple. The basal leaves are spoon-shaped, tapering into long petioles. Long hairs are present on all green parts of the plant; those on the involucral bracts and adjacent stem are woolly and blackish-purple. Fruits are yellow-ribbed and hairy, with white pappus bristles.

Range: throughout the Rockies, excluding Washington, Oregon, and New Mexico.

A squat perennial growing on rocky slopes in high alpine areas, Woolly Fleabane is anchored by long taproots and has short stems, seldom over 4 inches (10 cm) tall. The small leaves, in a basal rosette, are rounded at the apex and often 3-toothed. Up to nearly 1¼ inches (3 cm) in diameter, the daisy-like head has numerous and unusually long ray flowers, which are normally white but occasionally a pale lilac. Disk flowers are yellow. Upper portions of the involucral bracts and upper stems are a dark purple. Loose, branching hairs entirely cover the leaves, stems, and involucral bracts; this densely woolly covering gives the plant its common and species names. Fruits are dry achenes with white bristles.

Range: Alberta, British Columbia, Montana, Wyoming, and Colorado.

Woolly Fleabane
Erigeron lanatus

ASTER FAMILY
Asteraceae

Although considered a troublesome weed in some localities, Oxeye Daisy is a strikingly beautiful Eurasian invader whose blossoms brighten roadsides and other areas impacted by man. Usually growing in patches, the erect stems, 8-24 inches (20-60 cm) tall, are simple or forked near the top. The daisy-like blossoms have a solid center of yellow disk florets, with a depressed center, surrounded by a row of 15 to 30 shining white ray flowers. Its flower heads are open during the day but close at night. The petioled basal leaves are oblong to spoon-shaped with coarsely toothed margins; the upper stem leaves are clasping and also have toothed margins. These leaves may be hairless or sparsely hairy. To assist in future colonization, huge quantities of dry-ribbed achenes, without a pappus, are produced after the flowers fade.

Range: throughout the Rockies.

Oxeye Daisy
Leucanthemum vulgare
[Chrysanthemum leucanthemum]

ASTER FAMILY
Asteraceae

Arctic Sweet Coltsfoot
Petasites frigidus

ASTER FAMILY
Asteraceae

The flowering stems, 12–16 inches (30–40 cm) tall, appear early in the season, well before the triangular- to heart-shaped basal leaves develop. The heads consist of clusters of numerous small, white to purplish flowers. Within a few days the flowers are succeeded by seed-bearing tufts of whitish hairs, not unlike the "puff" of dandelions. After the seeds disperse, the leaves, dark green above and pubescent and whitish beneath, grow from the same fleshy underground rootstock that gave rise to the flowering stems earlier in the season. The leaves are lobed to about one-quarter to one-third of their width. Young leaves and flowers may be eaten raw as salad or cooked as a potherb; Native Americans used dried stems and leaves as a salt substitute. Arctic Sweet Coltsfoot grows in moist meadows and along brooks and streams in the alpine and subalpine zones.

Range: throughout the Rockies, excluding Utah and New Mexico.

White Prairie Aster
Symphyotrichum falcatum
[Aster falcatus]

ASTER FAMILY
Asteraceae

White Prairie Aster is a branching perennial with extensive running rootstocks, thus it can form large patches. The daisy-like flowers are ¾–1¼ inches (2–3 cm) across with white ray flowers, yellow disk florets, with tawny, bristle-tipped bracts below. From 12–32 inches (30–80 cm) high, the stems are densely hairy as are the linear to linear-oblong leaves. White Prairie Aster, a late summer and autumn bloomer, is fairly common in dry foothills and the montane zone.

Range: throughout the Rockies, excluding Oregon.

Hooker's Townsend Daisy is an almost stemless plant growing from a deep woody root. Stalkless flower heads are borne among a rosette of lance-shaped leaves, which are sharply pointed and covered with fine, silvery hairs. White to pink ray flowers surround the yellow disk florets. The involucral bracts have a green midrib and most have white margin hairs. This plant may be expected on prairies and dry hillsides, but it is conspicuous only when flowering in the early spring.

Range: throughout the Rockies, excluding Washington, Oregon, and New Mexico.

Hooker's Townsend Daisy
Townsendia hookeri

ASTER FAMILY
Asteraceae

An introduced weed, Scentless False Mayweed is an annual to short-lived perennial, growing to about 3 feet (1 m) from an extensive fibrous root system. Stems are highly branched with fern-like, very finely divided, alternate leaves. Showy daisy-like flowers are numerous with as many as 3,000 flower heads per plant. Long, white, 3-lobed ray flowers surround the yellow disk florets that are slightly domed at maturity. Both the flowers and florets are capable of producing seeds, which may number up to 200,000 per plant. Mature seeds are dark brown to black-brown and have 3 distinctive ridges. Roadsides and other disturbed places in the plains and foothills are favored habitat for Scentless False Mayweed.

Range: throughout the Rockies, excluding Oregon and New Mexico.

Scentless False Mayweed
Tripleurospermum perforata

ASTER FAMILY
Asteraceae

Buttecandle

Cryptantha celosioides

BORAGE FAMILY
Boraginaceae

All green parts of Buttecandle are densely covered with rather bristly white hairs, often giving it a gray appearance. The somewhat spoon-shaped lower leaves have rounded or sharp tips, while the upper leaves are linear. Small flowers cluster in the axils of the leaves over the upper two-thirds of the stem. The flowers, showy white with yellow centers, have a sweet perfume. The calyx is very bristly, and the nutlet is ridged on the back. This plant grows on dry hillsides and prairies, sometimes densely.

Range: throughout the Rockies, excluding Utah and New Mexico.

Lancepod Draba

Draba lonchocarpa

MUSTARD FAMILY
Brassicaceae

The drabas, or whitlow grasses, have cross-like flowers each with 4 sepals and 4 petals. In addition, they have 6 stamens, 2 being shorter than the others and on opposite sides of the pistil. Identification at the species level affords many difficult problems for flower lovers as well as expert botanists. Seed pod and hair-type characteristics must often be studied for certain determination. This particular species is a dwarf, matted plant less than 3 inches (8 cm) high. It has small hairy leaves and clusters of tiny white flowers set on top of a short stem. Rocky areas and scree slopes are favored habitats.

Range: throughout the Rockies, excluding New Mexico.

Alpine Smelowskia
Smelowskia calycina

MUSTARD FAMILY
Brassicaceae

This densely tufted perennial is widespread on scree slopes and rocky crests at high elevations. The blue-gray basal leaves may be lance-shaped or deeply cleft into several lobes; stem leaves are smaller and finely dissected. Both leaves and stems are fringed with hairs. Short racemes of creamy white flowers bloom at the stem tips, but these racemes elongate as the fruits develop. The resulting pods are dark-colored, slender, and pointed at both ends. Alpine Smelowskia is often infected by an invading rust fungus whose mycelium extracts food from the host plant and, in the process, causes flower abortion and disfiguration of leaves. The rust becomes evident on the leaves and stems as numerous brown, pimple-like protuberances that soon become powdery [inset].

Range: throughout the Rockies, excluding New Mexico.

Red Elderberry
Sambucus racemosa

HONEYSUCKLE FAMILY
Caprifoliaceae

Red Elderberry is a conspicuous shrub up to 9 feet (3 m) tall, often growing in large clumps. It has fast-growing, pithy, partly hollow stems. Each large compound leaf consists of 5 to 7 sawtooth-edged leaflets. The cone-shaped terminal clusters of small, creamy white flowers, held erect like torches, are strongly and sweetly scented. Bright scarlet berries that grow where the flowers once bloomed prolong this plant's charm. A multitude of birds feast on the berries, and deer, elk, and moose browse this shrub heavily. The berries can be used for making jelly and wine. Both the roots and stems are poisonous; children have been poisoned when stems were hollowed out and used as blowguns. Red Elderberry inhabits stream banks, moist woods, and thickets.

Range: throughout the Rockies.

Squashberry
Viburnum edule
HONEYSUCKLE FAMILY
Caprifoliaceae

Until the brilliant scarlet fruits are framed in a mat of snow or the leaves turn to crimson-purple, this common shrub of the woodlands tends to get overlooked. It is a straggly shrub, 3–6 feet (1–2 m) tall, whose mature leaves are maple-shaped while younger leaves are pointed and lance-shaped. The tiny, white, 5-parted flowers are arranged in flat-topped showy clusters between pairs of leaves along the stem. The fruits are juicy and acidic and contain a large, flattened stone. They hang on the tree after the leaves fall, providing a valuable food source for birds. Frequently the fruit ferments on the shrubs, resulting in many a tipsy bird. In addition to being favored by birds, these edible fruits make a tasty, tart jelly. The fruits also have a delicate fragrance, which wafts through the air on pleasant autumn days.

Range: throughout the Rockies, excluding Utah and New Mexico.

Fendler's Sandwort
Arenaria fendleri
[Eremogone fenderli]

PINK FAMILY
Caryophyllaceae

Fendler's Sandwort grows in mats from a woody base. Basal leaves are ascending or recurved and from ⅜–4 inches (1–10 cm) long; stem leaves are in pairs and reduced in size upward on the stem. All leaves are very narrow, bluish-green, and tapered to slender points. Stems are topped with 3 to 35 flowers in an open cyme. The white petals are oblong to spoon-shaped with stamens rising above them. The veined sepals taper to a slender point. A wide-ranging plant in the southern Rockies, Fendler's Sandwort grows from sagebrush plains to the alpine zone.

Range: Wyoming, Utah, Colorado, and New Mexico.

Another delightful little plant of exposed alpine ridges, Bering Chickweed is of low stature and often forms matted clumps. The stems are 2–10 inches (5–25 cm) tall, hairy, and sticky. The cheery white flowers have 5 petals, each with a prominent cleft at the tip. Smaller than the petals, the sepals have translucent margins and are often tinged with purple. The sessile leaves, covered with silky hairs, are said to resemble mouse ears. When fully mature the fruit is a cylindrical capsule.

Range: throughout the Rockies.

Bering Chickweed
Cerastium beeringianum

PINK FAMILY
Caryophyllaceae

Twinflower Sandwort is one of several "chickweeds" in the Rockies. Identification requires time, patience, taxonomic keys, and a hand lens to determine their genus and species. Twinflower Sandwort is matted low to the ground; the basal leaves are less than ⅜ inch (1 cm) tall and the stems seldom taller than ¾–2½ inches (2–6 cm). The wide-spreading flowers are white with 5 rounded petals, 10 stamens, and 3 styles borne on slender stems above moss-like leaves. Petals of the flowers are longer than the blunt-tipped, purple-tinged sepals. Mats of Twinflower Sandwort, up to 20 inches (50 cm) wide, may be found on gravelly slopes and meadows in the subalpine and alpine zones.

Range: throughout the Rockies.

Twinflower Sandwort
Minuartia obtusiloba

PINK FAMILY
Caryophyllaceae

Maidenstears; Bladder Campion
Silene vulgaris

PINK FAMILY
Caryophyllaceae

An introduced perennial weed, Maidenstears has deep roots that allow it to survive on roadsides, in gravel pits, and in other disturbed places. A conspicuous feature of the plant is the inflated sepal tube, marked by a network of dark veins. The corolla is formed by 5 deeply bilobed petals, which spread out like a wheel just beyond the rim of the sepal tube. The stems may be up to 3 feet (1 m) tall and branched from the base, the lower branches sometimes spreading horizontally before ascending. The opposite, lance-shaped leaves are produced from swollen leaf nodes. This rapidly spreading plant may crowd out some desirable native species.

Range: throughout the Rockies.

Longstalk Starwort
Stellaria longipes

PINK FAMILY
Caryophyllaceae

Longstalk Starwort is a tufted perennial with blue-green, lance-shaped leaves, which are sessile and opposite. Its stems, flowers, and leaves are generally rigidly erect, in contrast to several other Chickweeds. The white flowers may be solitary at the end of the straight stalks or with 1 or more flowers from branches at the leaf axils below the terminal flower. There are only 5 petals, but they are so deeply cleft there appear to be 10. This plant inhabits exposed rocky ridges and slopes within the alpine zone. The young leaves of the plant may be chopped and eaten raw or cooked. They are rich in vitamin C and iron. Several species of Chickweed are found in the Rocky Mountains. They are not always easily identified because they tend to be highly variable.

Range: throughout the Rockies.

Field Bindweed
Convolvulus arvensis

MORNING-GLORY FAMILY
Convolvulaceae

A beauty and a beast all in one, Field Bindweed is a vigorous weak-stemmed trailing or climbing vine reaching 5 feet (1.5 m) or more. Its petunia-like flowers have 5 petals that are fused at the base and flared at the open end. Flowers, ¾–1¼ inch (2–3 cm) across, are white or pale pink and grow on short stalks. This introduced weed has triangular leaves with lobes that point outward at the base and small bracts that are separated from the flower and often appressed to the stem. The petioled leaves are alternate, ¾–2½ inches (2–6 cm) long, with pointed tips. In spite of its beauty, it is a major pest when it occurs on cultivated land, twining around and over other plants by using its tendrils for support and exhausting soil nutrients. Its deep, twisting underground rhizomes make it especially difficult to eradicate. Field Bindweed is often mistaken for Hedge False Bindweed (*Calystegia sepium*), but the latter has triangular leaves with a square (truncate) base and large bracts beneath the flowers. Both are noxious weeds. Tenacious and ubiquitous, Field Bindweed can be found in meadows, fields, waste ground, and woodlands from the foothills to the montane zone.

Range: throughout the Rockies.

Bunchberry Dogwood
Cornus canadensis

DOGWOOD FAMILY
Cornaceae

The 4 white "petals" of the Bunchberry Dogwood are actually bracts surrounding a central cluster of inconspicuous greenish flowers. Later the bracts fade to a brownish color and the flowers develop into clusters of bland-tasting, cardinal-red berries that are eaten by grouse and other birds. The plant is 3–8 inches (8–20 cm) in height, with a whorl of 4 to 6 dark green leaves, whose tips are sharply pointed. In autumn the leaves turn to brilliant shades of red and purple. The dried leaves may be used for smoking. Bunchberry Dogwood grows as individual plants or in dense colonies among the mosses and fallen needles of spruce and pine forests.

Range: throughout the Rockies, excluding Utah.

Redosier Dogwood
Cornus sericea ssp. sericea

DOGWOOD FAMILY
Cornaceae

This willow-like shrub, between 3–9 feet (1–3 m) tall, often forms nearly impenetrable thickets along streams and rivers and in moist forests. The reddish bark, which becomes a much brighter red when subjected to winter frost, is distinctive. The heavily veined leaves, dark green above and paler beneath are egg-shaped with rounded bases and pointed ends. These leaves handsomely set off the flat-topped clusters of small, greenish-white flowers. Each flower has 4 small sepals, 4 spreading, oval-shaped petals, 4 stamens, and a club-shaped pistil. By early autumn the clusters of globular white fruit, often tinged with blue, contrast with the brilliant plum-colored leaves and deep-red branches. Native Americans used the branches for weaving baskets, and the inner bark served in a tobacco mixture and for making tea.

Range: throughout the Rockies.

Red Fruit Bearberry
Arctostaphylos rubra

HEATH FAMILY
Ericaceae

Red Fruit Bearberry is a prostrate shrub, usually less than 4¾ inches (12 cm) tall, with reddish bark that is papery and shredded. Its urn-shaped, white flowers are often in bloom as the leaves open. When ripe, the drupe-like berries are a bright red with 5 stony nutlets inside. Although they are edible, the berries are seldom used. The spatula-shaped leaves are about 1½ inches (4 cm) long, toothed, and with conspicuous veins. Turning flame red in the autumn, the leaves add a splash of color to the alpine habitat where Red Fruit Bearberry is found. A similar species, Alpine Bearberry (*A. alpina*) has a coarser leaf with hairs on the margins and black berries. Red Fruit Bearberry is a circumpolar species.

Range: Alberta and British Columbia with a skip to Wyoming.

Often associated with Pink Mountainheath and Yellow Mountainheath, Western Moss Heather, a dwarf evergreen shrub, occurs in mats that carpet the ground near the timberline and below moist snowbed slopes well into the alpine region. The ends of the branches bear a profusion of nodding, bell-shaped, snow-white flowers, sometimes tinged with rose. Red-tipped sepals add a touch of color to each bell. The petals of the perfect little bells are slightly rolled back from the rim, which helps distinguish this plant from Yellow Mountainheath, whose petals are constricted near the rim. Minute scale-like leaves are arranged in 4 distinct rows and overlap one another like fish scales or cedar leaves. The stalks are curved when they bear the flowers, but become erect as the seed capsules mature. Because of its high resin content, this plant can be used as fuel for fires. Its branches are reported to produce a golden-brown dye. White Arctic Mountain Heather (*C. tetragona*) looks very similar except for a deep groove that runs the length of the lower leaf surface.

Range: Alberta, British Columbia, Washington, Oregon, Idaho, and Montana.

Western Moss Heather
Cassiope mertensiana

HEATH FAMILY
Ericaceae

Bog Labrador Tea is a much-branched, aromatic evergreen shrub, 12–32 inches (30–80 cm) tall that grows in mossy bogs and moist coniferous woods. Its leaves are a distinguishing feature. They are narrowly oblong, thick and leathery, dark glossy green above and rusty and woolly beneath, with downward-rolled margins. Numerous small white flowers, with stamens that rise from the center of each bloom, are clustered at hairy branch-tips. The stalks are erect when in flower but drooping in fruit. When crushed the leaves have a spicy aroma, redolent with the tang of the moist woods and bogs in which they grow. Ledol, a toxic compound, is found in the leaves, along with other narcotic substances. The leaves have long been used as a substitute or additive for tea, and those substances may produce restorative effects similar to caffeine. Native Americans extracted oil for tanning skins and to make a lotion to relieve the itch of insect bites. Where their ranges overlap it is easy to confuse Bog Labrador Tea and Western Labrador Tea (*L. glandulosum*). The latter lacks the rusty-brown hairs on the underside of the leaves.

Range: Alberta, British Columbia, Washington, Oregon, and Idaho.

Bog Labrador Tea
Ledum groenlandicum

HEATH FAMILY
Ericaceae

Cascade Azalea
Rhododendron albiflorum

HEATH FAMILY
Ericaceae

Of all shrubs that inhabit the cool, moist, mature montane and subalpine forests, Cascade Azalea, a deciduous bush, has one of the largest flowers, ¾–1 inch (2–3 cm) across. These white to creamy white flowers are shaped like a cup, with the petals joined to one another for about half of their length. There are 10 pale yellow stamens, hairy at their bases. The flowers, produced singly or in clusters of 2 or 3, are borne on branches of the previous season's growth. The calyx is deciduous as a unit with the corolla, so the forest floor may be covered with what looks like intact white flowers. Tufts of rather thin, lance-shaped leaves, shiny green above and paler beneath, with smooth margins, grow at the ends of the branches. These branches are seldom more than 3 feet (1 m) tall and are sparsely covered with reddish-brown glandular hairs. With the approach of autumn the leaves turn spectacular shades of bronze, crimson, and orange before they fall.

Range: throughout the Rockies, excluding Wyoming, Utah, and New Mexico.

American Licorice
Glycyrrhiza lepidota

PEA FAMILY
Fabaceae

American Licorice is a coarse perennial, 12–40 inches (30–100 cm) tall, arising from a thick rootstock that has a slight licorice flavor. Leaves consist of 11 to 19 pale green leaflets with conspicuous yellow-brown glands on the lower surface. Numerous showy yellowish-white flowers are borne on short stalks in dense racemes. Reddish-brown fruits, which are densely beset with short hooked prickles and which persist on the stem through the winter, follow them. The rootstocks were roasted and eaten by Native Americans, who used the plant for a number of other purposes including remedies for fever, toothaches, and earaches. This plant occurs throughout the aspen parkland and prairies on moist slopes, coulees, river banks, and slough margins.

Range: throughout the Rockies.

Inset photo by George Scotter

White Sweetvetch is a herb 12–24 inches (30–60 cm) tall, usually with a single erect stem growing from a stout, somewhat woody, perennial rootstock. Its leaves consist of 9 to 17 leaflets, which have obvious veins. The small, creamy white flowers are in a rather open cluster at the end of a stalk that arises from the upper leaf axils. Drooping seedpods, about 1 inch (2.5 cm) long, replace the flowers. As with Utah Sweetvetch, the constrictions between each seed in the pod easily distinguish this hedysarum from milkvetches and locoweeds, whose flowers may look similar but whose pods are shaped more like those of garden peas. This unmistakable plant grows in dense clumps along stream banks, in moist woods, and occasionally in alpine sites. White Sweetvetch is a very important food plant for bears. They eat the roots in spring and fall.

Range: throughout the Rockies, excluding Utah, Colorado, and New Mexico.

White Sweetvetch
Hedysarum sulphurescens

PEA FAMILY
Fabaceae

The white to creamy flowers of Whitish Gentian are funnel-shaped and usually in terminal pairs. The calyx has 5 pointed lobes about ¾ inch (2 cm) long. These lobes are strongly mottled or streaked with purple on the outside and have purple dots on the inside. Its stems, up to 8 inches (20 cm) tall, are yellowish-green with linear-oblong leaves that are single veined. A late summer bloomer, Whitish Gentian grows in alpine and subalpine meadows. *Algida* is Latin for "cold" and an apt description for the habitat in which this plant grows.

Range: Montana, Wyoming, Utah, Colorado, and New Mexico.

Whitish Gentian; Arctic Gentian
Gentiana algida

GENTIAN FAMILY
Gentianaceae

Richardson's Geranium
Geranium richardsonii

GERANIUM FAMILY
Geraniaceae

Richardson's Geranium, 12–32 inches (30–80 cm) high, is one of the most appealing plants found in aspen glades along the lower slopes of the mountains. The shapely leaves accentuate the open, gleaming white petals, often with pink or purple veins. The long-petioled, opposite leaves are sparsely hairy, deeply lobed, and split into 3 to 7 toothed divisions. When ripe, the long-beaked capsule splits into 5 portions lengthways from the bottom, and does so with enough force to catapult the seeds some distance from the parent plant, thus reducing competition with future generations of geraniums.

Range: throughout the Rockies.

Lewis' Mock Orange; Syringa
Philadelphus lewisii

HYDRANGEA FAMILY
Hydrangeaceae

Lewis' Mock Orange, the state flower of Idaho, is an erect, deciduous shrub up to 9 feet (3 m) tall. Captain Meriwether Lewis first collected it in Idaho and the specific name honors him. Syringa is another commonly used name. On mature plants the reddish brown bark checks in strips and eventually flakes off, revealing grayish bark beneath. The leaves are opposite each other on the stem and are oval to egg-shaped with 3 major veins from the leaf base. Each flower has 4 petals enclosing numerous yellow stamens and a single pistil. The common name, Lewis' Mock Orange, is derived from the sweet-scented, orange-blossom aroma of the flowers. This shrub is widely used for horticultural purposes. Lewis' Mock Orange is found on rocky slopes, forest edges, and in open Ponderosa Pine and Douglas-fir forests.

Range: Alberta and British Columbia, Montana, Idaho, Washington, and Oregon.

This densely hairy perennial grows from a stout rootstock, producing stems 6–16 inches (15–40 cm) high. The leaves are smooth-margined and lance-shaped, with conspicuous lateral veins that converge toward the tip. As suggested by the common name, they appear a dull gray, being covered with dense, fine, fuzzy hairs and long, flattened, coarse hairs. Numerous flowers in separate dense clusters are located at the top of each branching stem. Although mostly cream-colored to nearly white, the flowers may occasionally be pinkish or bluish. The filaments are usually bearded, protruding out of the flower. Silverleaf Phacelia is common on dry, exposed rocky slopes at middle elevations.

Range: throughout the Rockies, excluding New Mexico.

Silverleaf Phacelia
Phacelia hastata

WATERLEAF FAMILY
Hydrophyllaceae

Often splashed by the water that drips from melting snows, Sitka Mistmaiden is one of the alpine glories of the Rockies. The basal leaves have 5 to 9 lobes, and the petioles are about twice as long as the blades; there are few, if any, stem leaves. The frail stems seem scarcely strong enough to lift the delicate blossoms above the large, kidney-shaped leaves. The white to cream-colored flowers, each with a vivid golden-yellow eye, add a charming contrast to the rock crevices in which they grow. The 5 petals are funnel-like at the base, with rounded lobes forming about mid-length. The stamens have white anthers and are uneven in length, while the strap-like sepals are purplish-green. Numerous seeds are contained within the 2-valved fruit.

Range: Alberta, British Columbia, Washington, Oregon, Idaho, and Montana.

Sitka Mistmaiden
Romanzoffia sitchensis

WATERLEAF FAMILY
Hydrophyllaceae

Gunnison's Mariposa Lily
Calochortus gunnisonii

LILY FAMILY
Liliaceae

Growing from deeply buried, fleshy bulbs, the unbranched stems of Gunnison's Mariposa Lily are 4–12 inches (10 to 30 cm) tall. Leaves are grass-like, entire, parallel veined, rolled inward making a trough, and reduced in size upward on the stem. Stems often terminate in a single flower but occasionally more. Goblet-shaped flowers are upward facing with 3 translucent, narrow, greenish sepals and 3 broad petals that range in color from white, cream, pink, or purple. The lower interior has a broad crescent of yellow hairs above an elliptically shaped glandular structure on each petal. A deep purple band often separates the hairy part of the petal from the upper portion. Native American people and European settlers dug the nutritious bulbs and used them like potatoes or dried and ground them for flour. Winding Mariposa (*C. flexuosus*) and Sego Lily (*C. nuttallii*), the state flower of Utah, share a somewhat similar range within the Rockies. These lovely plants are found in meadows, open woods, and shrublands from the montane to subalpine zones.

Range: Montana, Wyoming, Utah, Colorado, and New Mexico.

Bride's Bonnet; Bluebead Lily
Clintonia uniflora

LILY FAMILY
Liliaceae

Bride's Bonnet challenges most mountain flowering plants to surpass its charm and simple, delicate beauty. The slender stem, about 6 inches (15 cm) tall, bears 1 (occasionally 2) saucer-shaped, 6-pointed, pure white flower with a crown of golden anthers. The plant has 2 or 3 large, glossy green basal leaves. Both the stems and leaves are clothed with fine white hairs. A shiny, deep blue, bead-like berry succeeds the short-lived flower, which in its own way is as elegant as the blossom it replaced. This attractive lily prefers a mossy habitat in the shade of coniferous forests.

Range: Alberta, British Columbia, Washington, Oregon, Idaho, and Montana.

Feathery False Lily Of The Valley has arching or erect stems up to 3 feet (1 m) tall that arise from a fleshy underground stem. The large, sharply pointed, oval to broadly lance-shaped leaves either clasp around the stem or are attached by short petioles. These prominently veined leaves are a handsome setting for the terminal cluster of many minute white flowers. The flowers have long stamens and a redolent fragrance. Pea-sized, bright red berries, often dotted with purple, mature later in the season. This lovely plant is common in moist, shaded woodland habitats.

Range: throughout the Rockies.

Feathery False Lily of the Valley

Maianthemum racemosum
[*Smilacina racemosa*]

LILY FAMILY
Liliaceae

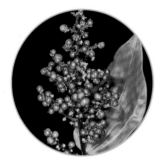

Each unbranched stem of this elegant little plant supports 7 to 13 stiffly arranged, pale blue-green leaves. The leaves are strongly veined and they zigzag up the stem. A few to several widely spaced flowers are borne at the tip. The star-shaped flowers are of the purest white and they have 6 petals, which are longer than the stamens. The fruits of this plant take the form of berries which are at first greenish, marked with 3 red stripes, but nearly black when ripe. The powdered root was reportedly applied to wounds to help in the clotting of blood. Starry False Lily Of The Valley is widespread and can be seen in woodlands and open meadows.

Range: throughout the Rockies.

Starry False Lily of the Valley

Maianthemum stellatum
[*S. stellata*]

LILY FAMILY
Liliaceae

Roughfruit Fairybells
Prosartes trachycarpa

LILY FAMILY
Liliaceae

This common woodland plant has crinkly-edged, veiny leaves, almost as wide as they are long, which clasp around the stalks. From 1 to 4 whitish to greenish-yellow flowers droop from the tips of the slender stalks. The flowers are like little bells in bud, but they are much more ragged when fully open. They give way to bright orange-red berries with wart-like projections on the surface. Although other lily species produce poisonous fruit, these berries are edible either cooked or raw. Roughfruit Fairybells bloom in spring and early summer.

Range: throughout the Rockies.

Western Featherbells; Bronze Bells
Stenanthium occidentale

LILY FAMILY
Liliaceae

Western Featherbells have grass-like leaves that emerge from an onion-like bulb. The bell-shaped flowers, greenish and flecked with purple, have 6 sharply pointed tips that twist backward, exposing the interior of the blossom. Ten or more flowers hang gracefully from each stem, 12–20 inches (30–50 cm) tall. The fruit is a sharp-pointed, erect pod. The tangy fragrance from the flowers of this curiously charming plant can be enjoyed in the moist, shaded woodlands where it is found.

Range: Alberta, British Columbia, Washington, Oregon, Idaho, and Montana.

This plant has a widely branching zigzag stem. Numerous sharply pointed, parallel-veined leaves encircle the stem at each angular bend. These graceful, glossy leaves often conceal the 1 or 2 dainty little flowers dangling on curving thread-like stalks from the axil of each of the upper leaves. Each white to greenish-yellow flower has strongly reflexed petals and sepals. Shiny orange or red berries, which are oblong and contain numerous seeds, replace the flowers. Claspleaf Twistedstalk favors moist, shaded forests at middle elevations.

Range: throughout the Rockies.

Claspleaf Twistedstalk
Streptopus amplexifolius

LILY FAMILY
Liliaceae

A distinctive feature of this plant is the upper portion of the flowering stem, which is glandular and sticky. White flowers are clustered at the tips of the stems, their dark anthers conspicuous against the white of the petals. Erect, plump, reddish seed capsules develop after the flowers fade. The 3 or 4 leaves are basal and grass-like and about half the length of the stems. Search for Sticky Tofieldia along the edges of open bogs or ponds. Scotch False Asphodel (*T. pusilla*) grows in similar habitats, but its stems are thinner and are not sticky.

Range: Alberta, British Columbia, and Oregon.

Sticky Tofieldia
Triantha glutinosa
[Tofieldia glutinosa]

LILY FAMILY
Liliaceae

Pacific Trillium
Trillium ovatum

LILY FAMILY
Liliaceae

Pacific Trillium is one of spring's showiest woodland wildflowers. The genus name *Trillium* refers to the 3 leaves, 3 petals, and 3 sepals. Each stem, 8-16 inches (20-40 cm) tall, produces a single, striking white flower that turns pink through purple with age. This flower is regally perched above a ring of 3 broadly ovate leaves, which are sharply tipped. The fruit is a fleshy green pod with winged ridges. This interesting plant favors damp, protected habitats with rich soil in lowland forests.

Range: throughout the Rockies, excluding Utah and New Mexico.

California False Hellebore
Veratrum californicum

LILY FAMILY
Liliaceae

A robust member of the lily family, California False Hellebore is a coarse perennial growing 3-6 feet (1-2 m) tall from thick rootstocks. Leaves are numerous, alternate, broadly elliptic, sessile, 8-12 inches (20-30 cm) long, 2¾-5 inches (7-13 cm) broad, and strongly sheathed at the base. Stems are densely hairy upward, but the lower foliage is glabrous. The inflorescence at the top of the central stem is a dense branching panicle 12-24 inches (30-60 cm) long. Flowers are 6-parted and can be white, yellowish, or greenish tinged. Fruits contain yellowish, winged seeds. California False Hellebore is toxic to humans and livestock, causing congenital deformities as well as abortion. This deadly plant is found in swamps, seeps, stream bottoms, wet meadows, and moist woodlands from the montane to subalpine zones.

Range: throughout the Rockies excluding Alberta, British Columbia, and Colorado.

Once seen, Common Beargrass's torch-like cluster of hundreds of small creamy white flowers rising from the large tuft of stiff, grass-like leaves will not be forgotten. A dense basal clump of sharp-edged evergreen leaves, 16–20 inches (40–50 cm) long, rises from a thick rootstock. The spectacular stem, unbranched for 20–48 inches (50–120 cm) of its length, is covered with shorter needle-like leaves and holds aloft the great plume of flowers, each of which is a miniature lily. The lowermost flowers are the first to open. Position of the flowers varies with the stage of growth: in bud they are pressed to the stem; in bloom they stand out at a sharp angle; and in fruit they are again erect along the stem. Some flower stalks exhibit knee-like curves; these are thought to occur during long rainy periods when the head is bowed down and the stalk matures in that position. Individual plants may be sterile for several years, with flowers present only 1 to 3 times in a 10-year period. Native Americans are reported to have used the leaves for weaving hats, capes, and baskets. Rocky Mountain goats eat the mature leaves, bears graze the softer leaf bases in the early spring, and bighorn sheep, deer, and elk feed on the flower clusters and stems. Common Beargrass is found on dry hillsides, coniferous forests, avalanche slopes, and subalpine meadows.

Range: throughout the Rockies, excluding Utah, Colorado, and New Mexico.

Common Beargrass
Xerophyllum tenax

LILY FAMILY
Liliaceae

Mountain Deathcamas
Zigadenus elegans

LILY FAMILY
Liliaceae

This handsome plant, from 12–24 inches (30–60 cm) tall, grows from a blackish-coated bulb 2¾–6 inches (7–15 cm) below the ground surface. Its V-shaped, smooth, grass-like leaves are slightly curved lengthwise and somewhat bluish-green in color. The stems are slender, often pinkish, and terminate in a graceful spray of dainty greenish- to yellowish-white flowers. These 6-parted flowers are ⅜–¾ inch (1–2 cm) across, and both sepals and petals have round, greenish glands near the base. Though an attractive plant to look at, the flowers smell foul. The mature capsule has 3 lobes and many seeds. Like other members of this genus, it contains an alkaloid and all parts can be poisonous to humans and grazing animals. Mountain Deathcamas may be found in open meadows from low elevations to alpine areas.

Range: throughout the Rockies.

Meadow Deathcamas
Zigadenus venenosus

LILY FAMILY
Liliaceae

Meadow Deathcamas is of considerable interest and charm without being spectacular in any way. Its narrow, green, grass-like leaves, sheathing at the base, form loose tufts from which rise stems 8–16 inches (20–40 cm) tall, carrying racemes of greenish white to creamy white flowers. This plant can be distinguished from Mountain Deathcamas by its much more compact spike of smaller flowers. The onion-like bulb is extremely poisonous, especially to sheep. Native Americans and early settlers sometimes confused these bulbs, often with deadly results, with those of Small Camas, a staple spring food. For that reason Meadow Deathcamas plants were regularly dug out and destroyed in some of the favorite camas-gathering areas. Mashed bulbs of this plant were used as an external cure for boils and rheumatism and in easing pain caused by bruises and sprains. Flowering in the early summer, Meadow Deathcamas is a fairly common plant on prairies and moist meadows.

Range: throughout the Rockies.

White Checkerbloom spreads easily by rhizomes and seeds, growing straight and slim, 20–35 inches (50–90 cm) tall. Lower leaves are rounded with 5 or more lobes and toothed; upper leaves are deeply divided into 5 or more narrow lobes. The hollyhock-like flowers are white to cream, 2 inches (5 cm) across, with red stamens. Salt Spring Checkerbloom (*S. neomexicana*) has rose-magenta flowers and is more widely distributed. This attractive and conspicuous plant is at home in riparian areas such as wetlands, wet meadow, and the edges of streams from the montane to subalpine zones.

Range: Wyoming, Colorado, Utah, and New Mexico.

White Checkerbloom
Sidalcea candida

MALLOW FAMILY
Malvaceae

An easily recognized aquatic to semi-aquatic perennial, Buckbean has 3-parted elliptical leaflets at the top of procumbent stems growing from creeping rootstocks. The leaflets are about 2 inches (5 cm) long and 1 inch (2.5 cm) broad. Flowers are borne on long, leafless stalks, 6–14 inches (15–35 cm) high, rising above the leaves and rendering them very conspicuous. Arranged in spikes of 10 to 20, the funnel-shaped flowers are outwardly white or pink-tinged, and inwardly white, conspicuously fringed with hairs, and with red stamens. The rank smell of the flowers attracts bees, beetles, and flies to ensure pollination. Seed capsules contain many buoyant yellow-brown seeds. Wetlands such as ponds, bogs, wet meadows, and lake margins at low to mid elevations are favored habitats for Buckbean.

Range: throughout the Rockies.

Buckbean
Menyanthes trifoliata

BUCKBEAN FAMILY
Menyanthaceae

Pinesap
Monotropa hypopithys

INDIAN PIPE FAMILY
Monotropaceae

There is no chlorophyll in Pinesap, so its root system is parasitic on saprophytic fungi in the forest humus as a source of nourishment. The entire plant is straw-colored to white, occasionally pink to reddish. Its unbranched fleshy stems have leaves that have been reduced to small scales. Each nodding, urn-shaped flower has 4 or 5 petals and 4 or 5 sepals; the terminal flower is the largest, with 5 petals, while the lower ones are smaller, generally with 4 petals. The broad stigma protrudes beyond the petals and the stamens are usually double the number of petals. As the flowers mature they change from a hanging to an erect position. This unique and curious plant is rare. Search for it in deeply shaded pinewoods.

Range: throughout the Rockies, excluding Utah.

Indianpipe
Monotropa uniflora

INDIAN PIPE FAMILY
Monotropaceae

Strange and exquisite, the ghostlike Indianpipe has lost the green pigment of the plant world. Like tiny shepherds'crooks, its white stems rise 4–10 inches (10–25 cm) above the leaf litter. They bear solitary bell-shaped flowers that droop downward. The translucent white flowers, rarely pinkish, are waxy to the touch. As the seeds ripen the stem straightens and becomes enveloped in a habit of black. Its leaves are reduced to colorless scales along the stem. Not rushing through its life cycles with the first warmth of spring like many of its neighbors, Indianpipe loiters and is not seen before summer. This eerie and unusual wildflower's nourishment is derived from fungi that digest dead organic matter in the soil. A fugitive from strong sunlight, Indianpipe is found in moist, deeply shaded woods from the foothills to the subalpine zone.

Range: Alberta, British Columbia, Montana, Idaho, Washington, and Oregon.

Tufted Evening-primrose is a low, tufted perennial growing from woody roots. Stems, if present, are very short. The radiating basal leaves are fleshy, 4-10 inches (10-25 cm) long with winged stalks, lance to spoon-shaped, wavy-edged, and generally toothed and hairy. Fragrant, cup-shaped blossoms, up to 3 inches (8 cm) across, are white on opening but soon fade to pink. Flowers have 4 heart-shaped petals that have slight indentations at the tips, 4 hairy sepals that reflex downward from the petals, a 4-parted stigma lobe on the end of the style, and 8 stamens. The flowers have long floral tubes that may appear to be stems. The showy flowers open late in the day to attract night-flying moths for pollination. Lasting only until the following morning, the flower wilts and turns pink. This appealing plant grows in dry, open sites, often with clay soil, from the plains to the subalpine zone.

Range: throughout the Rockies, excluding British Columbia.

Tufted Evening-primrose
Oenothera caespitosa

EVENING PRIMROSE FAMILY
Onagraceae

This exquisite orchid arises from thick, fleshy roots in bogs and moist, cool coniferous woods. A single elliptic or oval leaf cradles a slender, leafless stem 4-10 inches (10-25 cm) high. Commonly, 3 to 8 flowers are spaced along the upper end of the stem. A distinguishing feature of this flower is the white, tongue-like lip, speckled with minute dots of magenta. The lip is 3-lobed, the middle lobe being the largest and having a notch at the end. It is covered by a rose- to white-colored bonnet formed by the sepals and 2 lateral petals. The spur is stout and slightly curved.

Range: Alberta, British Columbia, Idaho, Montana, and Wyoming.

Roundleaf Orchid
Amerorchis rotundifolia
[Orchis rotundifolia]

ORCHID FAMILY
Orchidaceae

Mountain Lady's Slipper
Cypripedium montanum

ORCHID FAMILY
Orchidaceae

Among the showiest of orchids in the Rockies, Mountain Lady's Slipper occurs in open woods. This relative of Greater Yellow Lady's Slipper grows at higher elevations. Rising from a cord-like rhizome, the stems bear 4 to 6 hairy leaves. These lance-shaped leaves clasp the stem and have numerous parallel veins that converge at the pointed tips. At the top of the stem, up to 3 widely spreading, delightfully scented flowers develop. Both the sepals and petals are richly marked with brown. The thin, pointed petals are spirally twisted. The lip is the most distinctive feature of the flower, being a luminous white slipper or pouch, delicately veined at the base with purple. There are also colorful spots of purple within the slipper and a yellow tongue extends outward from above the slipper's opening.

Range: throughout the Rockies, excluding Utah, Colorado, and New Mexico.

Sparrowegg Lady's Slipper
Cypripedium passerinum

ORCHID FAMILY
Orchidaceae

This small-flowered plant was given the name *passerinum*, meaning "sparrow-like," because the flower forms an inflated and sac-like pouch that is spotted like a sparrow's egg and about the same shape and size. The pouch is white, rarely pink, with bright purple dots on the interior. The sepals are short, stubby, and greenish in color. The stems, which are 6–14 inches (15–35 cm) tall, grow from a fibrous rootstock and have large, prominently veined, clasping leaves. Both stems and leaves are covered with soft hairs. This little gem will be found in deep mossy coniferous forests, on gravel outwashes, and on the borders of ponds and streams. Picking this flower is particularly destructive: the flower quickly wilts, while the plant dies.

Range: Alberta, British Columbia, and Montana.

The gleaming white flowers of this graceful orchid are ¾–1¼ inch (2–3 cm) wide. Twenty or more of them will be clustered 28–40 inches (70–100 cm) above the ground, near the top of a smooth stem. The lip of the flower, conspicuously widened at the base, narrows toward the tip. A spur, usually as long as the lip, projects backward from the rest of the flower. Two yellow stamens enhance the waxy whiteness of the flower. Scentbottle is strongly perfumed, like a blending of cloves, vanilla, and mock orange. The rather succulent leaves, up to 8 inches (20 cm) long, decrease in size up the stem. Bogs, wet ditches, and seepages are favored habitats for this regal beauty.

Range: throughout the Rockies.

Scentbottle; Tall White Bog Orchid
Platanthera dilatata
[Habenaria dilatata]

ORCHID FAMILY
Orchidaceae

Hooded Lady's Tresses are one of the most common orchids in the Rocky Mountains. A characteristic feature is the crowded flower spike, which is so tightly twisted as to produce 3-ranked rows of overlapping, creamy white flowers. Like other orchids, each flower consists of 3 sepals and 3 petals, with the stamens and pistil combined into one unit. The upper sepals and petals are united into an overhanging hood that looks like the peak of an old-fashioned sunbonnet. Some flower lovers feel that the spiral spike bears a fanciful resemblance to neatly braided hair; hence the common name. Check this quaint orchid's flowers for a strong vanilla-like scent. The broad grass-like leaves, 2–6 inches (5–15 cm) long, are mostly near the base of the stem. This plant is found in wet meadows, seepage areas, and on damp grassy slopes.

Range: throughout the Rockies.

Hooded Lady's Tresses
Spiranthes romanzoffiana

ORCHID FAMILY
Orchidaceae

Crested Pricklypoppy
Argemone polyanthemos

POPPY FAMILY
Papaveraceae

A sun-loving annual or biennial, Crested Pricklypoppy grows from a deep taproot and produces a stout, upright prickly stem about 3 feet (1 m) tall. Leaves are alternate, bluish-green, up to 8 inches (20 cm) long, thick textured, glaucous, clasping, and with sharp, yellow spines on the margins and along the main veins on the underside. The spectacular flowers are up to 5 inches (12 cm) across with 4 to 6 satiny, snowy white petals and many golden stamens. The stem, when broken, will ooze a sticky, bright yellow-orange sap. This plant is poisonous, but seldom grazed due to its spines. Highly visible, Crested Pricklypoppy prefers disturbed areas with sandy soil from the plains to foothills.

Range: throughout the Rockies, excluding Alberta, British Columbia, and Oregon.

Cushion Phlox;
Alpine Phlox
Phlox pulvinata

PHLOX FAMILY
Polemoniaceae

This compact perennial grows on stems less than 4 inches (10 cm) tall. Cushion Phlox has sticky, hairy foliage that forms cushion-like mats, as suggested by its specific name *pulvinata* meaning "cushion-like." A single flower is borne atop each short stem. The 5 petals are usually white or pale blue and unite into a funnel-shaped tube at the base and flare open at the top. Cushion Phlox inhabits rocky, sun-washed areas mainly in the alpine zone. In some parts of the Rockies it may share its alpine habitat with two other white flowered phlox. Flowery Phlox (*P. multiflora*) has longer leaves and Dwarf Phlox (*P. condensata*) has shorter leaves.

Range: throughout the Rockies excluding Alberta and British Columbia.

American Bistort is a perennial with thick and knotted rhizomes. While the stem leaves are much reduced in size and sessile, the dark green basal leaves are lance-shaped with long petioles. The red stems are erect, from 8-24 inches (20-60 cm) tall. The clustered flowers are white with a blush of pink and broadly funnel-shaped, with red stamens and pink bracts; they have an unpleasant scent. Some Native Americans so prized the rhizomes for soup and stews that tribes fought over the right to live in areas that contained the plant. When roasted over a campfire, the rhizomes provided a nutritious, nut-like snack. The tart-tasting leaves and stems are also edible. Bears enjoy the rhizomes, and deer and elk graze the leaves and stems. Moist to wet meadows and stream banks from the montane to alpine zones are preferred habitats for this interesting, useful, and often abundant plant.

Range: throughout the Rockies.

American Bistort
Polygonum bistortoides

BUCKWHEAT FAMILY
Polygonaceae

A slender, unbranched perennial, 4-5 inches (10-13 cm) tall, Alpine Bistort grows from a starchy, edible rootstock. There is a cluster of petioled basal leaves, which are lance-shaped, dark green, and shiny. Stem leaves are few and small in size. White or pink flowers with protruding, fuzzy-looking stamens cluster on the stem. *Viviparum* means "to bring forth live young" and refers to the tiny pinkish-purple bulblets on the lower part of the stem, each capable of producing a new plant while still attached to the parent. The rootstocks may be eaten raw or cooked, and are said to taste like almonds. Leaves may be included in salads or cooked as a potherb. A yellow dye can be produced from the stem. Alpine Bistort is a common plant in alpine meadows and at the margins of lakes and streams.

Range: throughout the Rockies.

Alpine Bistort
Polygonum viviparum

BUCKWHEAT FAMILY
Polygonaceae

Lanceleaf Springbeauty
Claytonia lanceolata

PURSLANE FAMILY
Portulacaceae

These attractive and abundant plants grow from small underground corms about ¾ inch (2 cm) in diameter. The plants have several green to reddish stems with 2 opposite lance-shaped leaves on each. From 3 to 15 flowers, clustered on a one-sided raceme, bloom above the succulent leaves. Each flower has 5 petals, cupped in 2 sepals. Slightly notched at the top, the petals are white to pink in color and attractively streaked with rose or purple veins that join at the base. As suggested by its name, this is one of the earliest flowers to bloom, sprouting as the snowbanks retreat from the valley floor, though it will not be seen on alpine slopes until later. The dense mounds of emerald-green leaves and star-shaped flowers are soon concealed by the vigorous growth of other forbs and grasses. The corms used to be dug in the spring by Native Americans and were eaten as we would potatoes. Grizzly bears and smaller animals, as evidenced by numerous diggings, know these buried treasures as well.

Range: throughout the Rockies.

Alpine Springbeauty
Claytonia megarhiza

PURSLANE FAMILY
Portulacaceae

As the scientific name *megarhiza* suggests, this plant grows from a fleshy, swollen taproot rather than from a corm. Alpine Springbeauty in bloom is very similar to Lanceleaf Springbeauty, but may be distinguished by its tufts of spoon-shaped, reddish-green, basal leaves. The exquisite pink to white flowers are often obscured by narrow stem leaves. Both the leaves and stems are usually tinged with red. This glamorous and rather rare plant, confined to alpine scree slopes, flowers in mid-summer.

Range: throughout the Rockies.

Sweetflower Rockjasmine is a small perennial, which grows in tufts at intervals along a creeping stem, producing crowded rosettes of very small linear leaves covered with stiff hairs. These miniature rosettes of tiny leaves support a short stem that bears at its summit a compact cluster of dainty, sweet-scented flowers. The flowers are a soft creamy white with a yellow, orange, or pinkish eye at the center. This tiny plant prefers open slopes, meadows, ledges, and screes from subalpine to alpine elevations.

Range: throughout the Rockies, excluding Washington, Oregon, and Idaho.

Sweetflower Rockjasmine
Androsace chamaejasme
PRIMROSE FAMILY
Primulaceae

Tiny and delicate, Pygmyflower Rockjasmine is often masked by larger plants and is easily missed. This annual has a basal rosette with numerous leaves that range from sparsely to densely hairy. Anywhere from 3 to 20 flowering stalks, 4–8 inches (10–20 cm) tall, rise above the basal rosette. The minute flowers are white, often with a pink tinge. The corolla has a short tube that spreads out to a saucer shape at the open end. Flowering plants can be found throughout the growing season. Pygmyflower Rockjasmine is widespread, particularly on disturbed soil, from the plains to the alpine zone.

Range: throughout the Rockies.

Pygmyflower Rockjasmine; Northern Fairy Candelabra
Androsace septentrionalis
PRIMROSE FAMILY
Primulaceae

Single Delight
Moneses uniflora

SHINLEAF FAMILY
Pyrolaceae

Less than 4 inches (10 cm) tall, this small perennial has a basal rosette of rounded, veiny, and shallowly toothed leaves. Each leafless stalk supports one winsome nodding flower. Each flower has ivory-white petals, 10 greenish stamens, and a conspicuously long style extending from the center. Note the wavy petal margins. It is worth getting down on your hands and knees to discover the lovely fragrance of the flower. Although the flower nods while in bloom, the fruit lengthens and straightens to an upright brown capsule when mature. This delightful, large-flowered plant grows in mossy carpets within coniferous forests.

Range: throughout the Rockies.

Red Baneberry
Actaea rubra

BUTTERCUP FAMILY
Ranunculaceae

This perennial herb, 20–40 inches (50–100 cm) tall, is better known for its berries than for its flowers. Scores of very small flowers, with 3 to 5 white petal-like sepals and 5 to 10 white petals, form a rounded cluster on an elongated stalk. Neither sepals nor petals remain for long, and they fall at the slightest touch. The conspicuous fruits, about the size of a pea, come in two color phases, a lustrous coral-red and a startling ivory-white. These fruits are surrounded by large handsome leaves; they are thin, delicate, and 3-parted with many deeply saw-toothed, pointed leaflets. All parts of the plant, including the berries, contain a poisonous compound. Native Americans are reported to have boiled the roots and used the decoction to treat coughs and colds and also to treat sick horses. This woodland dweller may be found in moist coniferous forests.

Range: throughout the Rockies.

Another elegant member of the alpine community, this plant flowers near the edge of retreating snowbanks. A cluster of petioled, deeply dissected basal leaves grows from a thick, branched rootstock. Midway up the stem there is a collar of similar but smaller leaves. Fine woolly hairs protect all above-ground parts of the plant. The striking flowers are creamy white inside and tinged with pastel blue on the outside. Each solitary flower, which is short-lived, consists of 5 to 7 sepals and numerous pistils and stamens; there are no petals. The transitory flowers are soon replaced by tiny woolly "thimbles" containing round, black achenes.

Range: Alberta, British Columbia, Washington, Oregon, and Idaho.

Drummond's Anemone
Anemone drummondii

BUTTERCUP FAMILY
Ranunculaceae

Like all anemones, Pacific Anemone possesses no petals, only sepals. But the sepals display a joyous array of colors ranging from white, yellowish, or red on the inside to bluish or reddish on the outside. Deeply divided, feathery, basal leaves and a collar of 3 stem leaves complement these varied hues. Leaves, petioles, and flowering stems are densely hairy. The 5 to 10 blunt-tipped sepals give way to a seedhead of woolly achenes. Pacific Anemone is wide ranging, from dry grassy slopes to lowland and alpine meadows. It blooms from spring through early summer.

Range: throughout the Rockies.

Pacific Anemone; Wind Flower
Anemone multifida

BUTTERCUP FAMILY
Ranunculaceae

Smallflowered Anemone
Anemone parviflora

BUTTERCUP FAMILY
Ranunculaceae

Smallflowered Anemone prefers moist soils from lowland floodplains to stream banks above the timberline. The stalk is 6–8 inches (15–30 cm) tall and supports a single flower. The flower has 5 or 6 creamy white sepals, which are always hairy and usually tinged with blue-purple on the back. The oval-shaped fruiting cluster is covered by dense, white, woolly hair. The basal leaves are few in number, long-petioled and divided into 3 leaflets, which are cleft about halfway and have blunt teeth on the margins. Bracts on the elongating stalk have 3 lobes and are deeply cleft. Depending on the altitude, the plant may flower from June through August.

Range: throughout the Rockies, excluding New Mexico.

White Marsh Marigold
Caltha leptosepala

BUTTERCUP FAMILY
Ranunculaceae

These white flowers, commonly tinged with blue on the back, brighten marshes, stream banks, and seepage slopes below melting snowbanks near the timberline. Each flower is composed of 5 to 10 petal-like segments that appear at the end of a smooth, hollow, pinkish stem. The open flower measures up to 1½ inches (4 cm) across and has a bright yellow center composed of stamens and pistils. A perennial, the plant has soft green, somewhat fleshy, heart-shaped leaves, mostly at the base of the stem. The seeds are borne in top-shaped clusters of papery pods. Despite its harmless appearance, this plant is known to be poisonous to livestock.

Range: throughout the Rockies.

These large, creamy white flowers, with a bluish cast underneath, open early in the spring, as their leaves are beginning to emerge. Borne on woolly stems, the flowers brighten the slopes with their showy cups, half-filled with stamens that wreath their centers like golden crowns. Gray-green feathery leaves below the bloom expand during the summer. The sepals soon fall and are followed by a tousled top of plumed seeds at the tip of now tall stems. The plants are sometimes called "towhead babies" because of the fuzzy appearance of the fruiting heads. The fall winds carry away the seeds, whose feathery tails act as parachutes in the dispersal to new habitats. White Pasqueflower is a characteristic plant of wet alpine meadows and clearings in the timberline zone where snow remains late.

White Pasqueflower; Towhead Babies
Pulsatilla occidentalis
[Anemone occidentalis]

BUTTERCUP FAMILY
Ranunculaceae

Range: Alberta, British Columbia, Washington, Oregon, Idaho, and Montana.

Bright little white flowers, often flecked with gold at the base, are buoyed above the water surface on short stalks. This aquatic buttercup has 2 types of leaves. The submerged ones are divided into thread-like filaments while the few floating ones, when present, are deeply cleft into 3 to 5 lobes. In addition to the yellow flecks at the base of the petals, numerous stamens and pistils attract insects that pollinate the flowers. White Water Crowfoot sometimes entirely covers shallow ponds, lakes, ditches, and streams with its showy blossoms.

Range: throughout the Rockies, excluding Colorado and New Mexico.

White Water Crowfoot
Ranunculus aquatilis

BUTTERCUP FAMILY
Ranunculaceae

American Globeflower
Trollius laxus

BUTTERCUP FAMILY
Ranunculaceae

This handsome plant has individual, snowy white flowers, about 1½ inches (4 cm) across, with golden centers. Lacking petals, these flowers consist of 5 to 10 petal-like sepals, bright yellow stamens, and green pistils. The undersides of the sepals have a rose-green tinge, which is most easily seen when the flowers are partly closed. At this stage they look like small globes, as suggested by the common name. The glistening, rich green leaves, deeply 5- to 7-parted, are mostly at the base of the stem. The top-shaped pod contains several seeds. American Globeflower is common in wet alpine meadows and along marshy borders of alpine and subalpine streams.

Range: throughout the Rockies, excluding New Mexico.

Snowbrush Ceanothus; Deerbrush; Wild Lilac
Ceanothus velutinus

BUCKTHORN FAMILY
Rhamnaceae

Known by several common names, Snowbrush Ceanothus is a beautiful, evergreen shrub 6-9 feet (2-3 m) tall and sprawling to 15 feet (5 m) across. It often forms thickets from basal sprouts. Young branches are smooth and light green, contrasting with the grayish-brown bark on the older branches. The egg-shaped, glossy green leaves are shiny above and have a velvety covering of hairs below. The upper surface of the leaves, buds and new growth exude a sticky substance with a sweet, spicy odor, especially when rubbed or when the weather is hot. Creamy white flowers in dense clusters up to 4¾ inches (12 cm) long adorn the ends of the branches, giving rise to the name Snowbrush Ceanothus. Hundreds of individual flowers are loosely arranged in clusters. Individual flowers have 5 sepals, 5 stamens and 5 hooded petals and 1 pistil with a 3 lobed stigma. Snowbrush Ceanothus produces heat-resistant seeds that are stimulated to germinate following fire. Bacteria in the root nodules of this shrub allow it to convert nitrogen from the air into a form useful to plants. Look for Snowbrush Ceanothus in moist to dry forest openings in the montane to lower subalpine zones, especially in recently burned areas.

Range: throughout the Rockies, excluding New Mexico.

Saskatoon Serviceberry
Amelanchier alnifolia

ROSE FAMILY
Rosaceae

Saskatoon Serviceberry is a shrub or small bushy tree, 3–24 feet (1–8 m) tall, often spreading by stolons and forming dense colonies. The reddish-brown branches become gray with age. The oval leaves are ¾–2 inches (2–5 cm) long, just a little longer than broad, with margins coarsely toothed on the outer half. Fragrant clusters of showy white flowers appear in late May or early June. The 5 petals are linear to oblong and are slightly twisted. When mature, the apple-like fruits, about ⅜ inch (1 cm) in diameter, become dark purple and are sought by both people and wildlife. They were regarded as the most important plant food of the Blackfoot people, being used fresh in soups, stews, and pemmican, and being dried for winter. Dried berries from this shrub were common articles of trade and the wood was prized for making arrows. Today the delicious berries are renowned for making excellent pies and preserves. Bears, chipmunks, squirrels, and a host of birds also relish the fruits. All of the native ungulates are fond of the leaves and twigs. Saskatoon Serviceberry is a common shrub in coulees, bluffs, and open woods.

Range: throughout the Rockies, excluding New Mexico.

Eightpetal Mountain-avens

Dryas octopetala

ROSE FAMILY
Rosaceae

Eightpetal Mountain-avens is one of the most abundant and attractive flowers of the alpine zone. It grows close to the ground, forming an evergreen mat in gravelly or stony dry places, and it blooms soon after the snow melts. Numerous creamy white flowers, with many yellow stamens, are contrasted against the low mat of leaves. The flowering stems rise 2½–6 inches (6–16 cm) above the matted leaves, depending on the degree of protection from the elements. Each flower has 8 petals, hence the name *octopetala*. As with the Drummond's Mountain-avens, the persistent styles lengthen into long feathery tails that serve as parachutes in spreading of the seeds. The rough-surfaced, leathery leaves have scalloped edges and are dark green above, with the underside coated by dense white hairs. Eightpetal Mountain-avens is superbly adapted to its rigorous environment. For example, the deeply anchored root and leathery leaves help the plant withstand winds at high elevations, while root nodules store nitrogen in a habitat where nutrients are generally washed out of the soil by melting snow. Both the blooms and the seed plumes can be used to produce a vivid green dye.

Range: throughout the Rockies, excluding New Mexico.

Virginia Strawberry

Fragaria virginiana

ROSE FAMILY
Rosaceae

The snowy white petals of the Virginia Strawberry contrast with their yellow centers and are accentuated by the plant's many-toothed, green leaflets. The Wild Strawberry is not unlike its cultivated cousin except that the flowers and fruits are generally smaller, and its fruit has an even more delectable flavor than the cultivated variety. Virginia Strawberry fruits are eaten by a number of birds and mammals, which disseminate the seeds in their droppings. Virginia Strawberry is common from the montane to the alpine region, but while it blooms profusely in the subalpine and alpine region, it frequently does not set fruit because of the cold nights and short growing season. Fresh or dried leaves from this plant can be used to prepare a tea which, being rich in vitamin C, is reported to prevent colds.

Range: throughout the Rockies.

Partridgefoot
Luetkea pectinata

ROSE FAMILY
Rosaceae

Extensive mats of this dwarf evergreen shrub are formed as it creeps on strawberry-like runners over the ground. Its leaves are crowded in basal tufts, and continue alternately up the 2–6 inches (5–15 cm) of the stem. The leaves are small, smooth, and deeply cleft into two, 3-parted sections. Small white (occasionally cream) flowers, with 4 to 6 pistils and about 20 stamens, cluster at the tips of erect stems. Some velvety green mats, which may be more than 3 feet (1 m) across, produce hundreds of such stems. Partridgefoot is generally a rare plant on the east side of the Continental Divide, but it is common in moist, shady areas around the timberline on the west side.

Range: Alberta, British Columbia, Washington, Oregon, Idaho, and

Tall Cinquefoil
Potentilla arguta

ROSE FAMILY
Rosaceae

Tall Cinquefoil is a densely hairy perennial growing from a central taproot. Stems are stout, 12–35 inches (30–90 cm) tall, and covered with sticky brown hairs. The toothed leaves are cleft into 7 to 11 leaflets and are covered with white hairs. The common name Cinquefoil means, "5-leaved." Most of the leaves are basal, although a few alternate along the stem. Several clusters of flowers are borne at the apex of the plant, with smaller ones on the side. Individual flowers have 5 white to cream petals, 5 green sepals, numerous golden stamens and a golden button in the center. Each flower is about ¾ inch (2 cm) across and resembles a strawberry blossom. Tall Cinquefoil is a common plant on a variety of dry and rocky soils in grasslands and woods.

Range: throughout the Rockies.

Chokecherry
Prunus virginiana

ROSE FAMILY
Rosaceae

Chokecherry is a conspicuous white-flowering shrub or small tree, up to 30 feet (10 m) tall, which is common in thickets, in open woods, and along streams. Attached by stout petioles, the leaves are 2–4 inches (5–10 cm) long, egg-shaped to broadly oval, with sharp, marginal teeth. The 5-petaled flowers, about ⅜ inch (1 cm) across, are borne in thick cylindrical clusters 2–6 inches (5–15 cm) long. There are about 20 stamens and they extend conspicuously beyond the petals. When ripe the fruit is less than ⅜ inch (1 cm) in diameter, has become red-purple to black, and is nearly all stone. These small cherries make excellent jelly, pancake syrup, and wine. Most people find the fresh fruits too bitter, but songbirds and mammals relish them. Native Americans used the berries in soups and stews and for mixing with pemmican. Other parts of the plant served several medicinal purposes. Deer, elk, and moose eat leaves and twigs of the shrub.

Range: throughout the Rockies.

American Red Raspberry
Rubus idaeus

ROSE FAMILY
Rosaceae

There is little need for a long description of this wild relative of the cultivated raspberry that frequents our gardens. While the plant is a perennial, flowers and fruits are produced only on second-year canes. This woody shrub has compound leaves composed of 3 to 7 oval-shaped leaflets which are white and pubescent beneath and dark green above, with coarsely toothed margins. Beware of the arching, reddish-green stems, from 20–60 inches (50 cm to 1.5 m) tall, because they are armed with prickles. The clusters of white flowers, with numerous stamens, later yield deliciously sweet, red fruits (numerous drupelets around a central core in proper botanical language). These were important sources of food for Native Americans, early explorers, and settlers. Jam from the fruit is excellent and tea brewed from the leaves is most acceptable. Several kinds of wildlife also relish the fruit. This widespread shrub may be particularly abundant in disturbed areas such as roadsides, recent burns, and stream banks where it may form dense tangles.

Range: throughout the Rockies.

Unlike the closely related raspberry, this vigorous shrub does not have prickles or spines. Between 20–80 inches (50–200 cm) tall, it has large leaves, each with 3 or 5 lobes and with jagged-toothed margins. These rich green, maple-like leaves enhance the background for the attractive white blooms with their central boss of golden stamens. There are usually 3 to 5 flowers in clusters at the ends of the branches. The bright red fruit, which looks like a flat raspberry, is edible but rather tasteless and very seedy. Thimbleberry often forms thickets on avalanche slopes and along the margins of forests.

Range: throughout the Rockies.

Thimbleberry
Rubus parviflorus

ROSE FAMILY
Rosaceae

Spireas are very showy shrubs found in the wild as well as in home gardens. White Spirea has cinnamon-brown bark on its erect stems, which are from 12–35 inches (30–90 cm) tall. The leaves are shiny green above and paler beneath, egg-shaped, and deeply notched toward the tips. The white flowers, occasionally tinged with pink, are only weakly scented. They are gathered in nearly flat-topped clusters about 1½ inches (4 cm) across. The flowers soon turn brownish and after fertilization give way to small, dry, pod-like fruits. White Spirea grows in clearings and on rocky slopes in the montane zone.

Range: throughout the Rockies, excluding Utah, Colorado, and New Mexico.

White Spirea
Spiraea betulifolia

ROSE FAMILY
Rosaceae

Northern Bedstraw
Galium boreale

MADDER FAMILY
Rubiaceae

Northern Bedstraw is one of the most common roadside and woodland plants. Its dense clusters of tiny, fragrant white flowers are familiar to many. The cross-like flowers, clustered at the tops of stems, each have 4 spreading petals that are joined at the base, but there are no sepals. Each flower produces a 2-parted fruit, splitting into separate bristly achenes at maturity. The smooth stems are square in cross section and bear whorls of 4 narrow, lance-like leaves, each with 3 veins. Some Native Americans used the roots of this plant to dye porcupine quills red and yellow. As suggested by the common name, the dried, sweet-smelling plants were once used to stuff mattresses.

Range: throughout the Rockies.

Bastard Toadflax
Comandra umbellata

SANDALWOOD FAMILY
Santalaceae

This erect, blue-green perennial grows from a white, creeping rootstock. Numerous lance-shaped leaves, often delicately flushed with pink, hug the 4-12 inch (10-30 cm) stem. The greenish-white sepals are separate above and fused into a small funnel below. There are no petals. The flowers are in rounded or flat-topped clusters at the summit of the stems. Bastard Toadflax is a parasite that takes its food from the roots of other plants. It is common in open pinewoods, prairie grasslands, and on gravelly hillsides.

Range: throughout the Rockies.

The basal rosette of leathery, dark glossy-green leaves and the bright red-purple seed capsules are the arresting features of this plant, rather than the flowers. The spoon-shaped, evergreen basal leaves are 1¼–2½ inches (3–6 cm) in size with toothed margins. Up to 3 very small leaves clasp the rigid stem, 4–16 inches (10–40 cm) tall. The small white to pink flowers, each with 10 long stamens, form a dense cluster at the top of each reddish-purple stalk. As the flowers fade, attractive seed capsules develop. Fireleaf Leptarrhena is common along stream banks and on moist slopes in alpine and subalpine habitats.

Range: Alberta, British Columbia, Washington, Oregon, Idaho, and Montana.

Fireleaf Leptarrhena
Leptarrhena pyrolifolia

SAXIFRAGE FAMILY
Saxifragaceae

The creeping rhizomes of Naked Miterwort give rise to basal clusters of long-petioled, kidney- to heart-shaped leaves with crinkly, toothed margins, and erect flowering stems. Reaching a height of 8–12 inches (20–30 cm), the stems are leafless, with a few yellowish-green flowers resembling tiny pinwheels. A hand lens may be needed to appreciate the superb beauty of the small flower. The 5 petals are delicately fringed threads strung between the unbranched sepals and the 10 stamens, like finely crafted jewels. When opened, the 2-valved capsule contains tiny, shiny, black seeds, not unlike a miniature nest with a clutch of eggs. This dainty beauty is widespread in moist, shaded spruce forests.

Range: Alberta, British Columbia, Washington, and Montana.

Naked Miterwort;
Bishop's Cap
Mitella nuda

SAXIFRAGE FAMILY
Saxifragaceae

Fringed Grass of Parnassus
Parnassia fimbriata

SAXIFRAGE FAMILY
Saxifragaceae

The snowy white, buttercup-like blooms of Fringed Grass of Parnassus are borne singly on stems 6–14 inches (15–35 cm) tall, with a clasping leaf-like bract about halfway up the stem. The showy flower has 5 petals, each with 5 to 7 conspicuous green veins and fringed lower edges. A rosette of glossy green, kidney- or heart-shaped leaves spread from a perennial rootstock. Five white, fertile stamens alternate with 5 gland-tipped, sterile ones, which are yellow in color. The plant's fruit is a many-seeded, 4-valved capsule. Favorite haunts of the plant are wet mossy areas along creeks, springs, and lakeshores in valleys to above the timberline, where it is often found in dense colonies.

Range: throughout the Rockies.

Wedgeleaf Saxifrage
Saxifraga adscendens

SAXIFRAGE FAMILY
Saxifragaceae

This very small alpine plant, growing along mossy brooks or below snowbeds, often escapes notice. It may flower when less than ¾ inch (2 cm) tall and the mature stems are not more than 3 inches (8 cm) high. The reddish basal leaves, growing in a dense rosette, are wedge-shaped, as the common name implies, with the narrow portion at the point of attachment. The broad end may be entire or with 3 lobes, the middle one usually the largest. There are usually several smaller leaves along the stem. The small bell-shaped flowers have white, green-veined petals, which are about twice as long as the reddish-purple sepals. All green parts of the plant are glandular and hairy.

Range: throughout the Rockies, excluding New Mexico.

This densely matted or cushion-like plant has small leathery, lance-like leaves, overlapping each other. They are fringed with long hairs and each terminates in a sharp spine. The stiffly erect, dark brown flowering stems support a few small leaves and a number of branches. There are numerous star-shaped flowers, which are borne on a flat-topped cluster about 6 inches (15 cm) above the mat of evergreen leaves. The 5 white petals are speckled with purple, orange, or yellow spots so small that the beauty of this flower can best be appreciated only if the admirer gets down on hands and knees. Yellowdot Saxifrage is a common inhabitant of rock crevices and scree slopes from mid to high elevations.

Range: throughout the Rockies.

Yellowdot Saxifrage; Prickly Saxifrage
Saxifraga bronchialis

SAXIFRAGE FAMILY
Saxifragaceae

Redstem saxifrage is usually found embedded in mosses that border small stream banks in alpine and subalpine regions. The purple-colored stems, 4–12 inches (10–30 cm) tall, each bearing 1 to several tiny white, star-shaped flowers, contrast prettily with their mossy surroundings. At maturity the sepals are reflexed and the white petals are marked with 2 greenish-yellow blotches that later fade. Brownish, 3-pointed, erect capsules later replace the flowers. The leaves of this plant are coarsely toothed and fan-shaped, growing in clumps from a long rootstock.

Range: Alberta, British Columbia, Washington, Idaho, and Montana.

Redstem Saxifrage
Saxifraga lyallii

SAXIFRAGE FAMILY
Saxifragaceae

Threeleaf Foamflower

Tiarella trifoliata

SAXIFRAGE FAMILY
Saxifragaceae

Large maple-like leaves characterize this perennial herb, which is 4–16 inches (10–40 cm) tall and has a loose spray of delicate white or creamy white flowers. The long-petioled basal leaves, from 1¼–3 ½ inches (3–9 cm) across, arise from a rootstock. They have 3 to 5 lobes with prominent double-toothed margins. The flowering stem, with gland-tipped, white hairs on the upper portion, bears a similar but smaller leaf. A dozen or so flowers, usually in groups of 3, are arranged on the delicate stalks well above the leaves. Threeleaf Foamflower's small lacy flower consists of 5 pinkish-white sepals, 5 white to creamy petals, 1 pistil with 2 long styles, and 10 protruding stamens. The white filaments of the stamens are a conspicuous feature; 5 are longer than the calyx lobes and 5 are shorter. The seedpod has a rather odd shape and has been compared to a tiara worn by royalty, thus giving rise to the generic name *Tiarella*, meaning little tiara. Search for large clumps of this dainty beauty in sheltered places in woods, especially along streams.

Range: Alberta, British Columbia, Washington, Oregon, Idaho, and Montana.

Rocky Mountain Snowlover

Chionophila jamesii

FIGWORT FAMILY
Scrophulariaceae

A distinctive perennial, Rocky Mountain Snowlover is tiny, no more than 2–4 inches (5–10 cm) tall. Basal leaves are fleshy and spatulate; stem leaves are smaller and stalkless. Erect to leaning stems are typically minutely hairy. Blossoms are arranged in an unusual 1-sided cluster of up to 8 flowers. The white tubular corolla, ¾ inch (2 cm) long, and the greenish-white calyx are flattened in a unique manner, a characteristic only of this genus. In autumn, rosettes of leaves turn red, adding color to their harsh landscape. Tweedy's Snowlover (*C. tweedyi*) with pink to lavender flowers grows in similar habitats in Montana and Idaho. Rocky Mountain Snowlover is a high alpine plant found in snowbed communities and on gravelly soils near rivulets and streams.

Range: Wyoming and Colorado.

The lousewort group is known for the unusual shape of its flowers, and the 2-parted flower of Coiled Lousewort is the most spectacular of them all. Bright creamy-white flowers are scattered along a stem 3-4 inches (8-10 cm) tall. The long, downward-coiled, upper lip of the corolla tube is curved like a shepherd's crook and twisted sideways near its tip. The upper lip is partially enclosed by the 2 lobes of the lower lip. The fern-like basal leaves are toothed, and stem leaves alternate, decreasing in size towards the top of the plant. These feathery leaves are green and often wine-tinged. Small clumps of this showy plant are found in alpine meadows and on open slopes below the timberline.

Range: throughout the Rockies, excluding Colorado and New Mexico.

Coiled Lousewort
Pedicularis contorta

FIGWORT FAMILY
Scrophulariaceae

Curiously shaped, asymmetric flowers are the most notable feature of Sickletop Lousewort. The flowers, white with a wash of yellow or purple, are 2-lobed. The hood-like lip (galea) is strongly arched and tapers into a slender down-curved beak. The lower lip is 3-lobed, the center one being smaller and with a pair of raised ridges. In addition to several flowers in a terminal raceme, some lower flowers may be present on stalks from the leaf axils. This plant has a clump of stems, 6-20 inches (15-50 cm) tall, arching outward in bouquet-like clusters. Early in the season the slightly serrated leaves are wine-colored and gradually change to green with the production of chlorophyll. Basal leaves are generally lacking or much reduced in number. Sickletop Lousewort is generally found in coniferous forests and dry open sites from the montane to the subalpine.

Range: throughout the Rockies.

Sickletop Lousewort; Parrot's Beak
Pedicularis racemosa

FIGWORT FAMILY
Scrophulariaceae

Tobacco Root
Valeriana edulis

VALERIAN FAMILY
Valerianaceae

A perennial growing from a long stout taproot, Tobacco Root may be up to 3 feet (1 m) tall. Basal leaves are numerous, linear or widest above the middle and tapering gradually to a narrow base, entire, and 2¾–16 inches (7–40 cm) long. Stem leaves are opposite, in 2 to 6 pairs, smaller upward on the stem, clefted, and almost stalkless. White to yellowish flowers in elongated compound clusters are balanced on the upper stem. Although raw roots are poisonous, they were cooked and eaten by some Native Americans. The cooked roots are reported to smell like "dirty socks." Tobacco Root favors moist meadows and openings in Quaking Aspen and mixed conifers from the foothills to the lower subalpine zone.

Range: throughout the Rockies, excluding Alberta.

Sitka Valerian
Valeriana sitchensis

VALERIAN FAMILY
Valerianaceae

This herbaceous perennial is 16–31 inches (40–80 cm) tall and has somewhat succulent, squarish stems arising from a foul-smelling, fleshy rootstock. Large opposite leaves are divided into 3 to 7 coarsely toothed lobes, with progressively shorter petioles up the stem. The small but numerous tubular flowers are crowded into a nearly flat-topped cluster at the top of each stem. Buds and young flowers are pale lavender-pink, the flowers later fading to white. The floral tubes are slightly notched into 5 equal lobes, and 3 stamens and an even longer pistil protrude from the mouth of each flower. After the first frost, the vaguely unpleasant odor emitted by the flowers becomes overpowering. When mature, the flat, single-seeded fruits are crowned with numerous feathery bristles that carry seeds far afield on the mountain breezes. Native Americans used the rootstocks as food and also as medicine for stomach ailments; the plant was also used in a tobacco mixture. Several animals eat the leaves and stems of Sitka Valerian and its flowers attract large numbers of insects.

Range: Alberta, British Columbia, Washington, Oregon, Idaho, and Montana.

Canadian White Violet is a charming little flower known to many as the trumpeter of early spring. The petals are white to violet, with yellow at the base. Distinctive purple lines that converge on the lower petals guide bees and other insects to the sweet nectar within. The slender stems have several heart-shaped leaves, which form a suitable background for the subtly fragrant flowers. When the seedpods ripen they open with a sudden twist that shoots the seeds some distance away, a habit that reduces competition by the seedling with the parent plant for space, nutrients, and moisture. The leaves and flowers may be eaten raw in salads, boiled as potherbs, or used to thicken soup. The flowers can be candied for use as cake decorations. Canadian White Violet is often found in dense colonies in rich, moist deciduous forests.

Range: throughout the Rockies.

Canadian White Violet
Viola canadensis

VIOLET FAMILY
Violaceae

Blooming against a background of the previous year's brown foliage, the familiar blossoms of White Violet are a welcome sign of the arrival of spring. Individual small white flowers, with the lower petal often streaked with purplish veins, arise on slender leafless stems from a fleshy rootstock. The kidney-shaped leaves have blunt tips and their margins are wavy and toothed. The long, purplish seed capsules split open when ripe, expelling the brown seeds. Like other violets, both the flowers and leaves are edible and the leaves are a good source of vitamins A and C. This small violet may be found in damp shaded woodlands and meadows.

Range: throughout the Rockies, excluding Oregon, Utah, and New Mexico.

White Violet
Viola renifolia

VIOLET FAMILY
Violaceae

He is happiest who hath power to gather wisdom from a flower.

— Mary Howitt

YELLOW & CREAM

**Owl's-claws;
Orange Sneezeweed**

Hymenoxys hoopesii

ASTER FAMILY
Asteraceae

page 103

Dawson's Angelica; Yellow Angelica

Angelica dawsonii

CARROT FAMILY
Apiaceae

This distinctive plant grows 12–40 inches (30–100 cm) tall. Its attractive leaves are divided into 3 segments with finely-toothed, lance-shaped leaflets that are 1¼–2½ inches (3–6 cm) long. The tiny yellow flowers burst out in different directions from the top of the hollow stem like fireworks. Dawson's Angelica grows in moist meadows or along stream banks in the montane and subalpine zones.

Range: endemic to extreme southwestern Alberta, southeastern British Columbia, Idaho, and northwestern Montana.

American Thorow Wax

Bupleurum americanum

CARROT FAMILY
Apiaceae

American Thorow Wax is the only member of the carrot family without divided leaves. Clustered mainly near the base, basal and stem leaves are long and narrow with no teeth on the margins and prominent parallel veins. The smooth stems, 4–12 inches (10–30 cm) tall, bear umbels of 2 to 9 ray flowers. The compact, tiny flowers have petals that are bright yellow with very small bractlets. Its flattened fruits are brown and oblong with raised ribs. Some members of this genus are among the most prized plants used by Chinese herbalists. American Thorow Wax can be found on gravelly hillsides in the montane grasslands to talus slopes near the tree line.

Range: throughout the Rockies, excluding Washington and Utah.

A dwarf alpine plant of screes, Sandberg's Biscuitroot grows close to the ground, except for the flower stalks, which may elongate up to 8 inches (20 cm). The bright green leaves have petioles and the blades are finely divided like those of parsley. The main umbel, with bright yellow flowers, may be 1½ inches (4 cm) wide; there are smaller secondary umbels. Individual flowers are tiny, but numerous within a compound umbel. Oblong fruits with narrow marginal wings soon replace the flowers.

Range: Alberta, British Columbia, Idaho, and Montana.

Sandberg's Biscuitroot
Lomatium sandbergii

CARROT FAMILY
Apiaceae

Growing from an elongated taproot, Nineleaf Biscuitroot's strap-shaped, blue-green leaves are divided and clustered about the base. The flowering stem, 8–20 inches (20–50 cm) high, terminates in asymmetric, widespread umbels, from ¾–2 inches (2–5 cm) across with glossy, lemon yellow blossoms. The size of the umbels increases as the flowers give way to flattened seeds, which have marginal wings and parallel brown stripes on the back. Roots of Nineleaf Biscuitroot can be eaten raw or roasted. The flowers and upper leaves were dried and used to flavor meats, stews, and salads by Native Americans. *Lomatium* is Greek for a "fringe" or "border," referring to the winged edges of the seeds. The species name *triternatum* refers to the three sets of leaves each with three more divisions. This stately plant is found in grasslands, sagebrush steppes, woodland openings and meadows from the valley bottom to the subalpine zone.

Range: throughout the Rockies, excluding Colorado and New Mexico.

Nineleaf Biscuitroot; Prairie Parsley
Lomatium triternatum

CARROT FAMILY
Apiaceae

Meadow Zizia
Zizia aptera

CARROT FAMILY
Apiaceae

Meadow Zizia has yellow flower clusters that are held above their leaves like dainty umbrellas. The leaves are variable in shape and size. Basal leaves are long-petioled and heart-shaped; stem leaves are smaller, short-petioled, and divided into 3 leaflets. Stem leaves become progressively smaller along the stem until they become clefted leaflets. The somewhat flattened fruits are ribbed and greenish-brown in color. This member of the carrot family is most likely to be found in damp meadows up to the timberline.

Range: throughout the Rockies, excluding New Mexico.

American Skunkcabbage; Swamp Lantern; Yellow Arum
Lysichiton americanus

ARUM FAMILY
Araceae

A harbinger of springtime, American Skunkcabbage may burst through half-frozen soil or snowbanks to brighten still dormant swamps. The large, startling yellow, hood-like bract, called a spathe, encloses the spadix, a club-like stem on which the plant's minute and greenish flowers are clustered. The showy hoods gave rise to the generic name *Lysichiton* which is derived from Greek words meaning "loose" and "tunic." Elephant ear-sized leaves that may reach 55 inches (140 cm) in length and 27 inches (70 cm) in width follow the initial shoots. Despite its inelegant common name, the plant gives a skunk-like odor only when bruised or crushed underfoot. It provides food for hungry bears and deer. These water-loving plants grow in swamps, wet woods, and other low lying areas.

Range: British Columbia, Washington, Oregon, Idaho, and Montana.

The vivid yellow heads of Pale Agoseris are usually passed over as just another dandelion, but upon closer examination several differences are apparent. Pale Agoseris' leaves are narrower and much longer, while the leaf blades are smooth or faintly toothed rather than deeply incised. In addition, the bracts of the heads are broader and never turned back along the stem as they are in the introduced dandelion. The plant shares many characteristics with the Common Dandelion, including a long taproot, a rosette of basal leaves, a single yellow flower head borne on a long stalk, and a sticky, milky juice. The leaves and stems are usually blue-green with white hairs, or they may be nearly hairless. The flower heads, ¾–2 inches (2–5 cm) across, are yellow when young, but often turn pinkish at maturity. Pale Agoseris is a common species that is widely distributed in open habitats from the montane to the alpine zone.

Range: throughout the Rockies.

Pale Agoseris
Agoseris glauca

ASTER FAMILY
Asteraceae

Heartleaf Arnica is widely distributed in the Rockies. Its cheerful lemon-yellow flowers, 2–3 inches (5–8 cm) across, are among the most conspicuous of all mountain flowers, glistening above the heart-shaped lower leaves from which the common name was derived. The leaves have serrated edges. The stems may be 14–28 inches (35–70 cm) tall, often with one large flower head and two smaller lateral ones. Openings in coniferous woods are the favored habitat of this daisy-like flower.

Range: throughout the Rockies.

Heartleaf Arnica
Arnica cordifolia

ASTER FAMILY
Asteraceae

Snow Arnica
Arnica frigida spp. frigida
[Arnica louiseana]

ASTER FAMILY
Asteraceae

A tiny alpine plant with large, yellow, daisy-like flowers, Snow Arnica is found on open slopes and along brooks at high altitudes. Usually the flower head is borne singly (occasionally in twos or threes) at the top of a short, stout stem. The heads nod or hang in a graceful fashion just above the ground. The involucral bracts are nearly hairless except near the base. Oblong to broadly lance-shaped leaves, often toothed, are attached at the base of the plant by short petioles. Small stem leaves may also be present.

Range: Alberta and British Columbia.

Foothill Arnica; Shining Arnica
Arnica fulgens

ASTER FAMILY
Asteraceae

A fibrous-rooted perennial that sometimes grows vegetatively from rhizomes, Foothill Arnica has stems 8–20 inches (20–50 cm) tall, which are roughened with stiff short hairs. Narrow, 4–6 inch (10–15 cm) long, smooth, 3-ribbed leaves form a basal cluster; the opposite stem leaves become progressively smaller toward the top of the plant. Leaf axils are tufted with brown woolly hairs, an important characteristic in the identification of this plant. Each stem generally bears a single (occasionally 2 to 3) flower head about 2 inches (5 cm) wide. From 10 to 21 bright yellow-orange petals, hairy on both faces, surround the smaller disk florets. The involucre has 2 rows of blunt tipped, hairy bracts; the achenes have a tuft of grayish-white hairs. In Latin, the specific name *fulgens* means "shining" or "bright-colored," referring to the flowers. Although Arnicas, especially the flowers and roots, have a long history of herbal use, Foothill Arnica is considered toxic. This plant grows in damp depressions in grasslands and sagebrush scrub in the plains, foothills, and montane zones.

Range: throughout the Rockies.

Prairie Sagewort; Fringed Sagebrush
Artemisia frigida

ASTER FAMILY
Asteraceae

Pleasantly aromatic and very handsome, Prairie Sagewort is a low, mat-forming shrub, sometimes referred to as a "semi-shrub," generally 4-16 inches (10-40 cm) in height but rarely taller than 24 inches (60 cm). Woody stems are spreading and much branched while the upper stems are soft, erect, and leafy. Many finely cut, silvery-gray leaves grow from the upper stems. Several flower stems emerge from the basal leaves producing flower heads, less than ⅜ inch (1 cm) across, which contain only numerous tiny yellow disk florets. The silvery appearance is imparted by a cloak of silvery, silky hairs on the leaves and stems and woolly hairs on the flower bracts. Prairie Sagewort has a very adaptable root system, growing deep taproots where the water table is low and surface roots where water is more abundant. Prairie Sagewort is an important high protein food for several wildlife species, particularly for pronghorn, deer, and elk, as well as domestic livestock. *Frigida* is Latin for "cold," since the plant can grow in cold and dry climates of Alaska, northern Canada, Mongolia, and Siberia. This plant has the widest distribution of all members of the *Artemisia* genus. Prairie Sagewort is found on dry soils from the plains to the subalpine zone.

Range: throughout the Rockies, excluding Oregon.

White Sagebrush
Artemisia ludoviciana

ASTER FAMILY
Asteraceae

Only one of several species of sagebrush in the Rockies, this aromatic plant is about 16-28 inches (40-70 cm) tall, branching occasionally in the upper portion. Stems may be solitary, but this perennial has a tendency to form vegetative colonies that exclude other plants. Its alternate leaves vary from linear, narrowly ovate, to oblanceolate. They are sessile or with short petioles, up to 3 inches (8 cm) long and 1 inch (2.5 cm) across; most leaves are entire, but lower ones may be irregularly toothed or lobed. Like the stems, the attractive leaves have a silvery sheen from a dense mat of soft, white hair. Some of the upper stems terminate in narrow racemes or elongated panicles of flowers. Each nodding, yellow flower head contains hundreds of inconspicuous whitish-green disk florets. Deer and small mammals forage on White Sagebrush and birds enjoy the seeds. This plant favors dry, open areas in the montane to lower subalpine zones.

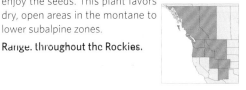

Range: throughout the Rockies.

Big Sagebrush
Artemisia tridentata

ASTER FAMILY
Asteraceae

Inset photo by Barry Gordichuk

Big Sagebrush is an erect, highly aromatic, evergreen species with a single or multi-stemmed, woody trunk. There are three widely recognized subspecies that range in size from 16 inches to 15 feet (40 cm to 5 m) on favorable sites. Young stems are smooth and silvery, but as the plant matures these stems turn grayer and the bark starts to grow in stringy strips that are dark brown or black. Principal leaves are ⅜-2½ inches (1–6.5 cm) long, 1/16-⅜ inch (2 mm to 2 cm) wide, wedge-shaped, and generally 3-toothed at the apex (hence the name *tridentata*). Flowering stems grow near the ends of the branches and numerous side branches that bear dense clusters of tiny yellow flowers in late summer. Up to a million tiny black seeds may be produced on a mature plant. Big Sagebrush is an important browse plant for a number of wildlife species including mule deer, elk, pronghorn, sage grouse, and many small mammals, in addition to domestic livestock. Many Native Americans used this plant as a source of fuel, in the construction of dwellings, and for several medicinal purposes. It is the state plant of Nevada. Big Sagebrush occupies a great variety of sites ranging from arid plains to mountain slopes at 11,100 feet (3,400 m) elevation.

Range: throughout the Rockies.

Arrowleaf Balsamroot
Balsamorhiza sagittata

ASTER FAMILY
Asteraceae

Arrowleaf Balsamroot, so named because it grows from a strong-smelling taproot, has clumps of arrowhead-shaped basal leaves up to 12 inches (30 cm) long and 6 inches (15 cm) wide. They are silver-gray in color, with a dense cover of woolly, white hairs on both sides. Bright yellow, sunflower-like blossoms, up to 4 inches (10 cm) across, are borne singly at the end of long stalks. Although generally shunned by domestic livestock, deer, elk, and mountain sheep graze Arrowleaf Balsamroot. Native Americans used to eat the stout starchy roots and tender young shoots. This striking plant blooms in early spring, spreading a carpet of yellow across the grassy slopes of the mountains and foothills.

Range: throughout the Rockies, excluding New Mexico.

Nodding Beggartick is a bushy annual that ranges in height from 4–40 inches (10–100 cm) or more. Its deep yellow flowers are ¾–1¼ inch (2–3 cm) in diameter with speckled or darker centers. The bracts, slightly reflexed, are a little longer than the ray flowers. Its dark green leaves are stalkless and clasping, from 2–7 inches (5–18 cm) long, toothed, and narrow. As implied by the common name, the flowers, although erect when new, commonly droop or nod at maturity. The specific name *cernua* means, "inclining the head, stooping," hence "nodding." *Bidens* refers to the prominent barbs on the seeds. An autumn walk through a patch of Nodding Beggartick may result in scratches on the skin or a horde of barbed nutlets adhering to clothes. This unloved plant is found in wet places such as stream banks, marshes, ditches, and wet meadows.

Range: throughout the Rockies.

Nodding Beggartick; Nodding Bur Marigold
Bidens cernua

ASTER FAMILY
Asteraceae

Tasselflower Brickellbush is distinctive with its triangular leaves and large drooping flower heads that are rayless. The showy disk florets range in color from creamy white to pale yellow and may be up to 2 inches (5 cm) long. The large heads, each comprising 20 to 40 flowers, appear to be too heavy for their slender stalks. Bracts at the base of the flower head are striped with green lines and the outer bracts are tipped with a well-developed slender appendage. The leaves are ¾–4 ¼ inches (2–11 cm) in length, toothed, triangular in shape, and on long petioles. Varying in size and luxuriance, this uncommon plant is found on exposed rocky slopes and stream banks in the montane and subalpine zones.

Range: throughout the Rockies.

Tasselflower Brickellbush
Brickellia grandiflora

ASTER FAMILY
Asteraceae

Yellow Rabbitbrush
Chrysothamnus viscidiflorus

ASTER FAMILY
Asteraceae

Photo by Barry Gordichuk

Yellow Rabbitbrush is a creeping, many-branched shrub reaching about 3 feet (1 m) tall with grayish-white bark and smooth stems. Leaves are alternate, linear to linear-lanceolate, narrow, and may be up to 2 inches (5 cm) long. They are pale green, hairless, sticky, and slightly twisted. The inflorescence is a dense, flat-topped to rounded-topped cyme with 5-flowered heads containing only disk florets. Their crowns become a bright, golden profusion of flowers in late summer. This glow gives rise to the Latin name *Chryso*, "golden," and *thamnus*, "bush;" *viscidiflorus* means "sticky-flowered." This wide-ranging plant is an important source of food for wildlife and livestock, particularly late in the year after more palatable species are depleted. Rubber Rabbitbrush (*Ericameria nauseosa*), which is common in similar habitats particularly at lower elevations, is easily distinguished by the white felt covering its twigs. Yellow Rabbitbrush ranges from the foothills to the subalpine zone.

Range: throughout the Rockies, excluding Alberta.

Parry's Thistle
Cirsium parryi

ASTER FAMILY
Asteraceae

Parry's Thistle is a biennial with entire basal and stem leaves that are darker green above and thinly pubescent, while the undersides are lighter green and hairless. They are unlobed or pinnately cleft with lobes and spiny margins. The ribbed stems are branched near the top with nodes ⅜–3 inches (1–8 cm) apart. Flower heads are loosely to densely clustered at the tip of the main stem and branches and also in the leaf axils. The corolla is generally pale yellow; the involucral bracts are lightly woolly. Parry's Thistle favors moist soils often in a shaded riparian understory in the montane zone.

Range: Colorado and New Mexico.

Another sturdy dweller of high elevations is Dwarf Alpine Hawksbeard. Anchored firmly in the soil by a long taproot, this little gem has bright yellow flower heads that look like flecks of gold among the scree and rocks in which it grows. A dwarf perennial, it has bluish-green leaves, with long petioles and spoon-shaped blades, forming a flat rosette tight against the ground. The short flower stems are barely elevated above the leafy rosette. Golden-brown fruits with white, downy tails soon replace the tiny yellow blooms. Only the fortunate wayfarer will find this lovely treasure, for it inhabits the high places where few people wander.

Range: throughout the Rockies, excluding New Mexico.

Dwarf Alpine Hawksbeard
Crepis nana

ASTER FAMILY
Asteraceae

This dwarf perennial plant produces bright golden-yellow flower heads, which, like those of several other alpine inhabitants, appear too large for the small size of the plant. The solitary flower heads may span ¾–1¼ inches (2–3 cm), while the stems are only ¾–6 inches (2–15 cm) tall. Bracts on the flower heads are purplish, or at least have a purplish tip, and are covered with woolly hairs. Deep green oval leaves branch on short petioles from the central rootstock in a small rosette. There may also be a few smaller stem leaves. With its 25 to 70 yellow ray flowers surrounding yellow disk florets, Alpine Yellow Fleabane is considered by many flower lovers to be the loveliest of the many fleabanes. Alpine Yellow Fleabane may be locally common on turfy alpine slopes.

Range: Alberta, British Columbia, and Washington.

Alpine Yellow Fleabane
Erigeron aureus

ASTER FAMILY
Asteraceae

Common Gaillardia; Brown-eyed Susan
Gaillardia aristata

ASTER FAMILY
Asteraceae

Across a grassland on a hot day in summer, there is nothing like a troop of showy Common Gaillardia to gladden the heart, for the big brown eyes seem to wink a friendly greeting as they sway in the breeze. The terminal flower heads, up to 3 inches (8 cm) across, consist of disk and ray flowers. Striking golden ray flowers, whose individual "petals" have 3-cleft tips, surround purplish-brown central disk florets. The lower leaves are lance-shaped and the others, on a stem 12–32 inches (30–80 cm) tall, are toothed. An abundance of grayish-green hairs covers the entire plant. Common Gaillardia is found on dry grasslands at low elevations.

Range: throughout the Rockies.

Fivenerve Helianthella; Little Sunflower
Helianthella quinquenervis

ASTER FAMILY
Asteraceae

Growing up to an eye-catching 5 feet (1.5 m), Fivenerve Helianthella grows on erect stems and usually in clumps. Long, strap-like leaves are basal and also on the stems; the blades are generally 5-nerved, giving rise to the specific name, *quinquenervis*. Nodding flower heads, 2–4 inches (5–10 cm) across, are usually borne singly atop the stem but occasionally there are smaller heads below. Sunny, lemon-yellow ray flowers surround the button of reddish-brown disk florets. The involucre has hairy margins and glands that secrete nectar rich in sucrose and amino acids. This nectar is gathered by ants, which in return protect the plants from other insects, thereby substantially reducing seed loss. Fivenerve Helianthella is scattered in woodlands from Quaking Aspen forests in the foothills to the subalpine zone.

Range: throughout the Rockies, excluding Alberta, British Columbia, and Washington.

A fast-growing annual herb, Common Sunflower is the only important crop to have evolved within the confines of North America. This plant hybridizes and is highly variable. Hairy stems, multistemmed or unbranched, may grow from 2½–11½ feet (0.7 to 3.5 m) tall. Lower leaves are opposite, large, heart-shaped, and irregularly toothed; upper leaves are alternate, egg-shaped, and long petioled. Flowering heads are terminal on the main stem, 4-16 inches (10–40 cm) in diameter, and sometimes drooping; heads on lateral branches are smaller. Each flower head consists of yellow outer ray flowers and numerous disk florets that are spirally arranged. The fruit that follows is a 1-seeded achene, familiar to us as a sunflower seed. The sharp-tipped, green bracts at the base of the flower head are egg-shaped. Flower heads turn to follow the sun as it passes. In Greek, *helios* means "sun" and *anthos* means "flower", thus sunflower. Archaeological excavations indicate that Native Americans grew domesticated forms of Common Sunflower by 1000 BC. In addition to being an important source of food, various tribes ascribed medical and magical powers to the plant and used it in their ceremonies. These plants are now cultivated worldwide for food, oil, fuel, and fiber. Common Sunflower is found in cultivated fields and other disturbed places from the plains to the foothills.

Range: throughout the Rockies.

Common Sunflower
Helianthus annuus

ASTER FAMILY
Asteraceae

Showy Goldeneye
Heliomeris multiflora var. multiflora

ASTER FAMILY
Asteraceae

Another member of the sunflower group, Showy Goldeneye is a perennial with several stems, 8–52 inches (20–130 cm) tall, arising from a short taproot or fibrous rootstock. Leaves are lance-shaped, with or without petioles, bristly, 1¼–4 inches (3–10 cm) long, and with a pointed tip. Except for the uppermost leaves, they are arranged opposite along the stem. Flower heads are borne at the ends of the stems with 8 to 16 showy yellow ray flowers surrounding a disk of yellow tubular florets. Distinguishing features, best seen with the aid of a hand lens, are the 4-sided achene and lack of a pappus. Showy Goldeneye is found along roadsides, disturbed areas, meadows, and forest openings from the foothills to the subalpine zone.

Range: throughout the Rockies, excluding Alberta, British Columbia, Washington, and Oregon.

Hairy False Goldenaster
Heterotheca villosa

ASTER FAMILY
Asteraceae

This much-branched perennial, growing from a woody taproot, may be erect, but it is more often sprawling. The upper gray-green leaves are entire, and narrowly to broadly lance-shaped; they grow alternately along the stem. The lower leaves wither early. All green parts of the plant are covered with soft white hairs. Rich golden-yellow, multi-petaled ray flowers and orange to brown tubular disk florets form heads at the end of each branch. Involucral bracts are overlapping, pointed, fuzzy, and slender. Hairy False Goldenaster prefers dry sandy soil with full exposure to the sun.

Range: throughout the Rockies.

Slender Hawkweed is a herb growing 4–12 inches (10–30 cm) tall in subalpine and alpine meadows and on rocky slopes in open coniferous woods. The basal leaves have long petioles and sparingly toothed margins. They vary from lance- to spatula-shaped. The erect flowering stem may have one or more leaves, but they are small and lack petioles. Three or more small heads with pale yellow ray flowers are produced on the stem. A black, woolly collar surrounds each flower head and protects the tender buds from penetrating frost and drying winds. As well, the stem and branches of the flowering part of the plant are covered with dense, gray down and long, black hairs. When ripe the fruit is chestnut-brown with white bristles.

Range: throughout the Rockies.

Slender Hawkweed
Hieracium gracile

ASTER FAMILY
Asteraceae

Owl's-claws is a perennial herb reaching to 3 feet (1 m). Lower leaves are alternate, egg-shaped, deeply veined, and up to 10 inches (25 cm) long; upper leaves are reduced in size, spatula-shaped, and sessile. Several flower heads are present on the upper portion of the stems. Narrow, open-spaced, drooping, yellow ray flowers, with 3-tooth tips, surround a mound of orange disk florets. The other common name, Orange Sneezeweed, is a reference to the allergic irritation caused by its pollen. This plant is toxic to livestock. Needing full sun and lots of moisture, Owl's-claws grows in wet meadows, open woods, and along streams from the foothills to subalpine zone.

Range: throughout the Rockies, excluding Alberta, British Columbia, and Washington.

Owl's-claws; Orange Sneezeweed
Hymenoxys hoopesii

ASTER FAMILY
Asteraceae

Nodding Microceris
Microseris nutans

ASTER FAMILY
Asteraceae

With only a casual glance Nodding Microceris might be mistaken for a dandelion, but it has very sharply pointed, narrow leaves, pappus bristles, and black hairs on the bracts that grip the flower head. This slender perennial, growing from a fleshy taproot, produces solitary heads on long unbranched, leafless stalks. The flower heads are nodding in bud, becoming erect in blossom. Their outer, pale yellow ray flowers, sometimes veined with purple, are longer than the inner ones. There are no disk florets. Like dandelions, the seeds are tipped with silvery-white, feathery "parachutes." This plant is fairly common in dry meadows and open woods at middle elevations.

Range: throughout the Rockies, excluding New Mexico.

Woolly Groundsel
Packera cana
[Senecio canus]

ASTER FAMILY
Asteraceae

Woolly Groundsel is a white woolly perennial, whose horizontal rootstock produces stems up to 16 inches (40 cm) tall. The clustered basal leaves have short petioles and no teeth. Leaves of the flowering stem, although variable, are smaller with toothed margins. In early summer the branching stems carry heads of bright yellow flowers in an open umbel. The involucral bracts are uniformly green. Green parts of the plant, and especially the underside of the leaves, are densely coated with hair. Although this plant is typical of the prairies, it may be found in dry and exposed sites almost to the timberline.

Range: throughout the Rockies.

Curlyhead Goldenweed is a perennial growing 8-32 inches (20-80 cm) tall. These stems may be pale green to reddish. The upright basal leaves are long and broad with a prominent light colored mid-vein; stem leaves are alternate, reduced in size upward and may be clasping. A large golden-yellow flower head tops each ¾-4 inch (2-10 cm) long, upright flower stem. Ray flowers are narrow and curled upward encircling the central disk florets. Key identifying factors are the large, rounded, overlapping bracts (phyllaries) below the flower head. *Pyrrocoma* is Latin for "reddish hair" or "tawny mane," referring to the pappus color; *crocea*, from the Greek for crocus, refers to the saffron color of the flower. Curlyhead Goldenweed grows along roadsides, in meadows, and openings in mixed forests in the montane zone.

Range: Wyoming, Utah, Colorado, and New Mexico.

Curlyhead Goldenweed
Pyrrocoma crocea
[Haplopappus croceus]

ASTER FAMILY
Asteraceae

The sombrero-shaped flower heads, resembling the high-centered and broad-brimmed hats worn during Mexican fiestas, are characteristic of Upright Prairie Coneflower. The bright yellow ray flowers, occasionally yellow and reddish brown near the base, are supported on long leafless stalks. Numbering from 4 to 11, the ray flowers are notched at the tips and droop. The disk florets open from the base to the top of a cylindrical receptacle and are covered by a gray scale prior to opening. For that reason the ¾-2 inch (2-5 cm) tall receptacle may appear dark brown on the lower portion and gray on the upper part. Upright Prairie Coneflower is a perennial rising from 12-35 inches (30-90 cm) high from a taproot. Leaves on the lower portion of the stem are alternate, stiffly hairy, and deeply cleft. It can be found in grasslands, sagebrush steppes, and foothills.

Range: throughout the Rockies, excluding Oregon and Washington.

Upright Prairie Coneflower
Ratibida columnifera

ASTER FAMILY
Asteraceae

Nodding Ragwort
Senecio bigelovii

ASTER FAMILY
Asteraceae

Nodding Ragwort is a fibrous-rooted forb with erect stems 12–32 inches (30–80 cm) tall. Both leaves and stems are tufted with cobwebby hairs, especially higher on the stem. Basal leaves are lanceolate to narrowly triangular, up to 8 inches (20 cm) long and 2½ inches (6 cm) wide, with petioles. Stem leaves are progressively reduced in size upward on the stem; they may be without petioles or clasping, sharply pointed at the tip, with entire or serrated margins. The upper surface of the leaf blade is hairless while the lower is pubescent. The terminal inflorescences with 1 to 8 distinctively nodding flower heads consist solely of myriads of tightly packed yellow disk florets. Even in full bloom the flower heads appear to be in the bud stage of development. Bracts of the involucre are a dark burgundy and are sparsely hairy. Nodding Ragwort occupies moist meadows in open Quaking Aspen and Spruce-fir forests from the montane to subalpine zones.

Range: Wyoming, Utah, Colorado, and New Mexico.

Dwarf Mountain Ragwort
Senecio fremontii

ASTER FAMILY
Asteraceae

Often growing in loose sprawling clumps on scree slopes of the alpine or subalpine zones, Dwarf Mountain Ragwort is a distinctive member of the genus *Senecio*. The leaves are somewhat fleshy, lance- to wedge-shaped, and have rather coarse, shallowly toothed margins. They occur alternately along the simple or sparsely branched stems. Relatively large, often wine-red, solitary heads form at the top of stems. Only a few bright yellow ray flowers are present in each head.

Range: throughout the Rockies.

A distinctive plant, Small Blacktip Ragwort is one of the multitudes of brilliant wildflowers that bedeck alpine meadows. The large, erect leaves vertically encircle stout stems that culminate in crowns of yellow blooms. At maturity, silken-haired seeds supplant the flowers and are spread near and far by the wind. The conspicuous black-tipped bracts are useful in identifying this species. For the Inuit, these bracts represented tears for the massacre of unsuspecting Inuit that took place in 1771 by Native American warriors who accompanied the explorer Samuel Hearne on his expedition to the Arctic Coast. Sir John Richardson first collected this plant near the massacre site, Bloody Falls on the Coppermine River, and named it *lugens* (from the Latin word meaning "to mourn").

Range: Alberta, British Columbia, Washington, Montana, and Wyoming.

Small Blacktlp Ragwort
Senecio lugens

ASTER FAMILY
Asteraceae

This ragwort is a coarse perennial with several tall, erect, and very leafy stems. The leaves are triangular, with long points, and they are borne singly along the stem, which is 24–48 inches (60–120 cm) tall. Large lower leaves, with jagged margins, have long petioles, but the smaller upper ones have no petioles and their margins have smaller teeth. The stems are smooth and generally purplish at the base, crowned with quite a showy terminal cluster of flowers. The open, flat-topped cluster may have only a few or many flower heads, each with 5 to 12 deep yellow rays. These plants are often found in large clumps or colonies along streams or in meadows of the subalpine region.

Range: throughout the Rockies.

Arrowleaf Ragwort
Senecio triangularis

ASTER FAMILY
Asteraceae

Canada Goldenrod
Solidago canadensis

ASTER FAMILY
Asteraceae

The golden glow of Canada Goldenrod is widespread in almost all Canadian provinces and U. S. states and signals the end of summer. Canada Goldenrod grows from creeping rhizomes, sending up stems 3 feet (1 m) or more tall. It has numerous alternate, lance-shaped stockless leaves that are only slightly reduced in size higher on the stem. Its terminal inflorescence is a pyramid-like panicle with yellow ray and yellow disk florets. The flowers are borne on one side of the branchlets, which often arch downward. Canada Goldenrod is a beautiful and variable plant found in meadows, open forests, along roadsides, and other disturbed sites from valley bottoms to the subalpine zone.

Range: throughout the Rockies.

Rocky Mountain Goldenrod
Solidago multiradiata

ASTER FAMILY
Asteraceae

Rocky Mountain Goldenrod has a woody rootstock and erect, leafy (often reddish) stems, which bear dense clusters of golden-yellow flower heads. Most often, 8 ray flowers surround 13 or more disk florets. The inner bracts of the flower head are much longer than the outer ones, although all are blunt-ended. The leaves, which are nearly spoon-shaped or lance-shaped, with deeply impressed midribs, occur in clumps at the plant's base and also along the stem. In addition, the basal leaves have white, hairy-margined petioles. Plants may be up to 16 inches (40 cm) tall, but are usually much smaller, around 2½ inches (6 cm), at high elevations. The flowers produce a gold to yellow dye. Certain species of goldenrod are believed to have wound-healing properties. This plant is common on dry, open slopes to above the timberline.

Range: throughout the Rockies.

Originally brought to North America as a decorative and medicinal herb, Common Tansy has escaped from herbalists' gardens and in many places is considered a noxious weed. This plant is a strong-scented herb with stout, erect, and reddish stems 16 inches (40 cm) to more than 40 inches (100 cm) tall. Its attractive leaves are alternate, pinnately divided, hairless, elliptical or egg-shaped, and about 4–8 inches (10–20 cm) long. Each leaflet is pinnately divided and fern-like, having its own teeth or lobes. The long-lasting flowers occur in somewhat flattened, terminal clusters called cymes. Each head has from 20 to 200 yellow, button-like disk florets; there are no ray flowers. Common Tansy contains volatile oil and the leaves and flowers are considered poisonous if consumed in large quantities. Its habitat includes pastures, and waste areas such as roadsides, ditches, and fencerows from the plains to the montane.

Range: throughout the Rockies.

Common Tansy
Tanacetum vulgare

ASTER FAMILY
Asteraceae

Most of the dandelions seen in the Rockies are the introduced Common Dandelion. There are a few native species, which are comparatively rare and usually found high in the mountains. More than 25 former species of dandelions have recently been lumped under the name of Common Dandelion. The general characteristics of dandelions are similar: heads of the brightest yellow; ray flowers on hollow stems; deeply toothed, lance-shaped leaves; milky sap in the stems and leaves; and a rounded seed head full of parachute-like seeds that drift far and wide. The leaves and flowering stems rise from a fleshy taproot. All parts of the dandelion may be used for food or drink. The greens are used as salad, potherb, or a tea; the roots roasted for a coffee substitute; and the blossoms fermented for wine. This plant has also been used for a host of medicinal purposes. Bears are particularly fond of the dandelion flowers, as evidenced by their yellow-stained muzzles during the flowering period. Common Dandelion can be found from valley bottoms to the open slopes of the alpine zone.

Range: throughout the Rockies.

Common Dandelion
Taraxacum officinale ssp. ceratophorum

ASTER FAMILY
Asteraceae

Graylocks Four-nerve Daisy; Old-Man-of-the-Mountain

Tetraneuris grandiflora
[Hymenoxys grandiflora]

ASTER FAMILY
Asteraceae

With flowers so large they often obscure the stems and leaves, Graylocks Four-nerve Daisy is a giant in the alpine habitat that it shares with other smaller wildflowers. The feathery leaves are mostly basal and 2¾-4 inches (7-10 cm) long. Leaves, stems, and involucral bracts are covered with cottony white hairs. The stout stems are 1¼-10 inches (3-25 cm) tall and each bears a single nodding flower head from 2-4 inches (5-10 cm) wide. Bright yellow petals with 3 teeth at the tip surround a wide, domed center of disk florets, which turn from yellow to tan with maturity. This plant may be vegetative and inconspicuous for years while storing sufficient energy to produce the huge flower heads; then they bloom, set seed, and die. It is worth any amount of effort to find enormous communal masses of Graylocks Four-nerve Daisy blooming in its high mountain habitat.

Range: Idaho, Montana, Wyoming, Utah, and Colorado.

Lyall's Goldenweed

Tonestus lyallii
[Haplopappus lyallii]

ASTER FAMILY
Asteraceae

Only those wayfarers with strong legs and keen eyes will find this sturdy mountain-dweller. It is a dwarf perennial, generally less than 4 inches (10 cm) high. The small lance-shaped leaves, ¾-2½ inches (2-6 cm) long, are hairy and often covered with a sticky coating. The leaves are clumped mainly at the base of the flower stem. The solitary flower head is a deep yellow and appears incongruously large compared to the rest of the tiny plant. Both the ray and disk florets are yellow, while the involucral bracts are purple-tipped and sticky. Lyall's Goldenweed forms small clumps on shaly slopes above the tree line and is easily confused with Alpine Yellow Fleabane, which is much more common. Lyall's Goldenweed, however, has sessile leaves in contrast to petiolate leaves on the latter.

Range: throughout the Rockies, excluding Utah and New Mexico.

Like a giant dandelion, this introduced biennial is a weed of roadsides and other disturbed places. The stout, stiffly erect plant, growing from a deep fleshy taproot, has bluish-green stems and grass-like leaves. When broken, Yellow Salsify leaves and stems exude a milky white latex. Often closing by early afternoon, the pale lemon-yellow ray flowers appear at the end of the stem, which is decidedly thickened below the flower head. There are 10 to 14 pointed involucral bracts, longer than the ray flowers. Perhaps more spectacular than the flower are the achenes with parachute-like attachments that form a globular ball. These are easily broken apart by the wind and the achenes are carried great distances.

Range: throughout the Rockies.

Yellow Salsify; Goatsbeard
Tragopogon dubius

ASTER FAMILY
Asteraceae

Strongly aromatic, Mule-ears is a native forb with stems up to 32 inches (80 cm) tall. Basal leaves are alternate, lance-shaped, 8–16 inches (20–40 cm) long and 2–6 inches (5–15 cm) wide with entire or toothed margins. The leaves resemble the ears of a mule, hence the origin of the common name. Sunflower-like blossoms comprised of 13 to 20 lemon-yellow ray flowers encircle the tubular yellow disk florets. The taproot of Mule-ears, which may reach 8 ¾ inches (22 cm) in circumference and a depth of over 5 feet (1.5 m), aids in survival during drought conditions. This plant is highly aggressive and often occurs in large dense stands, especially on clay soil. Sunflower Mule-ears (*W. helianthoides*), a similar plant but with white to cream ray flowers and more pubescence, hybridizes with Mule-ears where the ranges overlap.

Range: throughout the Rockies, excluding Alberta, British Columbia, and New Mexico.

Mule-ears
Wyethia amplexicaulis

ASTER FAMILY
Asteraceae

Creeping Barberry; Oregon Grape

Mahonia repens

BARBERRY FAMILY
Berberidaceae

Creeping Barberry is a spreading shrub, generally from 4–12 inches (10–30 cm) tall. Its holly-like leaves are waxy and leathery with prickly margins. Each leaf consists of 3 to 7 dark, glossy green leaflets. With the arrival of autumn, some of the leaves change to a flaming glory of red and purple. The handsome foliage is a suitable background for clusters of rich golden-yellow flowers. Each flower has 6 petals, 6 sepals, and 6 stamens. After the flowers' work is done, they are replaced by juicy blue berries that gleam amid the leaves. Native Americans ate the berries, extracted yellow dyes from the roots, and used the bark of roots as a medicine and tonic. Hollyleaved Barberry (*M. aquifolium*) is similar to Creeping Barberry, but ranging up to 60 inches (150 cm) tall. Creeping Barberry is at home on rocky slopes and in open forests.

Range: throughout the Rockies.

Narrowleaf Stoneseed; Narrow-leaved Puccoon

Lithospermum incisum

BORAGE FAMILY
Boraginaceae

Narrowleaf Stoneseed, a spring flowering herbaceous perennial, has an abundance of long, lemon-yellow, trumpet-like flowers, which make it a most attractive plant in bloom. The margins of the corolla are minutely fringed, giving rise to the name, *incisum*. Typically this plant grows low to the ground but may be as tall as 12 inches (30 cm). Its leaves are narrow, about ¾–2 inches (2–5 cm) long, and roughened with short, stiff hairs. The generic name comes from *litho,* meaning "stone," and *spermum* for "seed," referring to the bony white nutlets produced at maturity. The bark from the roots of Narrowleaf Stoneseed is reported to yield a bright purple pigment. It is most common on dry, open plains and foothills.

Range: throughout the Rockies, excluding Washington, Oregon, and Idaho.

This is a coarse perennial, up to 20 inches (50 cm) high, that is firmly anchored to dry slopes and grasslands by a large woody taproot. Numerous sharply pointed, lance-shaped leaves clasp the stem. The small flowers are not particularly showy, being lemon-yellow or greenish and partly hidden in the axils of the leaves near the top of the stem, but they have a strong and pleasing scent. Both the stems and leaves are covered with long white hairs. *Lithospermum* means "stoneseed," which is an apt description of the plant's extremely hard nutlets. For centuries some Native Americans used an extract of this plant for birth control. Natural estrogens in the plant suppress the release of certain hormones required for ovulation. The roots were used as food and as a source of red dye.

Range: throughout the Rockies, excluding New Mexico.

Western Stoneseed
Lithospermum ruderale

BORAGE FAMILY
Boraginaceae

Several drabas with pale to bright yellow flowers grow in the alpine region. They are low-growing, tufted plants with small cross-shaped flowers consisting of 4 sepals, 4 petals, 6 stamens, and 1 pistil. Discrimination between the various species is often difficult, but several of the high-elevation species are enchantingly lovely. This particular species is a matted plant scarcely 4–4¾ inches (10–12 cm) tall. It has numerous leaves, with branched hairs, and clusters of tiny yellow flowers at the ends of the stems. The flowers may be used to make dyes of cream, gold, and chartreuse.

Range: throughout the Rockies, excluding Colorado and New Mexico.

Payson's Draba
Draba paysonii

MUSTARD FAMILY
Brassicaceae

Common Twinpod
Physaria didymocarpa

MUSTARD FAMILY
Brassicaceae

Growing on fully exposed, dry, stony ground where there is little competition from other plants, Common Twinpod is anchored by a deep taproot. The cluster of fan-shaped basal leaves is mealy-white. Each leaf blade is blunt and shallowly notched, and densely covered with silvery hairs. The weak stems, often trailing on the ground, have much smaller leaves and support a short terminal cluster of cross-shaped, bright yellow flowers. Pairs of swollen seedpods, purplish-green in color, give the plant a distinctive character as they mature. Native Americans were reported to use the juice from the plant for sore throats, cramps, and stomach trouble.

Range: Alberta, British Columbia, Washington, Idaho, Montana, and Wyoming.

Brittle Pricklypear
Opuntia fragilis

CACTUS FAMILY
Cactaceae

Inset photo by George Scotter

With the most northern range of any cactus, this perennial lies flat on the ground and forms low mats or clumps that are 2–8 inches (5–20 cm) tall and 12 inches (30 cm) in diameter. Joints of the stem are rounded, globe- to egg-shaped and ¾–2 inches (2–5 cm) long. Areoles, from which the 1¼ inch (3 cm) long yellowish spines grow, are barbed with coarse, white hairs that are called glochids. The satiny, yellow flowers are solitary, 1¼–2 inch (3–5 cm) broad, with reddish filaments. Fruits are pear-shaped and usually somewhat spiny. The upper stem segments are easily detached and dispersed by animals to form new plants. Brittle Pricklypear may be confused with Plains Pricklypear (*O. polyacantha*) [inset]. The latter has flattened pads that do not readily detach, grows 3–6 inches (8–15 cm) tall, and can spread several yards (meters) in diameter. The flowers also tend to be larger and with a more reddish tint. Both species are found in dry grasslands from the plains to open montane forests.

Range: throughout the Rockies.

Limber Honeysuckle clambers over low shrubs and around the trunks of trees at low elevations. The trumpet-like flowers cluster in a shallow protective cup formed by 2 leaves that are joined at their bases. The upper leaf surface is bright green and smooth; the underneath is blue-green and downy. When the flowers first open they are yellow, changing to orange-red with age. The 5 petals are united into a funnel-shaped corolla tube, which has a swollen knob near the base where nectar accumulates. Insects puncture the knobs to access the reserve of sweets. On a calm day the sweet-scented flowers release a drifting trail of heavenly perfume. Red berries eventually replace the flowers within the cupped leaves.

Range: Alberta, British Columbia, and Wyoming.

Limber Honeysuckle
Lonicera dioica

HONEYSUCKLE FAMILY
Caprifoliaceae

Twinberry Honeysuckle is a bushy shrub 3–6 feet (1–2 m) tall. Its leaves are 2–6 inches (5–15 cm) long, elliptical to lance-shaped, veined, and bright green. The shrub is easy to recognize because the flowers, berries, and bracts are paired. The 2 dull yellow flowers, like little twin candles, are cupped by 2 green bracts. The 5 petals of each flower are fused into a funnel-shaped corolla tube; there are no sepals. As the flowers develop into shiny, inky-black berries, the bracts become deep maroon collars, which expand backward, exposing more of the twinberries. Although tasting disagreeable to people, the berries are eaten by birds and mammals. This sturdy shrub prefers rather damp, protected places within woodlands.

Range: throughout the Rockies.

Twinberry Honeysuckle
Lonicera involucrata

HONEYSUCKLE FAMILY
Caprifoliaceae

Scouler's St. Johnswort; Western St. Johnswort
Hypericum scouleri

MANGOSTEEN FAMILY
Clusiaceae

The showy yellow flowers of Scouler's St. Johnswort appear in a cluster near the end of the stem in an elongated, open inflorescence. The numerous stamens are upright when freshly opened then explode into lovely starbursts as they mature. The petals and sepals are edged with black dots. Unopened flower buds are conspicuously red tipped. The leaves are short and opposite with black dots on the margins, which can be seen with the aid of a hand lens. Spreading by rhizomes, the stems vary from 4 inches (10 cm) to more than 20 inches (50 cm) tall. This plant is a close relative of Common St. Johnswort (*H. perforatum*), an introduced noxious weed that is causing massive agricultural damage. Scouler's St. Johnswort is found in open, moist and boggy sites from the foothills to alpine elevations.

Range: throughout the Rockies.

Spearleaf Stonecrop
Sedum lanceolatum

STONECROP FAMILY
Crassulaceae

Like all species of *Sedum*, Spearleaf Stonecrop grows in clumps and has fleshy stems and leaves. The numerous basal leaves, almost round in cross-section, form a rosette. The petals are bright yellow, with sharp points, and they are distinctly separate right to the base. They form a compact cluster at the top of a stem that is 4-6 inches (10-15 cm) high. The long golden stamens are conspicuous. Both the succulent leaves and stems store water to ensure the plant's survival during drought. The young stems and leaves are reported to be good eating when cooked. Spearleaf Stonecrop grows on screes and thin gravelly soils from lower elevations to well above the timberline.

Range: throughout the Rockies.

Roundleaf Sundew
Drosera rotundifolia

SUNDEW FAMILY
Droseraceae

This unique inhabitant of sphagnum bogs is a carnivorous plant. Roundleaf Sundew has adaptations that allow it to capture and digest small insects and other invertebrates. This tiny plant has a diameter of 1¼–2 inches (3–5 cm) with a 2–10 inch (5–25 cm) tall inflorescence. Several insignificant, white but occasionally pink, 5-petaled flowers are borne towards the end of the slender stem that arises from the center of a rosette. At first the stem is coiled inward bearing a simple one-sided raceme, which straightens out as the flower expands. The shallow roots are poorly developed. The 8 to 15 club-shaped leaves are arranged in a basal rosette. Attached by a slender, hairy petiole about ⅝ inch (1.5 cm) long, the upper surface of the blade is densely covered by red glandular hairs, each with small enlargements at their free ends. The hairs and enlargements are called tentacles. Tentacles secrete sticky mucilage, loaded with a sugary substance to attract insects. They respond to the touch of an insect by bending inward to trap and hold the prey with the mucilage on the enlarged tips. In addition, the leaf blade may also close around the prey. The

tentacles secrete a protease and acid phosphatase for the enzymatic breakdown of the prey. Initial reaction begins within seconds and may be completed within minutes. Assimilation of the nutrients takes place only through the tentacles in contact with the prey and not through the surface of the leaf itself. By the practice of carnivory, these specialized plants acquire a source of nitrogen, phosphorous, and perhaps other elements in nutrient-poor environments. A close relative, English Sundew (*D. anglica*), at the bottom of the page, has erect leaves that are conspicuously more linear than those of Roundleaf Sundew. Although both species are often found in similar habitats, English Sundew prefers living closer to the waterline and in more lime-rich soils. Both thrive in wetlands such as marshes and fens and are associated with sphagnum bogs.

Range: throughout the Rockies, excluding Wyoming, Utah, and New Mexico.

Silverberry; Wolf Willow
Elaeagnus commutata

OLEASTER FAMILY
Elaeagnaceae

This shrub might have been designed by a silversmith; each leaf, tiny flower, fruit, and new stem or twig is covered with the same rich coating of silvery scales. The rusty-brown branches, from 3–9 feet (1–3 m) tall, are hung with oblong, silvery leaves, from 1¼–3 inches (3–8 cm) long, which are waxy and smooth-margined. Both surfaces of the leaves have the same striking silver color, sometimes with scattered brown scales beneath. Each small tubular flower is silvery on the outside and yellowish on the inside, with a strong, sweet scent. The fruits are dry and mealy and contain a single hard seed with 8 striped grooves. Like a tail, the remains of the flower hang onto the end of the silvery fruit. Native Americans resorted to the fruits, too dry and mealy for normal consumption, as a famine food; necklaces were made from the dry seeds. Silverberry is a distinctive shrub of deep coulees, stream banks, and hillsides.

Range: throughout the Rockies, excluding Oregon and New Mexico.

Russet Buffaloberry; Soapberry
Shepherdia canadensis

OLEASTER FAMILY
Elaeagnaceae

This common shrub, 5–8 feet (1.5–2.5 m) tall, grows in several habitats and is often the dominant species in the understory of pinewoods. Male and female flowers, borne in clusters on separate shrubs, appear on the brown scurfy twigs even before the leaves. The tiny yellowish flowers are inconspicuous; male flowers have 4 stamens while female flowers have none. In the fall, the female shrubs will be covered with small, translucent berries that range in color from shining yellow to red. The thick, leathery leaves are green and glossy on the upper surface, while the lower surface is covered with a white felt and sprinkled with rusty dots. All parts of the plant are covered with rust-colored, shiny scales. Although repulsive to most people, the berries are enjoyed by birds and mammals, being particularly important to grizzly bears and black bears. Whipped with a little water, the berries produce a pink, foamy drink that was much prized by many Native Americans. A berry crushed between the finger and thumb will reveal the soapy feel that results from the presence of the glucoside saponin, which is now used as a foaming agent in detergents.

Range: throughout the Rockies.

This dwarf evergreen shrub, 4-12 inches (10-30 cm) tall, often shares its habitat with Pink Mountainheath. Yellow Mountainheath has yellowish-green, bell-like flowers that are puckered at the open end. The flowers, flower stems, and young branchlets are covered with small sticky hairs—hence the species name *glanduliflora* (glandular flowers). Clusters of nodding flowers are produced on long stalks at the end of the stem. The small, round seed capsules are reddish-colored. There are grooves on the undersides of the needle-like leaves. Pink and Yellow Mountainheaths hybridize, and all degrees of variation may be found between the bell-shaped, rose cups of one parent and the vase-shaped, yellowish- to greenish-white flowers of the other. Watch for the many-flowered clusters near the timberline and in alpine meadows during the summer.

Range: throughout the Rockies, excluding Utah, Colorado, and New Mexico.

Yellow Mountainheath
Phyllodoce glanduliflora

HEATH FAMILY
Ericaceae

A highly variable species, Field Locoweed has flowers that are usually whitish-yellow, but white, blue, pink, and purple ones are not too uncommon. Many flowers are borne on stems up to 12 inches (30 cm) high. Each leaf consists of 11 to 31 leaflets with silky hairs on both surfaces. Both the stems and leaves branch from a stout, multiple base. Black and white hairs cover the 1½ inch (4 cm) long seedpods. Domestic livestock that eat these plants appear to suffer mental disorders, hence the name "locoweed." A yellow dye may be produced from both the leaves and the blossoms. Field Locoweed is common on prairies and in open woodlands.

Range: throughout the Rockies, excluding New Mexico.

Field Locoweed
Oxytropis campestris

PEA FAMILY
Fabaceae

Prairie Thermopsis; Buffalo Bean

Thermopsis rhombifolia

PEA FAMILY
Fabaceae

Closely resembling a yellow-flowered lupine, Prairie Thermopsis is one of the most striking and colorful early spring flowers. Stout, branched stems of this perennial usually grow in large patches from running rootstocks. The 4-16 inch (10-40 cm) stems have alternate leaves, each with 3 egg-shaped leaflets ¾-1¼ inches (2-3 cm) long. Bright golden-yellow flowers cluster in a showy raceme from 2-4¾ inches (5-12 cm) long. The pea-like flowers are succeeded by grayish-brown, hairy pods, which are often curved in a semicircle and whose fruits are poisonous. Native Americans applied another common name, Buffalo Bean, to the plant because they used its flowering season as an indicator that buffalo bulls were in prime condition for spring hunting. Flowering in early spring, the plant is common in dry, sandy grasslands.

Range: throughout the Rockies, excluding Washington, Oregon, and Idaho.

Pointedtip Mariposa Lily; Three Spot Mariposa Lily

Calochortus apiculatus

LILY FAMILY
Liliaceae

Among the loveliest flowers, Pointedtip Mariposa Lily has 3 broad, fan-shaped petals, each with a small, roundish, purple-black gland at the base as well as 3 sepals and 6 stamens. The inner base surface of the creamy white petals is heavily bearded on the lower portion. The 3 sepals are shorter, much narrower, and sharply pointed. From 1 to 5 saucer-shaped flowers may occur on a single stem. The 3-winged fruit pods are invariably nodding. Usually a single gray-green basal leaf, linear and sharply pointed, arises from a dark brown, onion-like bulb. Mariposa, the Spanish word for butterfly, was the name given the plant since its wide-spreading petals resemble a butterfly hovering over a slender stem. The boiled bulbs, rich in starch, have the flavor of potatoes and were relished by some Native American tribes and early settlers when food was scarce. Sunny grasslands or forest openings at low elevations are the favored habitats for this plant.

Range: Alberta, British Columbia, Montana, Idaho, and Washington.

Standing out like splashes of gold against the white edges of melting snowdrifts, these flowers are some of the first harbingers of spring, impatient to brighten the slopes as the snowbanks retreat. The nodding yellow flowers are on stems 6–12 inch (15–30 cm) high. The 6 taper-pointed "petals" (actually 3 petals and 3 sepals) curl back, exposing 6 yellow stamens and the style to full view. Two large, broad, pointed leaves grow from the base of the plant; they are a shiny light green. After the petals and sepals fall, an erect, many-seeded capsule develops. Both black bears and grizzly bears eagerly eat the small, deep-set corms. Dense patches of Yellow Avalanche-lily can be found in open timberline forests and alpine meadows.

Range: throughout the Rockies.

Yellow Avalanche-lily; Glacier Lily
Erythronium grandiflorum

LILY FAMILY
Liliaceae

The strikingly beautiful flowers of Yellow Fritillary herald the arrival of spring. It grows from a small, scaly, white bulb about ⅜ inch (1 cm) across. The bulbs, 2–12 inches (5–30 cm) beneath the ground surface, reproduce asexually by forming grain-sized offsets. The stems stand 4–12 inches (10–30 cm) tall and carry from 2 to 6 blue-green strap-shaped leaves about 3 inches (8 cm) long. The flowers are narrowly bell-shaped with similar petals and sepals about ¾ inch (2 cm) long; they hang demurely like solitary bells from the end of their curved stems. The chromatic yellow flowers, etched faintly with fine purple lines; turn orange to brick-red on aging. After the petals and sepals fall off, the stems straighten out and place the stout, 3-parted fruits in an erect position. The bulbs and offsets were used as food by Native Americans and early explorers and are eagerly sought by small mammals. This charming plant inhabits sheltered grasslands and coulees at low elevations.

Range: throughout the Rockies.

Yellow Fritillary
Fritillaria pudica

LILY FAMILY
Liliaceae

Columbia Lily
Lilium columbianum

LILY FAMILY
Liliaceae

Oval-shaped bulbs up to 2 inches (5 cm) in diameter give rise to the stiff stems of Columbia Lily, which may reach up to 3 feet (1 m) or more. Whorls of 6 to 9 smooth, dark green, lanceolate leaves circle the stems at intervals. One or more flowers hang from stalklets near the top of the stem. Tepals, consisting of 3 petals and 3 sepals, are yellow-orange to reddish-orange and strongly reflexed. The inner portions of the petals are decorated with numerous maroon spots from the midpoint into the throat. Each downward-hanging flower is 2–3 inches (5–8 cm) across, with chocolate-purple anthers and a sticky stigma. Six-parted capsules that contain flat, brown seeds follow the flowers. The bulbs were highly prized by various Native American tribes; they were eaten after steaming or boiling to reduce bitterness, and also dried and stored for future use. Columbia Lily inhabits moist forests openings and clearings with a low shrub cover from the montane to subalpine zones.

Range: British Columbia, Washington, Oregon, Idaho, and Montana.

Yellow Pond-lily
Nuphar lutea

WATER-LILY FAMILY
Nymphaeaceae

What appear to be petals on Yellow Pond-lily are actually 6 showy, yellow sepals, sometimes reddish tinged. The numerous petals are yellow, inconspicuous, and hidden from view unless seen from directly above. Myriads of stamens surround the prominent lobed stigma in the center of the flower. Leaves of this perennial have a V-shaped notch at their base and may be wide or rather narrow, floating, or submersed in the water. Yellow Pond-lily reproduces from seed or spreads by rhizomes and can grow in water up to 12 feet (4 m) in depth. Each fruit is flat-topped and has numerous seeds. Still or slowly moving water in ponds, lakes, swamps, rivers, canals, and ditches are habitats for this aquatic plant.

Range: throughout the Rockies.

Photo by George Scotter

Introduced from Europe early in the 17th century, Hairy Evening-primrose is a taprooted biennial or short-lived perennial up to more than 3 feet (1 m) tall. Stems are erect and can be simple or branched and often sport stiff, reddish hairs. Stem bases have a rosette of leaves up to 6 inches (15 cm) long and 2 inches (5 cm) wide; upper leaves are shorter and narrower, alternate, and stalkless. All leaves are sharp-tipped, have short teeth, and appear grayish from a dense cover of pale hairs. Several flowers occur in a crowded, leafy cluster on branched or unbranched terminal spikes. The tubular flower has 4 bright yellow petals that fade to reddish or orange with maturity and 4 leaf-like, turned-down sepals. These flowers open in the late afternoon or evening for pollination by night-flying moths and usually wither the following day. Hairy Evening-primrose is a plant of open disturbed places such as roadsides, fence rows, and irrigation ditches in the plains and foothills.

Range: throughout the Rockies, excluding Alberta.

Hairy Evening-primrose
Oenothera villosa

EVENING PRIMROSE FAMILY
Onagraceae

The flowers of this interesting little orchid have greenish-yellow petals and sepals, and a whitish, 3-lobed lip, rarely with a few purple spots. The specific name *trifida* refers to the lip. The plant grows about 8 inches (20 cm) high. In place of leaves, there are a few overlapping bracts on the lower part of the greenish-yellow stem. The elliptic seedpods are large for the size of the flowers and they droop down and away from the stem at an angle. Yellow Coralroot has no roots but grows from rhizomes that are a branched lump of tissue with hairs, hence the name coralroot. As a saprophyte it lives off leaf litter on the forest floor. This perennial grows in shaded forest habitats and wet meadows.

Range: throughout the Rockies.

Yellow Coralroot; Early Coralroot; Pale Coralroot
Corallorhiza trifida

ORCHID FAMILY
Orchidaceae

Greater Yellow Lady's Slipper

Cypripedium parviflorum
[C. calceolus]

ORCHID FAMILY
Orchidaceae

This is one of the most exquisite of nature's creations. Both scientific names mean "slipper" or "small shoe," referring to the resemblance of the flower's satiny, sun-golden, and inflated pouch to a slipper. This bladder-like pouch is lined with purple streaks and spots that add even more to its beauty. The lateral petals may be quite variable in color, ranging from yellowish- or greenish- to purplish-brown; they are often spirally twisted. The perfumed flowers are supported on stems 12–24 inches (30–60 cm) tall. Large, prominently veined, clasping leaves provide an elegant background for the unique flowers. Greater Yellow Lady's Slipper grows as an individual plant or in crowded clumps in moist forests and mossy bogs. While it is common in some locations, it has disappeared from others because of its susceptibility to being picked.

Range: throughout the Rockies, excluding Oregon.

Rooted Poppy

Papaver radicatum
[P. kluanensis]

POPPY FAMILY
Papaveraceae

Not unlike the poppies in our home gardens and parks, the Rooted Poppy has 4 petals that form a cup. The petals enclose a star-shaped stigma, which is ringed by a crown of stamens. All visible parts of the plant, except for the flower, are covered with hairs. Hairs on the leaf blades and petioles are white while those on the oval bud are dark brown. The numerous 5-lobed leaves are all basal. As the sulphur-yellow petals grow older they often become pale green. The flat-topped ovary later develops into the familiar seed capsule, ringed with small openings at the top that allow the wind to scatter the many seeds. Rooted Poppy is by no means common even in its favorite habitat among the rocks and ledges at high altitudes.

Range: throughout the Rockies, excluding Washington and Oregon.

Alpine Golden Buckwheat is a low perennial, 3–8 inches (8–20 cm) in height, growing from a coarse woody taproot and a reddish-brown tufted root crown. Linear-oblong, basal leaves are grayish-green above and gray on the underside and hairy on both surfaces, especially the underside. Dozens of sulfur-yellow flowers crowd into fluffy clusters atop leafless stems. The slender stalks, encased with leaf-like bracts, radiate upwards from a central point to form the flower head or umbel. *Eriogonum* is derived from *erion*, "wool," and *gonu*, "knee or joint," referring to the pubescent and swollen joints found on many species of buckwheat. The species name *flavum* means "yellow," referring to the flower color. Alpine Golden Buckwheat is an unfortunate common name since this plant is found from dry sites in the grasslands to the alpine zone.

Range: throughout the Rockies, excluding Utah and New Mexico.

Alpine Golden Buckwheat
Eriogonum flavum

BUCKWHEAT FAMILY
Polygonaceae

Cushion Buckwheat is easily recognized even when flowers are not present. This mat-forming perennial has white, woolly, basal leaves about ⅝ inch (1.5 cm) long. The mats, growing near the ground, can be more than 10 inches (25 cm) across. The specific name *ovalifolium* refers to the usual leaf shape but it is highly variable. Handsome, creamy to sulphur-yellow, puffball-like flowers, which may be tinted bright pink to rose-red as they age, adorn the stems. Cushion Buckwheat is wide ranging from the plains and foothills to exposed alpine ridges. Some early prospectors considered Cushion Buckwheat to be an indicator of silver deposits.

Range: throughout the Rockies.

Cushion Buckwheat
Eriogonum ovalifolium

BUCKWHEAT FAMILY
Polygonaceae

Sulphur-flower Buckwheat

Eriogonum umbellatum

BUCKWHEAT FAMILY
Polygonaceae

Sulphur-flower Buckwheat is a perennial that grows from 4–12 inches (10–30 cm) tall. Its basal leaves, though variable in shape, are generally lance- to spoon-shaped. They are densely covered with white hairs beneath, but have a green upper surface. The stem leaves occur in a whorl at the top of the main stalk where it is divided into 6 or more smaller branches, creating the flower umbels. The umbrella-like clusters of flowers are greenish-white to pale sulphur-yellow, often flecked with a faintly rose flush as they age. Reportedly, the leaves may be boiled to make tea. This plant is widely distributed on exposed sites from low elevations to alpine ridges.

Range: throughout the Rockies, excluding New Mexico.

Fringed Loosestrife

Lysimachia ciliata

PRIMROSE FAMILY
Primulaceae

Fringed Loosestrife is an erect plant 12–40 inches (30–100 cm) high. Its green, opposite leaves are pointed at the end and rounded at the base. Both the leaf margins and the petioles are fringed with white hairs. Borne in the upper leaf axils, the large flowers have 5 bright yellow petals with somewhat unevenly pointed tips and reddish glandular bases. The 5 fertile stamens alternate with 5 sterile stamens. This plant prefers moist or boggy places in the montane zone.

Range: throughout the Rockies.

Growing from creeping stems or underground rhizomes, the leafy, erect, unbranched stem is hairless and reaches from 8–28 inches (20–70 cm). The sharply pointed, oval, stalkless leaves are willow-like, marked with tiny dark dots, up to 4 inches (10 cm) in length, and arranged in opposite pairs on the stem. Flowers originate from the lower leaf axils. The 5 yellow petals are purple dotted or streaked, while the yellow stamens are noticeably extended beyond the corolla. Usually growing in shallow water, Tufted Loosestrife is a plant of damp places such as bogs, fens, springs, marshes, and wet meadows.

Range: throughout the Rockies, excluding New Mexico.

Tufted Loosestrife
Lysimachia thyrsiflora

PRIMROSE FAMILY
Primulaceae

Lemon-yellow in color, occasionally with a dash of pink, the beautiful flowers of the Yellow Columbine nod at the ends of slender stems that lift them above the gracefully divided leaves. Each flower consists of 5 wing-shaped, petal-like sepals; 5 tube-shaped petals, each flaring at the open end and tapering to a distinctive projecting spur at the opposite end; 5 pistils; and numerous stamens. The leaves, which grow from the base of the plant, are compound, long-stalked, and divided into many small segments. The seeds are borne in a 5-parted pod which points upward at maturity. Boiled roots of this plant were used as a cure for diarrhea. Yellow Columbine may be locally common on rocky ledges and screes in the alpine zone, as well as in subalpine glades and along trail verges.

Range: throughout the Rockies, excluding New Mexico.

Yellow Columbine
Aquilegia flavescens

BUTTERCUP FAMILY
Ranunculaceae

Alkali Buttercup
Ranunculus cymbalaria

BUTTERCUP FAMILY
Ranunculaceae

This buttercup spreads over the ground by slender creeping stems or trailing runners, much like those of strawberries. The long-petioled leaf blades are egg- to heart-shaped, with scalloped margins. These characteristic leaves distinguish it from other buttercups with the same creeping habit. The flowering stems are leafless and have one to several small yellow flowers. Several small achenes, with short straight beaks and prominent longitudinal ribs, form a cylindrical seed head. Alkali Buttercup is a plant of muddy shores and brackish ponds.

Range: throughout the Rockies.

Eschscholtz's Buttercup
Ranunculus eschscholtzii

BUTTERCUP FAMILY
Ranunculaceae

This dainty but hardy dwarf buttercup will be seen only by those who venture near or above the timberline. Five bright yellow petals, 5 lavender-tinged sepals, and numerous stamens and pistils form the flower. The flower, about 1 inch (2.5 cm) across and appearing too large for such a small plant, emerges in the spring or early summer before the stems have reached their full length. As the seed cluster matures, the plant may reach 10–12 inches (25–30 cm) in height. The leaves are mainly basal, each 3- to 5-parted, and deeply toothed. Eschscholtz's Buttercup often grows in pools of water from melting snow, along streams and ponds, and in meadows.

Range: throughout the Rockies.

A tiny perennial plant, Pygmy Buttercup bears one to several single-flowered stems above its basal leaves. The leaves are deeply divided into 3 main lobes, with each lobe split again. The 5 yellow petals and 5 greenish sepals are about the same length. A head of short-beaked achenes soon replaces the flowers. This tiny plant may be found on moist alpine slopes and rocky ledges.

Range: throughout the Rockies, excluding Oregon and New Mexico.

Pygmy Buttercup
Ranunculus pygmaeus

BUTTERCUP FAMILY
Ranunculaceae

As the common name suggests, this plant is a flowering shrub. The woody stems may be either spreading or erect and from 12–50 inches (30–125 cm) in height. The brown bark of the stem peels off in long strips. The grayish-green leaves consist of 3 to 7 closely crowded leaflets, which are lightly hairy, often curled, with smooth margins. Golden-yellow, buttercup-like flowers bloom all summer, one of the longest blooming periods of any plant within the Rockies. Flowers tend to be small and pale at low elevations and much larger and brighter at high altitudes. Shrubby Cinquefoil is found over a wide range of habitats, from prairies to alpine slopes. Because of their great beauty, domesticated varieties are frequently grown in gardens as ornamental shrubs. When growing in abundance its presence indicates overgrazing by domestic livestock.

Range: throughout the Rockies.

Shrubby Cinquefoil
Dasiphora fruticosa
[Potentilla fruticosa]

ROSE FAMILY
Rosaceae

Drummond's Mountain-avens
Dryas drummondii

ROSE FAMILY
Rosaceae

Pale to bright yellow nodding flowers distinguish this handsome species, growing on slender stems 6–10 inches (15–25 cm) tall. There are 8 to 10 petals, which never open fully. The sepals are densely covered with a dark, bumpy coat of hairs. Silken plumes later replace the flowers as the styles become twisted into a shiny top. The tiny seeds await a wind to float them away on parachute-like styles to populate new habitats. The wrinkled, leathery evergreen leaves are dark green above, contrasting with the white, hairy lower surface. This plant has a tough woody stem from which slender branches spread above the ground to form mats of leafy stems. It is a common pioneer on gravel flats, rocky slopes, and roadsides in the montane zone, where the lack of competition allows it to form extensive carpets up to 6 feet (2 m) in diameter.

Range: Alberta, British Columbia, Washington, Oregon, Idaho, and Montana.

Oceanspray; Cream Bush
Holodiscus discolor

ROSE FAMILY
Rosaceae

Tall, billowing masses of flowers on this plant are a common sight in late spring or summer. Oceanspray is a deciduous shrub, with slender arching branches, reaching 21 feet (7 m) in wet, coastal forests, but only 3–9 feet (1–3 m) in the Rockies. The straight stems arising from the base were historically used for several purposes including arrow shafts and digging sticks. Leaves are alternate, egg-shaped to oblong, 1½–2¾ inches (4–7 cm) long, with prominent veins, and coarsely toothed or with shallow lobes. Numerous small, saucer-shaped flowers are borne in large, loose, cascading clusters up to 12 inches (30 cm) in length. The sweet scented cream to off-white flowers turn brown as they wither and persist into the next growing season as clusters of seeds. Oceanspray occupies habitats ranging from moist to dry in coniferous forests from the foothills to the montane zone.

Range: throughout the Rockies, excluding Alberta, Wyoming, and New Mexico.

Varileaf Cinquefoil is a common and highly variable plant that grows from the subalpine to high exposed rocky ridges. Its leaves are nearly all basal, each having 5 to 7 leaflets with forward-pointing teeth along the upper two-thirds of their margins. The slender flowering stalks are often reddish, and grow from 4-16 inches (10-40 cm) in height. Generally, 3 to 5 bright yellow flowers are well spaced near the stem tip. The plant may be either hairy or smooth. Depending on the elevation, the flowering period runs from May into August.

Range: throughout the Rockies.

Varileaf Cinquefoil
Potentilla diversifolia

ROSE FAMILY
Rosaceae

Snow Cinquefoil is a dwarf perennial with a stout stem-base and numerous small, 3-parted leaves that hug the ground in a dense cushion or mat. These silvery-green leaves are densely clothed with coarse grayish hairs, somewhat less dense on the top than underneath. The hairs reduce the intensity of the sunlight and protect the stomata from the full force of the winds, thus preventing excessive water loss. The stems, 4-8 inches (10-20 cm) tall, scarcely lift the golden-yellow flowers above the cluster of leaves. *Potentilla* is a large and notoriously difficult group to identify. Recognition of the genus is easy, however, as there is an extra set of 5 bracts below the 5 petals and 5 sepals. This silvery little cinquefoil, with its vivid splashes of golden blossoms, adds color to rocky and exposed slopes in the high alpine.

Range: throughout the Rockies.

Snow Cinquefoil
Potentilla nivea

ROSE FAMILY
Rosaceae

Antelope Bitterbrush
Purshia tridentata

ROSE FAMILY
Rosaceae

Antelope Bitterbrush is a rigid, deciduous shrub varying in growth habit from multiple-stemmed, low, decumbent, spreading forms to upright plants over 12 feet (4 m) tall. Leaves are alternate, typically clustered at nodes, 3-lobed or occasionally 3-toothed, and sometimes glandular. They are green to gray-green above and grayish-white below, pubescent on both surfaces, short-petioled, and with smooth, rolled-under edges. Borne singly on short spurs of the previous year's growth, flowers are abundant with small cream to yellow (occasionally white) flared petals with numerous stamens. Flowers soon fall and are replaced with black achenes that are a tempting source of food for resident rodents. Antelope Bitterbrush has long taproots that extend up to 15 feet (5 m) and a few shallow roots that sometimes have nitrogen-fixing nodules. Its long taproots and nitrogen-fixing capacity enable this shade intolerant shrub to survive on rocky, arid sites. Antelope Bitterbrush provides excellent browse for several species of wildlife and can be critical for deer, especially during the winter. Cattle, goats, and sheep also graze on this shrub. Distributed over 340 million acres (137 million hectares), Antelope Bitterbrush occurs on foothills, mountain slopes, mesas, and open woodlands to elevations of 11,400 feet (3,500 m).

Range: throughout the Rockies, excluding Alberta.

A rather common but inconspicuous plant, this wee herbaceous perennial prefers stable alpine slopes. Branching from a woody base, the stems terminate in clusters of 3-parted, wedge-shaped leaflets, each with 3 prominent teeth at the blunt end and white hairs on both surfaces. The leaves resemble miniature strawberry leaves. Heads are few-flowered and consist of 5 small, pale yellow petals, like dabs of butter, alternating with larger dark green sepals. There are only 5 stamens, an unusual feature in the rose family. Instead of producing juicy berries, Creeping Sibbaldia develops small achenes on a dry receptacle.

Range: throughout the Rockies.

Creeping Sibbaldia
Sibbaldia procumbens

ROSE FAMILY
Rosaceae

This is a robust plant, at home on rocky slopes and ledges and in dry meadows. The leathery leaves, slightly longer than broad, with lobed and toothed margins, are at the base of the plant. Some of the leaves turn bronze or deep red by early autumn. Leafless, wiry stems, 8–20 inch (20–50 cm) high, arise from a thick, scaly rootstock to support the bell-shaped flowers, which are cream to greenish-yellow. An ample store of nectar lures a myriad of insects to the undistinguished flower. Native Americans were reported to use a decoction of the root as a remedy for diarrhea and as an astringent for sores on horses.

Range: throughout the Rockies, excluding Utah, Colorado, and New Mexico.

Roundleaf Alumroot
Heuchera cylindrica

SAXIFRAGE FAMILY
Saxifragaceae

Yellow Mountain Saxifrage

Saxifraga aizoides

SAXIFRAGE FAMILY
Saxifragaceae

Loose mats or cushions of this sturdy little plant, standing out like splashes of yellow gold when in bloom, are found on moist sand, gravel, and stony debris to well above the timberline. The upright stems are 2–4 inches (5–10 cm) tall and crowded with fat, succulent leaves, linear in shape with an abrupt tip. A few pale yellow flowers, often spotted with orange, top small clumps of stems. The 5 long and narrow petals are slightly ragged at their tips. The 10 stamens have conspicuously large anthers and there is generally a pair of plump carpels. Depending on the species and the part of the plant used, saxifrages yield yellow-gold to greenish-yellow dyes.

Range: Alberta and British Columbia.

Whiplash Saxifrage; Spider Plant

Saxifraga flagellaris

SAXIFRAGE FAMILY
Saxifragaceae

Whiplash Saxifrage is a true alpine dweller. A distinctive feature of this plant is its radiating whip-like, arching runners, each terminating in a tiny rooting offset, not unlike a strawberry plant. The spider-like appearance of the runners gave rise to one of the common names. A solitary stem arises from compact basal rosettes of leaves; it is leafy and covered with glandular bumps. The basal leaves are ¼–⅜ inch (5–10 mm) long with bristle-like white hairs on the margins. The solitary stem generally produces 1 to 3 brilliant, golden yellow flowers, often with pink spots near the inner base. The Rocky Mountains contain a few of these jewels, which are highly valued by the wildflower enthusiast since they are difficult to find. Look for Whiplash Saxifrage on limestone areas on moist, turfy alpine slopes and ridges.

Range: throughout the Rockies, excluding Washington and Oregon.

Identification of the Indian Paintbrushes is often puzzling even to specialists because of the wide variability of characteristic features. Western Indian Paintbrush is one of the most distinctive species. Growing singly or in small clusters, the plant's stems, 4-16 inches (10-40 cm) tall, are often purple with sticky hairs. As with other paintbrushes, the actual flowers are small and usually hidden by the larger bracts that are often mistaken for the flower. These blunt bracts, covered with white hairs, are usually greenish-yellow or sometimes tinged with red when fresh, but turn dark green on drying. The corolla is lemon yellow when in bloom and black on drying. This is but one of several Indian Paintbrushes that splash a riot of color from the foothills to alpine meadows. The origin of the numerous Indian Paintbrushes is explained by a legend: A young brave became frustrated as he painted a sunset because he could not match the brilliance of nature. He prayed for guidance from the Great Spirit who gave him paintbrushes laden with the desired colors. After painting his masterpiece, the young brave left the spent brushes on the ground. From those brushes sprouted the multicolored Indian Paintbrushes that we so enjoy today.

Range: throughout the Rockies, except for Washington, Oregon, and Wyoming.

Western Indian Paintbrush
Castilleja occidentalis

FIGWORT FAMILY
Scrophulariaceae

Despite its reputation as a noxious weed, this Eurasian introduction is a striking plant. From 8-32 inches (20-80 cm) tall, the upright stems of this perennial grow from creeping roots. The gray-green leaves are alternate, narrow, and stalkless. Butter and Eggs has snapdragon-like flowers ¾-1¼ inch (2-3 cm) long, each with a long, tapered spur. The tube and corolla are lemon yellow with a brilliant orange pouch on the lower lip. This plant is found along roadsides and other disturbed areas. Dalmatian Toadflax (*L. dalmatica*) closely resembles and grows in the same disturbed habitats as Butter and Eggs. Dalmatian Toadflax is distinguished by broader leaves that clasp the stem.

Range: throughout the Rockies.

Butter and Eggs; Yellow Toadflax
Linaria vulgaris

FIGWORT FAMILY
Scrophulariaceae

Seep Monkeyflower
Mimulus guttatus

FIGWORT FAMILY
Scrophulariaceae

Seep Monkeyflower varies a great deal, but it is always spectacular. It may be an annual or a perennial, a ground-hugging dwarf or a robust plant 40 inches (100 cm) high; the stems may be erect or trailing; the leaves may be smooth or covered with soft hairs; and the lower flower lip may have a single large crimson spot or many smaller spots. These flowers are like snapdragons, ¾–1½ inch (2–4 cm) long, bright yellow, trumpet-shaped, with crimson to brownish-red dots on the larger lower lip. Also, the corolla tube is delicately haired and distinctly 2-lipped, with prominent ridges in the throat. The stem is succulent, hollow, and squarish, and the leaves are well spaced, growing in pairs on opposite sides of it. After the corolla has fallen, the whole calyx inflates until in fruit it is large and conspicuous. Sunny moist areas such as springs and mossy banks of mountain streams are favored habitats and this plant may dominate such areas with bright patches of shimmering golden blooms.

Range: throughout the Rockies.

Oeder's Lousewort
Pedicularis oederi [P. flammea]

FIGWORT FAMILY
Scrophulariaceae

Of the several louseworts that grow in the Rockies, this is one of the most attractive. The upright, reddish-purple stem is about 4 inches (10 cm) high. It bears a spike of fascinating flowers that look like miniature parrot bills. The lower portion of the lip is yellow and the upper portion purple to deep crimson. The leaves are pinnately divided and lacy. Although Oeder's Lousewort is rare, it is immediately noticeable because of its brilliant flowers. Search for it on calcareous alpine slopes.

Range: Alberta, British Columbia, Montana and Wyoming.

The stout, erect stems of Giant Lousewort grow 3 feet (1 m) or more tall. The fern-like basal leaves, 8-24 inches (20-60 cm) long, are pinnately divided into toothed lobes; stem leaves are similar but reduced in size upward on the stem. Flowers, interspersed among sharply pointed bracts, are a dingy yellow to greenish white, often with red streaks. The hooded upper lip and wider lower lip are almost touching. Large mammals occasionally forage on the young flower heads. Giant Lousewort prefers moist habitats in meadows and openings in Quaking Aspen and mixed conifers from the montane to lower subalpine zones.

Range: Wyoming, Utah, Colorado, and New Mexico.

Giant Lousewort
Pedicularis procera

FIGWORT FAMILY
Scrophulariaceae

The numerous tiny tubular flowers of this delightful plant are closely set in several compact whorls along the upper part of the slender stem, the top ring being largest. These rings of sulphur-yellow flowers contrast sharply with the paired green leaves below. Each flower has a tuft of long yellow hairs in its throat, which accounts for the common name. Yellow Penstemon graces open slopes from low elevations to above the timberline.

Range: Alberta, British Columbia, Washington, Oregon, Idaho, and Montana.

Yellow Penstemon
Penstemon confertus

FIGWORT FAMILY
Scrophulariaceae

Little Yellowrattle

Rhinanthus minor

FIGWORT FAMILY
Scrophulariaceae

Little Yellowrattle is partially parasitic on the roots of other plants, from which it extracts ready-made food. This practice sometimes visibly depresses the growth of grasses and other surrounding plants. The 20 inch (50 cm) tall flowering stems are erect and may be single or sparsely branched. The leaves are lance-shaped with toothed margins; they grow in opposite pairs, becoming smaller toward the top of the stem. The curious flowers, on a one-sided spike, have yellowish-green calyx tubes that are inflated but flattened along 2 sides and fringed with 4 short teeth. Golden yellow petals form a 2-lipped corolla; the upper lip is 2-lobed and hooded and the lower is 3-lobed. When ripe, the loose seeds in the swollen pods rattle as the wind blows the withering stems, hence the common name. Look for this unusual annual plant in grassy meadows and open woodlands.

Range: throughout the Rockies, excluding Wyoming and Utah.

Common Mullein

Verbascum thapsus

FIGWORT FAMILY
Scrophulariaceae

This Eurasian import grows about 3–6 feet (1–2 m) tall and is a biennial. From the first-year rosette of large velvet-like leaves surges the strong sentinel-like stalk during the second year. Over a period of many days, pleasant-smelling yellow flowers open up and down the flowering spike in no apparent order. The 3 upper stamens have densely hairy filaments while the 2 lower ones are smooth; all 5 have showy orange anthers. The pistil is prominent and club-topped. After flowering, the dead stem, changing to a dark brown color, may persist for many months. Common Mullein grows along roadsides and in other disturbed areas within the montane zone.

Range: throughout the Rockies.

This dwarf species has bright yellow flowers streaked with violet. The violet lines converge on the lower petals and guide insects to the nectar-secreting glands, which are enclosed within the spur. Both the basal leaves and flower stalks rise from a scaly rootstock. The roundish leaves are smooth with toothed margins, and they generally remain green through the winter. Candied flowers of this plant can be used for decorating cakes and pastries. Darkwoods Violet inhabits moist woods in the montane zone, especially sites with damp moss. It blooms early in the season.

Range: throughout the Rockies, excluding Utah, Colorado, and New Mexico.

Darkwoods Violet
Viola orbiculata

VIOLET FAMILY
Violaceae

The earth laughs in flowers.

— Ralph Waldo Emerson

GREEN

**Huron Green Orchid;
Northern Green
Bog Orchid**
Platanthera huronensis

ORCHID FAMILY
Orchidaceae

page 145

Elkweed; Monument Plant

Frasera speciosa

GENTIAN FAMILY
Gentianaceae

Photo by Katherine Darrow

Elkweed is a monocarpic plant, meaning that it only flowers once in its lifespan of 20 to 80 years and then dies. The plant, therefore, has two stages of life. Until the taproot stores enough energy for reproduction, Elkweed produces only large rosettes of leaves that are pale green, narrow, smooth, 10–20 inches (25–50 cm) long, and up to 7 inches (18 cm) wide. In flowering plants there are tiered clusters of leaves that become smaller upward on the tall, thick, unbranched stock. Numerous showy flowers on short stalks cluster around the junction of these leaves and the stock. Each flower has 4 slender sepals, 4 broad petals, joined at the base, that are pale green flecked with purple, 4 stamens, and some fascinating floral appendages. Each of the broad petals has a pair of elliptical green bumps, lined with myriads of minute glandular hairs, which are covered by a horizontal flap tipped in lavender. Flowering is unpredictable, almost totally absent in some years and in great abundance in others. This sporadic flowering may be a response to environmental factors or an insect avoidance system to help ensure a good seed set. When there is a total absence of floral colonies a build up of predator populations is prevented. During years of peak flower abundance, insect predators cannot respond rapidly enough to threaten seed production. The species name *speciosa* means "showy" or "beautiful," referring to the flower. The large taproot is edible raw, roasted, or boiled and is an excellent source of carbohydrates. Fruits are oblong and slightly flattened capsules about ¾–1 inch (2–2.5 cm) long. After death the straw-colored skeleton of the plant persists, giving rise to another common name, Monument Plant. White Frasera (*F. montana*), a similar but much smaller plant, is endemic to central Idaho. A robust and showy plant, Elkweed is scattered in grasslands, sagebrush communities, and forest openings from the foothills to the subalpine zone.

Range: throughout the Rockies, excluding Alberta and British Columbia.

Photo by Katherine Darrow

Its great size and beautiful foliage alone make Green False Hellebore an impressive sight. This robust herb, 3-6 feet (1-2 m) tall, grows from a thick rootstock, which produces only a single stem. The large, prominently ribbed leaves overlap one another up the stem, like shingles on a roof, until the tassels of flowers begin. Individually, the greenish-yellow flowers are disappointing, but massed together on long arching or drooping branches near the top of the spike, they are impressive. The 6-parted, star-shaped flowers have a musky odor. When young, all parts of the plant are highly poisonous to grazing mammals. Some Native Americans snuffed the dried root as a remedy for headaches. Green False Hellebore may be found from low elevation swamps to moist timberline meadows.

Range: throughout the Rockies, excluding Utah, Colorado, and New Mexico.

Green False Hellebore
Veratrum viride

LILY FAMILY
Liliaceae

While its flowers are not strikingly beautiful, this orchid attracts attention by the oddity of the long, tapering bracts that stand out from the flowering spike like little stakes. Among the bracts, and almost hidden by them, are the small, inconspicuous green flowers. Close examination of a flower reveals a spur and distinctive lip. The lip is spoon-shaped with 2 or 3 prominent teeth at the tip; the spur is about half as long as the lip. Several dark green, oval to lance-shaped leaves ascend the stem, becoming smaller as they merge into the floral spike. Longbract Frog Orchid grows in open woods and moist meadows almost to the timberline.

Range: throughout the Rockies, excluding Oregon and Idaho.

Longbract Frog Orchid
Dactylorhiza viridis
[Habenaria viridis]

ORCHID FAMILY
Orchidaceae

Western Rattlesnake Plantain
Goodyera oblongifolia

ORCHID FAMILY
Orchidaceae

As the species name implies, the evergreen basal leaves are oblong. They are quite striking, with a blue-green color and a broad white stripe down the center, sometimes with a whitish net-like pattern of veins extending beyond the middle of the blade. The robust downy spike is 8–14 inches (20–35 cm) tall, and bears from 10 to 30 small flowers in a loose one-sided raceme. These flowers are a drab greenish-white. The lip has a wide-open mouth pressed up almost against the overhanging hood. Look for Western Rattlesnake Plantain in coniferous forests at low elevations.

Range: throughout the Rockies.

Northern Twayblade
Listera borealis

ORCHID FAMILY
Orchidaceae

An inconspicuous orchid, Northern Twayblade is a delicate plant that grows in the rich humus of mossy coniferous forests. Two elliptical to oval, blunt-tipped leaves grow on opposite sides halfway up the stem. From 5 to 12 pale-green to yellowish-green flowers, with petals showing darker green mid veins, form a loose raceme. The sepals and lateral petals are awl-shaped while the prominent lip is broad, flat, platter-like, and deeply notched at the tip. A darker band of green marks the center of the otherwise translucent, pale-green lip, which is disproportionately long and wide at the tip. There are 2 small ear-like structures at the base of the lip.

Range: throughout the Rockies, excluding New Mexico.

A litter of needles under a cool coniferous forest is the favored habitat of Heartleaf Twayblade. From 2¾–6 inches (7–15 cm) tall, the stem has a pair of opposite leaves about midway along its length. These egg-shaped leaves are abruptly pointed at the tip. Tiny greenish-yellow flowers, with spreading sepals and petals, are in a loosely spaced raceme. The flower has a lip at the tip and two awl-like teeth at the base, which are best inspected with a magnifying glass.

Range: throughout the Rockies.

Heartleaf Twayblade
Listera cordata

ORCHID FAMILY
Orchidaceae

Much less showy than Scentbottle, in whose company it often grows, Huron Green Orchid often goes unnoticed because its overall greenish color blends with the surrounding vegetation. It is distinguished from Scentbottle by its small green or yellowish-green flowers, with a tongue-shaped lip and club-shaped spur. The flowers may be loosely to densely crowded on a spike 16–24 inches (40–60 cm) tall. In contrast to Scentbottle, the flowers are unscented or only weakly perfumed. The lance-shaped leaves clasp the stem and become progressively smaller upward until they merge into sharp-pointed bracts. This orchid is found near the timberline in wet meadows, bogs, wet forests, and along the borders of streams and ponds.

Range: Alberta, British Columbia, Wyoming, Colorado, and New Mexico.

Huron Green Orchid; Northern Green Bog Orchid
Platanthera huronensis [P. hyperborea]

ORCHID FAMILY
Orchidaceae

Bluntleaved Orchid
Platanthera obtusata
[*P. obtusata*]

ORCHID FAMILY
Orchidaceae

Its single, broadly-blunted, clasping leaf easily identifies this humble little orchid. The stem is 4-12 inches (10-30 cm) tall and bears a succession of uncrowded greenish-white flowers, usually fewer than 10. A distinctive hood, formed by the 2 lateral petals and the sepals, overhangs the narrow, strap-shaped lip like a flat-topped porch. The spur is tapered and curves slightly downward. Mosquitoes, with a selective taste for the nectar of this plant, are important in its pollination. Bluntleaved Orchid grows in the damp cool soils of bogs, mossy stream banks, and dense coniferous forests.

Range: throughout the Rockies, excluding New Mexico.

Sidebells Wintergreen
Orthilia secunda

SHINLEAF FAMILY
Pyrolaceae

This plant grows from long creeping rootstocks and often forms dense colonies in coniferous forests. Its one-sided arrangement of blossoms on the flowering stalk and lantern-shaped, greenish-white flowers are unmistakable. The many flowers are all arranged on the upper part of the stem, which bends gracefully downward, seemingly from their weight. Each flower has a long style with a knob-like tip that projects beyond the corolla and still is evident when the capsule forms. The flowering stem straightens as the many-seeded capsules mature. Sidebells Wintergreen leaves are olive-green, variable in shape, and have finely toothed margins. They retain their color throughout the winter, as suggested by the common name.

Range: throughout the Rockies.

As the common name suggests, this plant has whitish-green flowers rather loosely spaced around the 4-8 inch (10-20 cm) stem. These delicately fragrant flowers are large, nodding, and have 5 waxy petals. The clapper-like style is strongly curved; it protrudes with a distinct collar below the stigma. The anthers are yellow-tipped. Rounded seed capsules develop after the flowers wither. Leaves grow only at the base of the plant. They are long-petioled and broadly elliptical with olive green blades, very finely toothed. Like most wintergreens, this plant prefers the deep shade of coniferous forests.

Range: throughout the Rockies.

Greenflowered Wintergreen
Pyrola chlorantha

SHINLEAF FAMILY
Pyrolaceae

Its uniquely mottled leaves may identify this unmistakable but rare plant. The thick, glossy green leaves are strikingly marked on the upper surface with white streaks near the main veins. These pale areas, caused by a lack of chlorophyll, indicate the partially parasitic nature of this plant. From 2 to 20 yellowish-green flowers, often blotched with purple, grow on a single stem, from which they tend to hang sideways. The small sepals have a reddish color. This choice beauty grows in the shade of coniferous forests.

Range: throughout the Rockies.

Whiteveined Wintergreen
Pyrola picta

SHINLEAF FAMILY
Pyrolaceae

Western Meadow-rue
Thalictrum occidentale

BUTTERCUP FAMILY
Ranunculaceae

This is a dioecious species, which means that male and female flowers are found on separate plants. Male flowers (top photo) are greenish-purple with clusters of drooping stamens; female flowers (bottom photo) are greenish-white with 8 to 15 tiny pistils. There are no petals on the tassel-like flowers and the sepals are numerous but not conspicuous. The gracefully formed leaves are the plant's chief attraction. The stems, 12–40 inches (30–100 cm) tall, bear large bluish-green, prominently veined, compound leaves, which are divided 2 or 3 times into delicate, fan-shaped leaflets. Juice from this plant is acrid. Its roots were used as a source of yellow dye. In earlier times, the seed and foliage of the plant was given to horses as a tonic. Western Meadow-rue is common and widely distributed in moist woods, thickets, meadows, and along streams.

Range: throughout the Rockies, excluding Utah and New Mexico.

Stinging Nettle often forms dense patches from creeping rhizomes with stems growing to more than 3 feet (1 m) tall. The dark green leaves are opposite, triangular to almost egg-shaped, 2–6 inches (5–15 cm) long, ¾–3 inches (2–8 cm) wide, coarsely toothed, tapered at the tip, and clothed with stinging hairs on the underside. Formic acid from the tiny, needle-like hairs of the plant causes a stinging sensation and an irritating rash on bare skin. The acid is injected from the swollen base of the hair when the tip pierces the skin. Those hairs lose their stinging qualities as they dry or are cooked. Dangling clusters of tiny, greenish or greenish-white flowers arise just above where the leaves attach to the stem. The name *Urtica* is derived from the Latin *uro*, meaning, "to burn." Despite the stinging hairs, this plant has many medical uses including treatment of hypertension. Both a painful and useful plant, Stinging Nettle grows in moist, shady spots along streams and river bottoms from the plains to the subalpine zone.

Range: throughout the Rockies.

Stinging Nettle
Urtica dioica ssp. holosericea

NETTLE FAMILY
Urticaceae

*The more I think I know
about plants, the more
I realize I have yet to learn.*

— John Van Ast

PINK

Tall Fleabane
Erigeron elatior

ASTER FAMILY
Asteraceae

page 154

Spreading Dogbane
Apocynum androsaemifolium

DOGBANE FAMILY
Apocynaceae

Spreading Dogbane is a shrub 12–40 inches (30–100 cm) tall with freely branching, slender stems. When broken, the leaves and stems exude a milky sap. Bright green above and lighter and somewhat hairy beneath, the leaves are opposite, egg-shaped, with short pointed tips. Characteristically, these leaves droop during the heat of a summer day. Clusters of small, pink, bell-shaped flowers hang from the ends of the leafy stems. The petal lobes are spreading or bent backward and are often streaked with darker pink veins. Red pods, 3–4 inches (8–10 cm) long and filled with many hairy-tipped seeds, replace the sweet-scented flowers. This is a fairly common plant in thickets and wooded areas.

Range: throughout the Rockies.

Showy Milkweed
Asclepias speciosa

MILKWEED FAMILY
Asclepiadaceae

Showy Milkweed, often forming large clumps from its spreading rhizomes, is a coarse perennial reaching to 4 feet (120 cm). The leathery leaves are opposite, light-green, 4–8 inches (10–20 cm) long, oblong to ovate, with a pinkish midrib, and with pronounced cross veins. When broken the leaves and stem secrete a white, sticky substance that was responsible for its common family name. The tennis ball-sized flower heads grow on the upper portion of the stem. These globular umbels, 2–2¾ inches (5–7 cm) across, radiate from a central point on white, woolly branches, like miniature starbursts from fireworks. Individual flower structure in Showy Milkweed is most unusual, almost like an upside down flower. The 5 pink to pinkish purple petals and the 5 greenish sepals, which are concealed by the petals, are both reflexed strongly downward, exposing a large complex crown of male appendages consisting of long, tan, lance-shaped hoods with incurved horns that thrust upward and appear to be petals. These flowers have a strong, sweet fragrance. By late summer the flower clusters are replaced by large seedpods (follicles). These are 2¾–4 inches (7–10 cm) long, plump, and covered with hair and small, curved appendages. Eventually the pod

Showy Milkweed cont.

splits on one edge, releasing many seeds bearing long plumes of silky hairs to facilitate their dispersal by the wind. During World War II the pods were collected and the seeds were used as filler for aviation life jackets. The interdependence of animals and plants is clearly demonstrated by the relationship between milkweeds and monarch butterflies, well known for their long migrations. The monarch butterfly lays its eggs on leaves and the larvae feed exclusively on the foliage of plants in the milkweed family. Those leaves contain toxic alkaloids that accumulate in the tissues and are retained after pupation. As a result mature butterflies are not exposed to predation by birds because they are distasteful. The name of the milkweed family (Asclepiadaceae) and the generic name were dedicated to Asklepios, the Greek demigod of medicine and healing. The specific name *speciosa* means "showy" in Latin. Showy Milkweed is found on roadsides, fence lines, ditches and pastures in the plains and the montane zone.

Range: throughout the Rockies.

A pastel flush of rosy pink bracts among the many-flowered compact heads makes Rosy Pussytoes easy to identify. Its microscopic flowers are hidden in furry down so the flower heads have a fanciful resemblance to tiny pussytoes. This rather handsome species has a rosette of basal leaves, which are covered with woolly white hairs, somewhat spoon-shaped and blunt tipped. The leaves were used by Native Americans in smoking mixtures and were also chewed for their flavor. Dried flowers are long-lasting in floral arrangements. This is a common plant that grows in patches on open, dry slopes.

Range: throughout the Rockies.

Rosy Pussytoes; Pink Everlasting
Antennaria rosea

ASTER FAMILY
Asteraceae

Tall Fleabane
Erigeron elatior

ASTER FAMILY
Asteraceae

Growing 8-24 inches (20-60 cm) tall from rhizomatous roots, the erect stems of Tall Fleabane are sticky and hairy near the top. Leaves are light green and broader at the base than at the tapering and pointed tips; upper leaves clasp the stem. As many as 75 to 150 light lavender to pink ray flowers surround the yellow disk florets. There are 1 to 3 heads per stem. The whole plant is hairy and the nodding flower buds are especially fluffy looking. *Elatior* is Latin for "tall." Often growing in clumps, this eye-catching fleabane is a subalpine to alpine moist meadow dweller.

Range: Wyoming, Utah, Colorado, and New Mexico.

Spinystar; Ball Cactus
Escobaria vivipara
[Coryphantha vivipara]

CACTUS FAMILY
Cactaceae

Spinystar is a wide-ranging and highly variable species, with varieties of intergrades where the subspecies meet geographically. Stems, 1½-2¾ inches (4-7 cm) high, are succulent and overall globular in shape. The leaves have been reduced to sharp spines that radiate from the ends of nipple-like knobs (tubercles) that protrude from the main body of the cactus. Central spines are reddish and ⅜ inch (1 cm) long; lateral spines are shorter, and white with brown tips. Very showy reddish-pink flowers arise at the top of the stem. These are 1¼-2 inches (3-5 cm) across with fringed, lance-shaped petals and clusters of yellow stamens at the center. The green, fleshy berries that follow are edible and taste like gooseberries. The fruits turn brown on ripening. Spinystar is mainly a plant of the plains and the montane zone, but in New Mexico it may grow in areas up to 8,200 feet (2,500 m) in elevation.

Range: throughout the Rockies, excluding British Columbia and Washington.

Photo by George Scotter

One of the cold-hardiest species of cacti, Simpson Hedgehog Cactus can be 4¾–6 inches (12–15 cm) in diameter. The surface of the plant is covered with spirally arranged nipple-like tubercles that are conical and about ⅜ inch (1 cm) long. Areoles located on the tips of the tubercles contain 15 to 35 radial spines about ⅜ inch (1 cm) long and 5 to 11 central spines that are slightly longer and more widely spread. The fragrant flowers, with many pointed petals and numerous yellow stamens, are usually a rose-pink but can be yellowish to white. This plant is variable and several varieties are found over its range. During dormancy the plant can shrink below the soil surface. Preferring cooler and moister habitats than most cacti, Simpson Hedgehog Cactus grows in dry sandy soils in grassland, sagebrush, pinyon-juniper, and pine forest habitats from the foothills to the montane zone.

Range: throughout the Rockies, excluding Alberta and British Columbia.

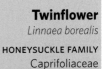

Simpson Hedgehog Cactus
Pediocactus simpsonii

CACTUS FAMILY
Cactaceae

Photo by Katherine Darrow

Of the thousands of plants known to Linnaeus, the father of modern plant nomenclature, Twinflower was his favorite. This elegant, sweet-scented, trailing evergreen is common in coniferous forests throughout the Rockies, but is easily overlooked. Its runners creep over the forest floor, lichens and moss, rotting logs, and stumps alike. At frequent intervals the runners give rise to Y-shaped stems 2–4 inches (5–10 cm) tall. Each fork of the stem supports at its end a demure, slightly flared, pink, trumpet-like flower, which hangs like a tiny lantern on a miniature lamppost. Within the trumpet are 2 long and 2 short stamens. The flowers emit an incredibly sweet perfume, which is most evident near evening. The plant's dry fruit has hooked bristles that readily become attached to the fur of mammals or the feathers of birds. The leaves, on opposite sides of the stem, are broadly elliptical with a few blunt teeth above the middle on each side. Some Native Americans are reported to have made tea from the leaves.

Range: throughout the Rockies.

Twinflower
Linnaea borealis

HONEYSUCKLE FAMILY
Caprifoliaceae

Deptford Pink; Grass Pink
Dianthus armeria

PINK FAMILY
Caryophyllaceae

This annual or biennial, 4–20 inches (10–50 cm) tall, is a European weed which appears to be increasing along roadsides and other disturbed sites. The narrowly lance-shaped leaves, almost grass-like, are fused basally around the stem. Pink to red flowers crowd the stem tips. Each of the 5 petals is attractively dotted with white and has a shallowly toothed tip. Deptford Pink flowers open only briefly during midday, being hidden by long hairy bracts having 5 pointed lobes during the remainder of the day. It is a relative of the carnations purchased from florists.

Range: throughout the Rockies.

Moss Campion
Silene acaulis

PINK FAMILY
Caryophyllaceae

Moss Campion is a perfect example of a plant adapted to withstand the fierce winds, intense sunshine, and extreme temperatures of the alpine region. These plants sometimes extend in a tight cushion for nearly 3 feet (1 m) over rock and thin topsoil. The bright green mats, looking like patches of moss, are spangled with flowers that vary from pale to bright pink to lavender (rarely white). They can be found from May through August, depending on the latitude and elevation. The small, 5-lobed tubular flowers appear to project from the mats without stems. The flowers are scented to attract night-flying insects, which cross-fertilize them. From up close the sharp-pointed leaves resemble conifer needles.

Range: throughout the Rockies.

This trailing or matted evergreen shrub has long branches with brownish-red, flaky bark and shiny green, leathery, oval leaves. Drooping urn-shaped flowers, pale pink in color, are at the ends of the stems. The dull red berries are edible, but they are dry and mealy. They are relished by bears and birds and were used by Native Americans in several different ways. Kinnikinnick, one of the common names for the plant, is a Native American word meaning "something to smoke;" the dried leaves were used as tobacco or mixed with it. The plant was also used in a tanning mixture and as a dye. Kinnikinnick is common and widespread on gravel terraces, in coniferous woods, and on alpine slopes.

Range: throughout the Rockies.

Kinnikinnick; Bearberry
Arctostaphylos uva-ursi

HEATH FAMILY
Ericaceae

This is a small evergreen shrub, usually less than 8 inches (20 cm) tall, with pink to rose-purple, saucer-shaped flowers that are borne in clusters at the end of red stalks. The showy flowers have 10 arched filaments, each bent and held in a crease in the corolla. At the slightest touch by an insect, the anthers snap inward and dust the visitor with a shower of golden pollen, thus ensuring cross-pollination when the insect moves to other flowers. The dark green, leathery leaves are rolled under along the margins and have a whitish lower surface. They contain andromedotoxin, which is poisonous to livestock. Gray and yellow dyes can be produced from the leaves. Look for this gorgeous plant in wet meadows, swampy places, and especially in peat bogs.

Range: throughout the Rockies, excluding New Mexico.

Alpine Laurel; Bog Laurel
Kalmia microphylla
[K. polifolia]

HEATH FAMILY
Ericaceae

Pink Mountainheath; Red Heather
Phyllodoce empetriformis

HEATH FAMILY
Ericaceae

Thick carpets of this evergreen shrub may cover the ground on alpine meadows and thinly wooded slopes near the timberline. Clusters of red or reddish-pink, bell-shaped flowers are borne on slender stalks at the stem tips. The sepals surrounding the flowers are a darker red. Leaves are blunt, linear, needle-like, and grooved on both sides; they are more numerous toward the ends of the branches. While not the true heather of Europe, this plant is well known by that name. Hikers in alpine areas should stop for a moment and inhale the subtle perfume from these cheerful bells.

Range: throughout the Rockies, excluding Utah, Colorado, and New Mexico.

Grouse Whortleberry; Grouseberry
Vaccinium scoparium

HEATH FAMILY
Ericaceae

Grouse Whortleberry is a low shrub, 4–8 inches (10–20 cm) tall, which often forms a dense ground cover on open mountain slopes near the timberline. Its angular branches remain green for several years. The rather small, bright green, oval-shaped leaves, with finely serrated margins, are deciduous. Small urn-shaped flowers hang downward from the leaf axils. These solitary flowers resemble waxen pearls of the softest pink, later turning into small edible berries that are bright coral-red. The juicy berries are attractive to birds, small mammals, and humans.

Range: throughout the Rockies.

Alpine Milkvetch
Astragalus alpinus
PEA FAMILY
Fabaceae

A low mat-forming herb, Alpine Milkvetch arises from creeping rhizomes that support delicate stems from 4–8 inches (10–20 cm) tall. These stems bear leaves with 13 to 25 leaflets, which are greenish in color, elliptical in shape, and have white, bristly hairs beneath and appressed hairs above. The flowers, borne in crowded clusters along the ends of the stems, are two-toned in color with the standard and tip of the keel a pale, bluish-violet to pinkish and the wings and rest of the corolla white. Sharply pointed at both ends, the pendulous pods are brown and densely covered with black hairs. A yellow to greenish-yellow dye may be produced from the flowers, leaves, and stems. This plant is rather common on stable scree slopes and meadows of the alpine zone and may occasionally be seen along streambeds in the valleys.

Range: throughout the Rockies.

Redstem Stork's Bill; Filaree
Erodium cicutarium
GERANIUM FAMILY
Geraniaceae

An introduction from Europe, Redstem Stork's Bill is an annual or biennial. Prostrate basal rosettes and upright often-leafy flowering stalks grow from a small taproot and a fibrous root system. The stalks range from 1¼–12 inches (3–30 cm) high, and originate in the axils of the leaves. Leaves are divided into fine, opposite leaflets that are deeply lobed and without petioles, similar to those of a carrot. Clusters of 2 to 8 flowers occur with each flower on its own stalk. Individual flowers are about ⅜ inch (1 cm) wide and consist of 5 bright pink to purple petals. These plants bloom profusely for many weeks in the winter to spring, depending on latitude, and continue blooming to a lesser degree into the autumn. Flowers open in the morning sun and may close in the afternoon, depending on the temperature. The upright fruiting structures are ¾–2 inches (2–5 cm) long and resemble a miniature stork's bill. At maturity, the fruit splits into 5 segments, each with a long, spirally coiled style attached to a seed. When moist, the style uncoils, driving the arrow-shaped fruit into the ground to a depth of up to 1 inch (2.5 cm). Considered to be a noxious weed in croplands, Redstem Stork's Bill can be a serious competitor causing economic losses. Large, communal masses of this plant may be found along roadsides and in croplands, dry plains, hillsides, and waste places, mostly at low elevations.

Range: throughout the Rockies.

Sticky Purple Geranium
Geranium viscosissimum

GERANIUM FAMILY
Geraniaceae

Sticky Purple Geranium, 12–24 inches (30–60 cm) high, blooms profusely for much of the summer. The flowers with their large, showy, rose-purple petals, strongly veined with purple, demand attention over their less strikingly garbed companions. The long-petioled leaves, deeply lobed and split into 5 to 7 sharply toothed divisions, are in opposite pairs along the stem. Sticky, glandular hairs cover the stems, leaves, and some flower parts. The seed capsule elongates into a long beak as it ripens, and eventually splits lengthways from the bottom up into 5 divisions, shooting the seeds away from the parent plant. Although most at home in the light shade of aspen groves, Sticky Purple Geranium also grows in exposed grasslands.

Range: throughout the Rockies.

Wax Currant
Ribes cereum

CURRANT FAMILY
Grossulariaceae

Wax Currant is an upright to spreading small shrub reaching to 5 feet (1.5 m) with an open crown. Deciduous leaves are alternate, often sticky, fan-shaped with 3 to 5 palmate lobes, ¾–2 inches (2–5 cm) long, dark green above, paler and glandular hairy below. Hanging singly or in small clusters, the whitish to pinkish flowers are urn-shaped since the calyx tube is slightly constricted below the reflexed lobes of the petals. The 5 small, spreading sepals are generally sticky and have glandular hairs. Fruits are bright red to yellow-red, spherical, waxy, and have numerous seeds. The species name, *cereum*, refers to the waxy appearance of the fruits that are eaten by birds and other wildlife. Native American people used the seedy and tasteless berries in making pemmican. Flourishing best in open or lightly forested areas, Wax Currant is found from sagebrush slopes to subalpine ridges.

Range: throughout the Rockies, excluding Alberta.

The onion-like essence that is released at the least bruising of its tissues proclaims the generic relationship of Nodding Onion. Its pinkish-lavender (rarely white) flower heads, nodding above grass-like leaves, suggest a number of little bells with the long style and stamens protruding beyond the petals. With maturity the nodding stalks rise until the dry capsules stand stiffly erect. The leaves are circular but not hollow. Both the leaves and flower cluster arise from a purple bulb with a black membranous coating. Native Americans and early settlers ate the bulbs and the leaves raw or used them as flavoring. This onion is common in grasslands and meadows from the montane to the alpine zones.

Range: throughout the Rockies.

Nodding Onion
Allium cernuum

LILY FAMILY
Liliaceae

A stout perennial with stems from 20–60 inches (50–150 cm) high, Streambank Wild Hollyhock closely resembles the cultivated hollyhock grown in gardens. The maple-shaped leaves, which decrease in size upward on the stem, are 3- to 7-lobed with coarsely toothed margins. All green parts of the plant are covered with fine hairs, like tiny silver stars. The leafy stems carry numerous whitish-pink to rose-purple flowers in the leaf axils and on stem tips. Smaller leaves separate these saucer-shaped flowers, which are up to 2½ inches (6 cm) across. The fruit is a hairy, globular pod that breaks open like the segments of an orange. Flowering during early summer, this handsome plant is found along highways and stream banks at low elevations.

Range: throughout the Rockies, excluding New Mexico.

Streambank Wild Hollyhock
Iliamna rivularis

MALLOW FAMILY
Malvaceae

Fireweed
Chamerion angustifolium
[Epilobium angustifolium]

EVENING PRIMROSE FAMILY
Onagraceae

In disturbed sites, such as along roadways or in burned-over forests, a galaxy of large, magenta (rarely white) flowers of this plant is likely to brighten the way during the summer. The flowers open from the bottom upward to the top of the spike, on a plant that is often up to 6 feet (2 m) high. Seedpods, mature flowers, and buds may all be present on a spike at the same time. This perennial has large, dark green, lance-like leaves, which are paler and veiny underneath. The seedpods are long and slender and produce numerous seeds with tufts of silky hairs for carrying them long distances in a breeze. The plant has several food uses: young shoots may be cooked like asparagus; young leaves, peeled stems, and buds may be added to salads or cooked in soup and stews; tea can be brewed from older leaves and flowers. This plant colonizes burned areas rapidly and helps control erosion. Fireweed is the floral emblem of the Yukon Territory.

Range: throughout the Rockies, excluding Oregon, Idaho, Utah, and New Mexico.

Dwarf Fireweed; River Beauty
Chamerion latifolium
[Epilobium latifolium]

EVENING PRIMROSE FAMILY
Onagraceae

Dwarf Fireweed resembles Fireweed in general appearance but it has shorter stems, generally less than 16 inches (40 cm), broader leaves, and larger, more brilliantly colored flowers. The stems bear waxy, bluish-green lance-shaped leaves with rounded tips. The flower parts are in fours, 4 sepals, 4 pink to rose-purple petals, and a deeply 4-lobed white style, and 8 stamens. Long, narrow capsules contain many tiny seeds, each with silken fluffy attachments, to be borne away by the wind until they find some favored niche. Flowers and buds of the plant may be eaten raw as a salad; its young leaves, when cooked, are an excellent substitute for spinach. The plant is also cooling and astringent and was used to promote healing of wounds; in powdered form it was used to stop hemorrhages. Yellow to green dye can be produced from the flowers. Dwarf Fireweed grows as a pioneer, often in dense colonies, on gravelly floodplains and river bars where the blue-green of the dense leaves and the waving masses of brilliantly colored flowers often obscure the stony ground beneath.

Range: throughout the Rockies, excluding New Mexico.

Pinkfairies
Clarkia pulchella

EVENING PRIMROSE FAMILY
Onagraceae

A unique annual in shape and color, Pinkfairies often grow in groups on 6-20 inch (15-50 cm) stems. Leaves, ¾-2¾ inches (2-7 cm) long and narrow and sometimes spatulate, are alternately placed on the stem with clusters growing in the leaf axils. The 4 magenta-lavender to rose-purple petals are 3-lobed, with the middle lobe twice as wide as the side lobes, and tapering to a long, claw-like base with a pair of short, blunt teeth. Petals grow above the elongated ovary, which has a white, 4-lobed stigma, dominating the center of the flower, and 4 stamens. Numerous seeds develop in the elongated capsules. The genus *Clarkia* is named after Captain William Clark; the species name *pulchella* means "beautiful," and indeed it is. Pinkfairies can be found on dry open sites, which may be seasonally wet, in valleys and foothills up to 6,000 feet (1,800 m).

Range: British Columbia, Washington, Oregon, Idaho, Montana, and Wyoming.

Marsh Willowherb
Epilobium palustre

EVENING PRIMROSE FAMILY
Onagraceae

As the common name would suggest, this plant grows in wet places such as bogs or beside mossy streams. The delicate slender stems, up to 16 inches (40 cm) tall, may be simple or sparingly branched. The paired leaves are oblong-ovate to lance-shaped. A few small, notched flowers, white to pink in color, droop at the end of the long stalks. The resulting fruit is a capsule 1¼-2 inches (3-5 cm) long, bearing seeds with a white tuft of hairs. The thread-like stolons issuing from the base of the plant are a useful field mark for Marsh Willowherb.

Range: throughout the Rockies.

Scarlet Beeblossom; Scarlet Gaura; Butterfly Weed
Gaura coccinea

EVENING PRIMROSE FAMILY
Onagraceae

A pretty little plant, Scarlet Beeblossom varies greatly in size, flower color, leaf characteristics, and the amount of hairiness. The slender stems, 4–12 inches (10–30 cm) tall, may be erect to decumbent. Its bluish-green leaves are alternate and vary in shape from linear to lanceolate to narrowly elliptic. They lack petioles and may have entire to shallow toothed margins and blunt to pointed tips. The spike-like raceme of flowers is initially white, quickly turning to scarlet. The flowers tend to open just before evening to attract night-flying insects for pollination. This plant is sometimes called Butterfly Weed because the 4 white-to-scarlet petals are twisted and move like wings in the slightest breeze. The stamens and style are long and look like insect antennae. Scarlet Beeblossom is found from the plains to the foothills.

Range: throughout the Rockies, excluding Oregon.

Fairy Slipper; Calypso
Calypso bulbosa

ORCHID FAMILY
Orchidaceae

Fairy Slipper is one of the loveliest of all the wildflowers within the Rockies. The drooping blossom of this orchid has a crown of rose-purple sepals and petals, all sharply pointed, twisted, and radiating upwards above the lip. The jewel-like lip or slipper is a wide, whitish apron streaked and spotted with purple and adorned with a cluster of golden hairs. There is a spotted double spur below the lip. The upper lip is broadly winged and also rose-purple. A single leaf, with parallel veins that converge at the tip, appears in the late summer and persists through the winter only to wither and disappear early the following summer. Both the leaf and stem grow from an ivory-colored corm with weak roots that are easily broken. Fairy Slipper is generally one of the earliest orchids to flower in the Rockies. It can be locally common among the mosses in shaded coniferous or aspen forests.

Range: throughout the Rockies.

Hooded Coralroot plants lack chlorophyll and therefore cannot manufacture their own food. They are parasites on the fungi that live among pine and spruce needles in coniferous forests. They do not have proper roots, but part of the stem is underground, where its short, thick fibers branch and interweave in a manner reminiscent of coral. Hooded Coralroot is the most striking member of its genus. Erect purple or yellow-brown stems, 6–16 inches (15–40 cm) high, terminate in a raceme of 10 to 25 large drooping flowers. The petals and sepals may be pinkish, yellowish, or nearly white, with 3 conspicuous stripes of deep red-purple. The lower petal or lip is broader and its stripes join into a solid purple, tongue-shaped tip.

Range: throughout the Rockies.

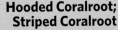

Hooded Coralroot; Striped Coralroot
Corallorhiza striata

ORCHID FAMILY
Orchidaceae

A little-noticed plant, Tiny Trumpet is an annual, 3–18 inches (8–45 cm) in height, with simple or branched reddish stems. Leaves are narrow, sharply pointed, entire, alternate on the stems, and about 2 inches (5 cm) long. Stems and leaves are both covered with tiny, glandular hairs. Small, pink (occasionally white to bluish) flowers are 5-lobed, trumpet-shaped, about ⅜ inch (1 cm) across, with 7 to 20 blossoms clustered into a head at the top of the stem. Tiny capsules bearing a few seeds, which become sticky when wet, replace the flowers. The generic name *Collomia* is Greek for "glue" referring to the sticky seeds; *linearis* is in reference to the narrow leaves. Tiny Trumpet is widespread in dry, open disturbed sites from the plains to the montane zone.

Range: throughout the Rockies.

Tiny Trumpet
Collomia linearis

PHLOX FAMILY
Polemoniaceae

Longleaf Phlox
Phlox longifolia

PHLOX FAMILY
Polemoniaceae

Longleaf Phlox is a more or less erect, 2-16 inches (5-40 cm) tall perennial growing from a taproot or underground branches. The base of the stem is often woody. Opposite, linear leaves, ¾-3 inches (2-8 cm) long, are well spaced along the stem and may be smooth to glandular or hairy. The sweetly scented flowers vary from white to pink and purple. There may be few to several flowers, with smooth or slightly ragged lobes, in clusters with leafy bracts at their base. A distinctive feature is the transparent membrane between the 5 short, green ribs of the calyx. This is best seen in the flower bud stage with the aid of a hand lens. Longleaf Phlox is scattered in dry, open rocky places on the plains and montane zone, occasionally to near the tree line.

Range: throughout the Rockies, excluding Alberta.

Alpine Mountainsorrel
Oxyria digyna

BUCKWHEAT FAMILY
Polygonaceae

Alpine Mountainsorrel forms dense rosettes with clusters of long-petioled, kidney-shaped, green and somewhat succulent leaves; there are several short upright leaves on each branched stem. The ends of the stems bear short sprays of rather insignificant green flowers. They are replaced in mid-summer by prominently winged, bright red fruits. The color is from the enlarged sepals that form thin, papery envelopes around each seed. They dangle from a slender stem and quiver in the wind like a Japanese lantern. In exposed alpine sites the whole plant often turns dark reddish-green. Good sources of vitamins A and C, the leaves may be used in salads and as a potherb in soup. This plant can reduce the itching of mosquito bites, and it produces a yellowish-green dye. Large ungulates, marmots, and pikas eat the leaves and stems, and lemmings like the fleshy roots. The leaves have a refreshingly sharp, salty taste. Alpine Mountainsorrel is a plant of the alpine region, particularly along streams, seepages, and crevices.

Range: throughout the Rockies.

Water Knotweed
Polygonum amphibium

BUCKWHEAT FAMILY
Polygonaceae

Water Knotweed grows from a running rootstock in the water or on the margins of drying ponds in the montane zone. Its leaves are of 2 types: if growing on land, the leaves are lance-like with short petioles; if floating on the water surface, they are waxy and broader with long petioles. This plant has a vast profusion of small, rose-red flowers in erect dense spikes. The small lens-shaped achenes are an important food for ducks.

Range: throughout the Rockies.

Alpine Lewisia;
Pygmy Bitter Root
Lewisia pygmaea

PURSLANE FAMILY
Portulacaceae

A widespread and variable deciduous perennial, Alpine Lewisia springs from a fleshy taproot the size and shape of a short carrot. Its dark-green leaves form rosettes and are linear-shaped to inversely spear-shaped. In addition, the succulent leaves are channeled and longer than the flower stalks. Each short flowering stalk, prostrate or sometimes erect, bears a single flower. Variable in color, the open, saucer-shaped flowers range from pink to white to deep purple. Each of the 5 to 9 petals may have darker veins running through them. Each flower has a green throat that holds a cluster of yellow stamens. Alpine Lewisia has the widest distribution of any Lewisia species. This charming plant grows in open, sun-kissed habitats at high elevations in short alpine turf or moist gravelly substrates.

Range: throughout the Rockies.

Bitter Root
Lewisia rediviva

PURSLANE FAMILY
Portulacaceae

Bitter Root is a small plant, ⅜–2 inches (1-5 cm) tall, with succulent, quill-like leaves that resume growing from fleshy taproots early in the year and generally shrivel and die by the time of flowering. Five to 10 stems on each plant produce spectacular flowers 1½–2½ inches (4-6 cm) across. Although pink is the most usual color for the 12 to 18 lance-shaped petals, color may range from white to almost red, with like-colored sepals and numerous stamens. These water lily-like flowers open only in bright sunshine. The petals soon dry up and blow away, leaving a tiny parasol-shaped capsule of jet-black seeds. Flowering occurs from early spring to summer, depending on elevation. Bitter Root has a rather storied history. Collected near today's Missoula, Montana, by Meriwether Lewis during the famous Lewis and Clark expedition, the plant now bears his name. Lewis's specimens were sent to the Academy of Natural Sciences in Philadelphia where the dried roots produced flowers a short time after being planted. The feat of coming back from what appeared to be dried death is what gave rise to the species name *rediviva*, meaning, "restored to life." Called *spetlem*, meaning "bitter" by Native Americans, Bitter Root was highly prized through the inland northwest as a source of food and as a valuable item for trade. The fleshy roots were gathered, peeled to remove the bitter skin, boiled, roasted, or dried for winter storage. Bitter Root was designated as the state flower of Montana in 1895. Inconspicuous except when in flower, this ground-hugging plant is found on dry, open, often rocky sites from the foothills to the subalpine zone.

Range: throughout the Rockies, excluding New Mexico.

Making up in beauty what it lacks in size, Mistassini Primrose is a small, delicate, but showy species that likes moist situations such as stream margins and wet meadows. Its leafless flowering stem, growing from a rosette of small, minutely toothed, oval leaves, is only 4–6 inches (10–15 cm) tall. A small open cluster of flowers is set at the top of the stem. Each flower looks like a miniature pinwheel with 5 deeply notched pink petals and a contrasting yellow eye. On occasion, the petals may be lilac or white. Dried sepals often cover the short-capsuled fruits.

Range: Alberta and British Columbia.

Mistassini Primrose
Primula mistassinica

PRIMROSE FAMILY
Primulaceae

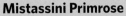

Pipsissewa is a low evergreen plant, 6–12 inches (15–30 cm) tall, with a long creeping rootstock. Its waxy, glossy green leaves are in whorls and have saw-toothed margins. A cluster of 4 to 8 pinkish and pleasantly fragrant flowers shaped like small shallow saucers droops gracefully on arching stalks near the tip of the stem. If turned upright, the 10 stamens can be seen, radiating like the spokes of a wheel around a fat green ovary. Fruits are roundish capsules, each holding numerous small seeds. Native Americans used the leaves of this plant in a tobacco mixture and as a substitute for tea. Pipsissewa prefers dry, shady coniferous forests.

Range: throughout the Rockies.

Pipsissewa; Prince's Pine
Chimaphila umbellata

WINTERGREEN FAMILY
Pyrolaceae

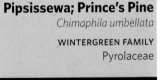

Liverleaf Wintergreen
Pyrola asarifolia

WINTERGREEN FAMILY
Pyrolaceae

This is the largest and showiest of the wintergreens in the Rocky Mountains. The plant has a rosette of basal leaves and a leafless flowering stem that is between 10–20 inches (25–50 cm) tall. The leathery leaves are large, roundish to kidney-shaped, with slightly wavy and sparingly toothed margins. They are a glossy dark green above, often purplish to reddish beneath, with reddish stalks. The leaves retain their color during winter, thereby giving rise to the name "wintergreen." Up to 20 fragrant flowers crowd the reddish, erect, flowering stem. The flowers are pink to purplish-red, cup-shaped, and each has a style that projects downward like a curved hook. This handsome plant is widespread on stream banks, in open coniferous forests, and occasionally in the lower alpine zone.

Range: throughout the Rockies.

Old Man's Whiskers; Three-flowered Avens
Geum triflorum

ROSE FAMILY
Rosaceae

Another harbinger of spring, the bright green, fern-like leaves of Old Man's Whiskers surround a stem crowned with three short-stalked flowers. In addition to basal leaves, the flowering stem has a cluster of leaves halfway up and another just below the nodding flowers. Soft hairs cover the whole plant. The urn-shaped flowers, mostly hidden by purplish-red sepals, open just enough to expose the cream to pinkish petals. Later the 3 nodding flower stalks grow erect as a mist of feathery plumes replaces the flowers and soon scatter on wind-blown parachutes. Old Man's Whiskers is a common perennial from dry grasslands to subalpine meadows. Native Americans used various parts of the plant as a tonic, perfume, or as a treatment for swollen eyes.

Range: throughout the Rockies.

Prickly Rose, the floral emblem of Alberta, is the best known and most easily recognized of all the flowering shrubs in the Rockies. Its sweet-scented, open-faced flowers, 1¼–2½ inches (3–6 cm) across, are bright pink or reddish-pink. The flower has 5 sepals and 5 somewhat heart-shaped petals surrounding a shower of yellow-gold stamens. The plant's alternate leaves are composed of 3 to 7 leaflets, which are thin, green, and lightly toothed. Many slender prickles arm the stems, which are 20–50 inches (50–125 cm) tall. Framed in a background of green leaves, the flower's glory is replaced in late summer by the scarlet, globose to pear-shaped fruits (rose hips). These remain on the stem throughout the winter, providing food for numerous birds and mammals. Rose hips are unusually high in vitamins A and C and can be made into jam, jelly, syrup, marmalade, and juice. Native Americans employed the leaves for tea and in salads, and the inner bark for smoking. The petals can be used to make a perfume or dried for a sachet or potpourri. At one time the dried fruits served as beads for necklaces. This species hybridizes freely with another common and very similar species, Woods' Rose (*R. woodsii*), and hybridization between the two makes identification difficult. Both grow on dry grassy slopes, open woods, roadsides, and riverbanks almost to the timberline.

Range: throughout the Rockies, excluding Washington, Oregon, and Utah.

Prickly Rose
Rosa acicularis

ROSE FAMILY
Rosaceae

Rose Meadowsweet; Mountain Spiraea
Spiraea splendens
[S. densiflora]

ROSE FAMILY
Rosaceae

A low shrub 20–35 inches (50–90 cm) tall, Rose Meadowsweet has dense, flat-topped flower clusters that are a deep rose-pink. The flowers are sweet-scented and have a fluffy appearance because the long stamens intermix with those of adjacent blossoms. Each branch has between 10 and 20 oval leaves ¾–1½ inches (2–4 cm) long, with rather small marginal teeth except near the base. The chestnut-brown outer bark of the branches peels off in thin, papery layers. Rose Meadowsweet is found in wet meadows and other boggy places near the timberline.

Range: throughout the Rockies, excluding Utah, Colorado, and New Mexico.

Splitleaf Indian Paintbrush
Castilleja rhexiifolia

FIGWORT FAMILY
Scrophulariaceae

Indian Paintbrushes hybridize easily so precise identification on the basis of color can be difficult. For example, Splitleaf Indian Paintbrush may have "flower" clusters that are crimson, magenta, rose-pink, purple, yellow or 2-toned as is shown here. As with other Indian Paintbrushes, their true flowers are rather small and nondescript. The job of attracting pollinators is taken over by colorful leafy bracts that conceal the actual flowers. The flowers are 2-lipped with the upper lip 4 to 5 times longer than the thickened lower lip. The corolla is generally less than 1 inch (2.5 cm) long, which helps separate it from Giant Red Indian Paintbrush with a corolla 1¼ inches (3 cm) or longer. The linear to lance-shaped leaves are normally entire, so the name *rhexiifolia*, meaning "splitleaf," seems inappropriate. Perhaps the name refers to the modified leaves or bracts that are generally lobed. This perennial plant grows 6–12 inches (15–30 cm) tall in clusters, and when massed together present a striking display. Splitleaf Indian Paintbrush is a fairly common plant of alpine and subalpine meadows and rocky slopes.

Range: throughout the Rockies.

This plant is restricted to the high alpine zone in the northern Rocky Mountains. One to several stems arise from a stout, almost white taproot. Small fern-like leaves grow from the base and extend over the whole length of the flowering stem, and both leaves and stems are covered with woolly hairs. Beautiful pink-rose, 2-lipped flowers are closely set along the elongated stem. The prominently arching upper lip of the corolla tube has a pair of sharp teeth near the tip, while the shorter, lower lip is 3-lobed.

Range: Alberta and British Columbia.

Langsdorf's Lousewort
Pedicularis langsdorfii [P. arctica]

FIGWORT FAMILY
Scrophulariaceae

*Flowers are the sweetest
thing God ever made
and forgot to put a soul into.*

— Henry Ward Beecher

RED, ORANGE & BROWN

**Summer Coralroot;
Spotted Coralroot**
Corallorhiza maculata

ORCHID FAMILY
Orchidaceae

page 182

Orange Agoseris
Agoseris aurantiaca

ASTER FAMILY
Asteraceae

This perennial plant, 4–20 inches (10–50 cm) tall, looks like a dandelion with reddish-orange flowers. Two or more rosettes of long, slender leaves with smooth or slightly toothed margins are produced from a woody taproot. The leafless stem is smooth except for white and woolly hairs under a solitary flower head. When fresh, the flowers are a burnt orange color, drying to deep pink or purple. Their outer floral bracts are narrow, often spotted with purple along the midrib. Tufts of long white hairs, like silken shuttlecocks, are attached to the end of each seed and ensure that they are scattered by the wind. A milky juice exudes from the stems and leaves when broken. Like the Common Dandelion, this plant can be used for salads, potherbs, and making wine. Orange Agoseris grows on open slopes and meadows to slightly above the timberline.

Range: throughout the Rockies.

Firewheel; Indian Blanket
Gaillardia pulchella

ASTER FAMILY
Asteraceae

The official state wildflower of Oklahoma, Firewheel is a vibrant colored annual, sometimes persisting as a biennial or perennial. Its branching stem is hairy and upright, growing to 24 inches (60 cm). Alternate leaves, 1½–3 inches (4–8 cm) long, with smooth to coarsely toothed or lobed edges, are mostly basal. Showy flower heads consist of ray flowers that are red with yellow tips while the central disk florets tend to be more red-violet. Each ray is 3-clefted with a tooth on the broad end of each cleft. Firewheel is heat and drought tolerant and is found on dry hillsides and roadsides in the plains and foothills.

Range: Colorado and New Mexico.

First introduced from Europe because of its brilliant, flame-colored flowers, Orange Hawkweed has become a nuisance in many places. Its extensive stolons can create a dense mat of plants that practically eliminates other more palatable species. Leaves are spatulate, up to 4¾ inches (12 cm) long, and almost exclusively basal. There are numerous short, black hairs on the stems and leaves, which exude a milky juice when cut or broken. At the top of the flowering stems, reaching 8–24 inches (20-60 cm) in height, are 5 to 30 composite flower heads. Handsome individual flowers are square-edged at the tips and usually red on the margins, merging into orange-colored centers. This aggressive plant is locally abundant in pastures and disturbed sites up to the lower subalpine zone.

Range: throughout the Rockies, excluding Utah and New Mexico.

Orange Hawkweed
Hieracium aurantiacum

ASTER FAMILY
Asteraceae

Growing from a stout rootstock, this perennial has stems up to 16 inches (40 cm) tall. The spade-shaped basal leaves, 1¼–4 inches (3-10 cm) long, are long-petioled and somewhat fleshy with coarsely toothed margins; leaves on the stem are cleft and sessile. Flowers heads, usually from 2 to 6 (rarely 10), have orange to reddish disk florets; ray flowers are inconspicuous or lacking. The involucral bracts are reddish-purple. Plump, red-brown seeds are produced later. Alpine Groundsel is found in moist alpine and subalpine meadows.

Range: throughout the Rockies, except for Oregon, Utah, and New Mexico.

Alpine Groundsel; Few-flowered Butterweed
Packera pauciflora
[Senecio pauciflorus]

ASTER FAMILY
Asteraceae

Montane Coneflower; Black Beauty
Rudbeckia montana

ASTER FAMILY
Asteraceae

An unusual and distinctive plant, Montane Coneflower grows 24–60 inches (60–150 cm) tall on stems that are leafy throughout. Lower leaves are grayish-green, deeply lobed, nearly heart-shaped, and with petioles; upper leaves are smaller and stalkless. The black to dark maroon flower heads are cone-shaped and 2 inches (5 cm) long at maturity. As the disk florets bloom in an upward direction, the dark cone is decorated with a myriad of golden stamens. The cone is surrounded at the base by green sepals. Ray flowers are absent. Often growing in large clusters, Montane Coneflower is at home in moist meadows in deciduous and coniferous forests in the montane and subalpine zones.

Range: Utah and Colorado.

Gypsyflower; Hound's Tongue
Cynoglossum officinale

BORAGE FAMILY
Boraginaceae

Inset photo by George Scotter

Gypsyflower is a biennial, tap-rooted weed. During the first year it forms a rosette with softly pubescent leaves 4–12 inches (10–30 cm) long and ¾–2 inches (2–5 cm) wide. Flower stems, 12–47 inches (30–120 cm) tall, are produced during the second year, or sometimes later. Stem leaves are shorter, stalkless, broadest near the base and narrower towards the tip. Cymes, solitary in the axils of the upper leaves, each bear from 10 to 35 flowers. Individual flowers are a dull red and broadly funnel-shaped. Each flower produces 4 triangular nutlets covered with hooked prickles (glochids), which facilitate dispersal by attachment to clothing and animals. This alien plant is not a favorite of ranchers because alkaloids contained within it are toxic to cattle and horses; in addition the nutlets accumulate on the faces of their animals as they forage, causing irritation. This rampant weed can be common in pastures, open forests, and waste places in the plains, foothills, and montane.

Range: throughout the Rockies.

Easily missed in its forest habitat, Oregon Boxleaf is an evergreen shrub. Its numerous opposite leaves are glossy-green, thick-textured, about ¾–1¼ inches (2–3 cm) long, with attractively serrated margins. Borne in the axils of its leaves, the tiny brick-red flowers are cross-shaped with flared petals. Although diminutive, the flowers have a pleasant fragrance. This compact shrub may grow prostrate or erect to a height of 8–24 inches (20 to 60 cm). Oregon Boxleaf is so handsome that it is greatly prized by florists for use in flower arrangements. Search for this plant in coniferous forests, clearings, and rocky openings mostly at middle elevations.

Range: throughout the Rockies.

Oregon Boxleaf; Mountain Lover
Paxistima myrsinites

BITTERSWEET FAMILY
Celastraceae

When in flower, Blite Goosefoot is readily overlooked since the stalkless, tiny, green flowers on a leafy stem blend with the other prevailing greens. The flowers have 5 sepals and no petals and are borne in clusters at intervals along the stem. At maturity the flower clumps enlarge into rounded masses of vivid crimson fleshy calyxes. To some people these crimson balls resemble ripe strawberries. Leaves are dark green, broadly arrow- or goosefoot-shaped. The raw leaves may be added to salads, and when cooked young leaves and stems are an acceptable substitute for spinach. Bright red juice squeezed from the fruits was a source of red dye. This widespread annual plant invades disturbed sites and waste places at low elevations.

Range: throughout the Rockies.

Blite Goosefoot; Strawberry Blite
Chenopodium capitatum

GOOSEFOOT FAMILY
Chenopodiaceae

Rusty Menziesia; False Huckleberry
Menziesia ferruginea

HEATH FAMILY
Ericaceae

This much-branched deciduous shrub may form thickets up to 6 feet (2 m) tall, particularly in cool, moist forests of the subalpine zone. The pale green leaves have wavy margins and grow in clusters alternately along the stems. Small salmon-colored to greenish-orange flowers hang by short stalks in drooping clusters beneath the leaves. The 4-lobed corolla is urn-shaped, while the 4 short but broad sepals are greenish and fringed with hairs. All of the above-ground parts of the plant are generally covered with rusty colored glands. While in flower Rusty Menziesia may be confused with Thinleaf Huckleberry (*Vaccinium membranaceum*), but the latter produces luscious berries while the former, alas, produces only an inedible 4-parted pod, which becomes erect as it ripens. This shrub is attractive in the autumn when its leaves turn a brilliant crimson-orange.

Range: throughout the Rockies, excluding Utah, Colorado, and New Mexico.

Prickly Currant
Ribes lacustre

CURRANT FAMILY
Grossulariaceae

Prickly Currant is an erect shrub in sunny openings but a spreading shrub in shade, growing to about 3 feet (1 m). The stems are covered with sharp prickles, with larger thorns at the nodes. The older bark on the stems is cinnamon-colored. Its maple-like leaves, 1¼–1½ inches (3–4 cm) across, consist of 3 to 5 deeply cut lobes that are toothed and may be smooth to sparsely hairy. The drooping racemes have 5 to 15 reddish, saucer-shaped flowers. Its fruit is dark purple to black and covered with gland-tipped bristles. Stream banks and moist woods are its favored habitats.

Range: throughout the Rockies, except for New Mexico.

The floral emblem of Saskatchewan, this strikingly beautiful lily may be up to 20 inches (50 cm) or more in height and has an upright flower with petals of orange or orange-red at the top of the stem. The petals are narrowly tapered and become golden toward the base while the inner basal portion is spotted with a maroon-wine color. The flowers, which may be 2½–4 inches (6–10 cm) across, are generally solitary but occasionally plants with 5 or more blooms are encountered. The leaves are narrow, pointed, and whorled. The egg-shaped fruit is ¾–1½ inches (2–4 cm) long, containing numerous flat seeds. The plant springs from a thick, scaly bulb. It is found in a variety of habitats from grasslands to open woodlands, usually at low elevations. Unfortunately, Wood Lily is often picked, and as a result it has disappeared from some localities.

Range: throughout the Rockies, excluding Washington, Oregon, Idaho, and Utah.

Wood Lily
Lilium philadelphicum

LILY FAMILY
Liliaceae

Scarlet Globemallow is a perennial forb with a stout woody taproot and spreading rhizomes. Freely spreading stems 3–12 inches (8–30 cm) in height may be decumbent, ascending, or erect. The short-stalked, alternative leaves are grayish-green, palmately divided with the segments irregularly lobed, and have entire margins. Both leaves and stems are covered with dense, star-shaped hairs. Orange flowers are clustered in terminal spike-like racemes. The flowers are saucer-shaped, ¾ inch (2 cm) across, with 5 shallowly notched petals and numerous stamens. *Coccinea* is derived from the Latin, *coccin*, meaning "scarlet," in reference to the color of the flowers. This forb provides forage for pronghorn, deer, and domestic livestock. In contrast to Scarlet Globemallow, Smallflower Globemallow (*S. parvifolia*) has triangular lobed leaves, long flower stocks, and is a larger plant. Drought tolerant, Scarlet Globemallow is found in dry, open areas from the plains to the montane zone.

Range: throughout the Rockies, excluding Washington.

Scarlet Globemallow
Sphaeralcea coccinea

MALLOW FAMILY
Malvaceae

Woodland Pinedrops
Pterospora andromedea

INDIAN PIPE FAMILY
Monotropaceae

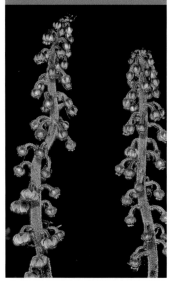

A saprophyte, Woodland Pinedrops may grow to 3 feet (1 m) tall. Dark purplish-red, scale-like leaves are massed near the base of the stout, reddish-brown stem, which is covered with sticky, glandular hairs. From 40 to 60 nodding flowers, usually yellowish to tan, are widely spaced along the stem. The calyx is deeply cleft into 5 lobes; the urn-shaped corolla also has 5 small lobes, which are slightly bent back. Woodland Pinedrops produce yellowish-pink capsules with an astronomical number of minute seeds that require exacting conditions to germinate and grow. Since the plant lacks chlorophyll, it cannot produce its own food and survives as a parasite on soil fungi. This interesting plant occurs in soils rich in decaying materials such as needle-strewn earth in coniferous woodlands in the montane and subalpine zones.

Range: throughout the Rockies.

Summer Coralroot; Spotted Coralroot
Corallorhiza maculata

ORCHID FAMILY
Orchidaceae

Lacking true roots, this saprophytic orchid has coral-like rhizomes containing symbiotic fungi that helps the plant to feed upon decaying organic matter in the soil and hence to absorb its nutrients. It has no need for chlorophyll and thus does not have green leaves. Alternate leaves on the stem are reduced to thin, semi-transparent sheaths. Stems 6-8 inches (15-20 cm) tall are usually purplish to reddish-brown. About 10 to 30 flowers are produced in an elongated cluster. The 3 sepals are brownish-purple while the 2 brownish side petals are slightly shorter than the sepals. The lip petal, with 2 prominent side lobes, is white and usually strongly spotted wine-red. Later, the spent flowers produce drooping, oval-shaped seedpods. A startlingly attractive albino form with yellow stems and white flowers but lacking spots, is occasionally encountered. *Corallorhiza* is Greek for "coral root" and *maculata* is Latin for "spotted." Summer Coralroot grows in organic humus layers under the dark canopy of trees in the montane and lower subalpine zones.

Range: throughout the Rockies.

One of the larger native orchids, Stream Orchid grows 12–40 inches (30–100 cm) tall from short rhizomes or seeds. Alternating on the stem, there are about 10 glossy, green, ovate-lanceolate clasping leaves, each 2–4 inches (5–10 cm) wide and reaching 12–20 inches (30–50 cm) long. From 12 to 20 flowers form a raceme arrangement along the upper portion of the stem, but only 2 to 3 open at a time. Flowers are about 2 inches (5 cm) across, and usually face the same direction. The 3 sepals are greenish-yellow with purple veins, forming a kind of cross; the 2 upper petals are reddish-brown with purple veins. The usually red lip is deeply 3-lobed, hinged in the middle, with yellow-brown to yellow with purple-veined lateral lobes. As with many orchids there can be significant color variation between individual plants. Part of the hinged lip vibrates with the slightest breeze, hence the other common name of Chatterbox. Stream Orchid requires porous soil and a constant source of water at the roots. It is found near beaches, bogs, hot springs, seeps, and streams.

Range: throughout the Rockies, excluding Alberta.

Stream Orchid; Chatterbox
Epipactis gigantea

ORCHID FAMILY
Orchidaceae

This attractive and rare poppy has bluish-green leaves that may be sparingly bristled or smooth. Each leaf blade has a petiole and is broadly ovate and deeply cleft. The flowering stems, 2½–4¾ inches (6–12 cm) tall, each produce a single, 4-petaled flower from orange-apricot to orange with a yellow base, generally drying pinkish. Although nodding when in bud, the flowers and bristly, many-seeded pods that follow are erect. Alpine Poppy grows on ridges and exposed scree slopes well above the timberline and is endemic to the Castle River wilderness and Waterton Lakes National Park in extreme southwestern Alberta, and Glacier National Park in Montana.

Range: Alberta and Montana.

Alpine Poppy; Pygmy Poppy; Alpine Glacier Poppy
Papaver pygmaeum

POPPY FAMILY
Papaveraceae

Scarlet Gilia; Skyrocket
Ipomopsis aggregata

PHLOX FAMILY
Polemoniaceae

One of the most widespread and common wildflowers, Scarlet Gilia has an attractive rosette of lacy, fern-like, basal leaves, up to 4 inches (10 cm) long, and leaves that gradually reduce in size upward on the stem. Both the leaves and stems, 8–40 inches (20–100 cm) tall, are sticky and covered with fine, white hairs. When crushed they emit an unpleasant skunk-like odor. Eye-catching, trumpet-shaped flowers are present in the upper leaf axils and at the tops of the sparsely leaved stems. The fiery red petals, with 5 flared lobes at the open end, are fused in a long, narrow tube. In some areas the flowers are pinkish with speckles on the lobes. The stamens and anthers protrude beyond the throat of the flower, which distinguishes it from Slendertube Skyrocket (*I. tenuituba*). The specific name *aggregata,* meaning "brought together," refers to the cluster of flowers. Scarlet Gilia is a favorite nectar source for hummingbirds. This biennial or short-lived perennial grows in dry meadows, open forests, and along roads in the foothills and montane zone.

Range: throughout the Rockies, excluding Alberta.

Western Columbine
Aquilegia formosa

BUTTERCUP FAMILY
Ranunculaceae

This graceful plant displays the regal beauty of its bloom above the fern-like foliage of its leaves. The daintily suspended flowers have 5 coral-red, wing-shaped sepals and 5 tube-shaped, yellow petals, each flaring at the open end and tapering to an orange-red spur at the other. Butterflies and hummingbirds are attracted by the vivid splash of flower color and by the nectar within the spurs. A central tuft of stamens and styles protrudes like a brush, to deliver and receive pollen from the visiting birds and insects. The plant's leaves are compound, long-stalked, and divided into many segments. Many seeds are borne in a head with 5 sections, which are erect at maturity. Favored habitats for Western Columbine are open woods and valleys as well as moist alpine and subalpine meadows.

Range: throughout the Rockies, excluding Colorado and New Mexico.

Easy to distinguish from other raspberries by its rose-red flowers and ground hugging habit, Arctic Blackberry can be found trailing over moss-covered ground from low elevation bogs to the alpine zone. The flowering stem and tufts of leaves rise from a slender creeping rootstock. From 2 to 5 leaves, divided into 3-parted leaflets with unevenly toothed margins, provide a pleasant contrast to the usually solitary terminal flower and the juicy red berry that follows. The slender pointed sepals are strongly reflexed, and the ribbon-like stamens are a similarly colored rose-red. The fruits are rather small, but sweet, aromatic, and richly flavored.

Arctic Blackberry; Arctic Raspberry
Rubus arcticus
[R. acaulis]

ROSE FAMILY
Rosaceae

Range: throughout the Rockies, excluding Idaho, Utah, and New Mexico.

One of the most striking wildflower groups found in the Rockies, Indian Paintbrushes are often difficult to distinguish because of overlapping variation in many characteristics. Giant Red Indian Paintbrush, for example, is an extremely variable species. Although known for their bright red "flowers," the color can vary from orange to scarlet to purple to even white or yellow. The colorful parts of the plant are not actually petals but modified leaves called bracts. The true flowers are largely hidden within the fan-shaped bracts, which typically have 3 deep lobes. The flower is 2-lipped; the slender upper lip with a slightly hooked tip is much longer and arches over the broader, 3-lobed, lower lip. This 8–24 inch (20–60 cm) tall plant can be glabrous or with long, woolly hairs, and sticky to the touch. Its leaves are linear to lanceolate and entire except for those near the top of the reddish stem, which may have small lobes. Indian Paintbrushes are hemiparasites deriving some nutrients, water, and chemical defenses from host plants via a siphoning system in their roots. Unlike total parasites, they have green leaves and some or all of their requirements can be manufactured by photosynthesis without the assistance of host plants. Giant Red Indian Paintbrush is widely distributed in open and forested areas in the foothills and montane zone.

Giant Red Indian Paintbrush
Castilleja miniata

FIGWORT FAMILY
Scrophulariaceae

Range: throughout the Rockies.

You must not know too much or be
too precise or scientific about birds
and trees and flowers and watercraft;
a certain free-margin, and even vagueness—
ignorance, credulity—helps your
enjoyment of these things.

— Walt Whitman

PURPLE &
BLUE

American Vetch
Vicia americana

PEA FAMILY
Fabaceae

page 204

Chicory; Blue Sailors
Cichorium intybus

ASTER FAMILY
Asteraceae

An immigrant from Eurasia, Chicory was introduced for culinary purposes. Its blanched leaves are used for salad and the roots are harvested, roasted, ground and used as a coffee substitute or additive. Chicory is a bushy perennial, growing from deep taproots, with coarse, rigid stems reaching to 65 inches (170 cm). The dandelion-like leaves near the base are lanceolate, 3-10 inches (8-25 cm) long, pinnately toothed or lobed, and edged with small, sharp teeth: upper leaves are smaller and have clasping bases. The 1¼-1½ inch (3-4 cm) wide flower heads develop from the axils of the leaves and are made up only of ray flowers that are sky blue (rarely white or pink). Flowers close by noon or even earlier on dark days. If cut or bruised, the leaves and stems exude a milky sap. Chicory, a pretty sight to some passers-by and a noxious weed to others, inhabits gravel edges of roads, open waste places, ditches, and fields from the plains to the montane.

Range: throughout the Rockies.

Canada Thistle; Creeping Thistle
Cirsium arvense

ASTER FAMILY
Asteraceae

Introduced from Eurasia, Canada Thistle is a persistent perennial that grows vigorously, forming dense colonies from deep and extensive horizontal roots. Stems are 12-47 inches (30-120 cm) tall, ridged, and much branched above. The stalkless, alternate leaves are dark green, oblong or lance-shaped, with irregular spiny lobes. This is the only thistle with male and female flowers on separate plants. Disk flowers are variable in color from rose-purple to pink to occasionally white; it is without ray flowers. Involucral bracts below the flower heads are spineless. This aggressive weed inhabits disturbed areas in fields, along fence lines, and roadsides in the plains and foothills.

Range: throughout the Rockies.

Another Eurasian introduction, Bull Thistle is a much-hated but interesting weed. It is a stout-stemmed biennial, 20–60 inches (50–150 cm) tall, with an armor of sharp prickles. The dark green, hairy leaves are deeply cleft and very prickly. Numerous rose-purple flower heads, resembling shaving brushes, develop at the ends of the branches. The involucral bracts are cobwebby, each with a spreading yellow spine tip. This thistle is found along roadsides and other disturbed places.

Range: throughout the Rockies.

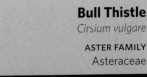

Bull Thistle
Cirsium vulgare

ASTER FAMILY
Asteraceae

Streamside Fleabane can be a biennial or perennial growing from fibrous roots. These slightly hairy plants are 6–16 inches (15–40 cm) tall and have multiple stems. The base of the stem bears most of the leaves. These are spear-shaped, about 2–4 inches (5–10 cm) long, and sparingly toothed at the tips. A few smaller and narrower leaves are present upward on the stem. Each stem has 2 to 5 flower heads that are ¾–1¾ inch (2–4 cm) across. The 125 to 175 ray flowers on each head are usually purple or pink, but occasionally white. The numerous disk florets on the central button are yellow. Flower heads have linear bracts with a brown mid vein. At maturity, the seeds are hairy and bear a double row of longer bristles. This fleabane is wide ranging, from the prairies, foothills, and open woods to the alpine zone.

Range: throughout the Rockies, excluding Oregon.

Streamside Fleabane; Manyflower Fleabane; Smooth Fleabane
Erigeron glabellus

ASTER FAMILY
Asteraceae

Subalpine Fleabane
Erigeron peregrinus

ASTER FAMILY
Asteraceae

Stems of this very charming perennial grow 12-28 inches (30-70 cm) high from a thick rootstock. Basal leaves are petioled and narrow, broadening toward their apex, while the stem leaves are smaller and stalkless. The winsome flower, resembling that of a daisy, has a yellow center of disk florets with a surrounding circle of between 30 and 80 deep rose-purple (sometimes pale pink or even white) ray flowers. The large flower heads are usually solitary, but smaller heads occasionally develop from the axils of the upper leaves. The involucral bracts are long, pointed, and usually green. Characteristics of the involucral bracts are important in distinguishing fleabanes from asters: bracts of fleabanes are uniform in length and arranged in 1 or 2 slightly overlapping rings while the bracts of asters are shingled and the outer ones are shorter than the inner ones. Subalpine Fleabane is common in damp subalpine and alpine meadows.

Range: throughout the Rockies.

Western Showy Aster
Eurybia conspicua
[Aster conspicuus]

ASTER FAMILY
Asteraceae

Western Showy Aster is a robust, erect perennial with a distinctive flat-topped to rounded inflorescence. The 12 to 35 ray flowers are usually violet to purple, occasionally with a pinkish tint. Disk florets are a dark yellow while the involucral bracts are in 5 overlapping rows with white, paper-textured bases and tapering to a pointed green tip that is bent outward. Leaves are quite wide, about half as wide as long, ovate in shape, and coarsely toothed; lower leaves are smaller and soon wither. Stems are generally 12-40 inches (30-100 cm) high. Western Showy Aster is found in forest openings in the foothills and lower mountain valleys.

Range: Alberta, British Columbia, Washington, Oregon, Idaho, Montana, and Wyoming.

The stems of this plant are often purplish, arising singly or in clusters from a creeping rhizome. The leaves are highly variable, but they are generally lance-shaped, hairy beneath but smooth above, with serrated margins. Broad-faced, lavender-blue to purple ray flowers are emphasized by a central boss of closely packed, tiny yellow disk florets. The involucral bracts are mostly green with purple margins and white hairs. Although basically an alpine plant, Arctic Aster can be found on gravelly river flats and other rocky areas.

Range: Alberta, British Columbia, Washington, Idaho, and Montana.

Arctic Aster
Erybia sibirica
[Aster sibericus]

ASTER FAMILY
Asteraceae

Blue Lettuce is a 12–36 inch (30–90 cm) tall, perennial herb often growing in patches from creeping rootstocks. When this plant is broken the sap is milky, giving rise to the name *Lactuca,* meaning, "milk." The leaves alternate on the stem and are lance-shaped to oblong. The upper leaves are entire while leaves on the bottom are prominently toothed. These hairless leaves are bluish-green with a waxy coating beneath. The showy blue flowers, about ¾ inch (2 cm) across, have 18 to 50 ray flowers in an open cluster, with no disk florets. The overlapping bracts are in 3 rows. The achene is short and rather stout with several veins on each face of the seed. The pappus is white with hair-like bristles. Blue Lettuce is most likely to be found in meadows, thickets, and other moist places from the plains to the foothills.

Range: throughout the Rockies.

Blue Lettuce
Lactuca tatarica

ASTER FAMILY
Asteraceae

Dotted Blazing Star; Dotted Gayfeather
Liatris punctata

ASTER FAMILY
Asteraceae

Dotted Blazing Star is a perennial growing from a taproot to 8–16 inches (20–40 cm) tall. Stiff, sandpapery leaves point strongly upward and are covered with tiny dots of resin; in botanical Latin, *punctata* means "with colored or translucent dots or pits." The bottom leaves are 4–6 inches (10–15 cm) long, but leaves get progressively smaller toward the top of the stem. The flower head is tightly packed in a cylindrical spike on the upper one-third of the plant. Each head is composed of 4 to 6 showy, tubular disk florets, each with 5 tiny petals, ranging in color from purple to rose, rarely white. The pistil of each disk floret has 2 purple, twisted appendages that give the flower head a feathery look. Each tiny 10-ribbed seed bears a plume of bristles. The willowy lavender spikes of this handsome member of the aster family occupy dry prairies, foothills, roadsides, and openings in montane forests.

Range: Alberta, Montana, Wyoming, Colorado, and New Mexico.

Clustered Sawwort; Purple Hawkweed
Saussurea densa

ASTER FAMILY
Asteraceae

A sturdy mountain dweller, Clustered Sawwort is found on rocky alpine slopes at medium to high altitudes. At first glance it looks like a deformed thistle. Its thistle-like flower heads are like tight balls of wool, from which protrude beautiful, dark bluish-purple disk florets. They are so densely clustered at the top of the short stem that the large, densely haired, saw-edged leaves are almost obscured. Clustered Sawwort stands 4–8 inches (10–20 cm) tall and is quite a giant in comparison with many of its floral companions on the rocky slopes where it grows. It takes a strenuous climb to reach the plant's habitat, but the pleasant fragrance of the flower is a compelling reward.

Range: Alberta, British Columbia, and Montana.

Smooth Blue Aster has leaves that are variable in size and shape. They are alternate, lanceolate to ovate to almost linear, and clasp the stem. They are also smooth and almost waxy or with a whitish bloom and can be up to 7 inches (18 cm) long and ¾ inch (2 cm) wide. Its inflorescence is an open panicle of several to numerous heads. The attractive and numerous blue to pale-lavender flowers with yellow centers occur in large, open heads atop the stems. Its overlapping involucral bracts are sharply pointed and whitish at the base. The stout, leafy stems are 16–40 inches (40–100 cm) tall and are reddish near the base. Smooth Blue Aster may be found in both dry and moist forests from the foothills to the montane zone.

Range: throughout the Rockies.

Smooth Blue Aster
Symphyotrichum laeve

ASTER FAMILY
Asteraceae

Blooming early in the spring, the showy flower heads of Parry's Townsend Daisy hug the ground, directly above a very short stem. The central disk florets are deep yellow, surrounded by broad ray flowers of violet to bluish-purple. The stems, spoon-shaped leaves, and involucral bracts are covered with stiff white hairs. Most of the leaves form a rosette at ground level. This attractive plant may be found in rocky or grassy places from low elevations to the alpine zone, the flowers appearing with the melting snow.

Range: Alberta, British Columbia, Oregon, Idaho, Montana, and Wyoming.

Parry's Townsend Daisy
Townsendia parryi

ASTER FAMILY
Asteraceae

Arctic Alpine Forget-me-not
Eritrichium nanum

BORAGE FAMILY
Boraginaceae

Photo by Katherine Darrow

The official flower of Grand Teton National Park, Arctic Alpine Forget-me-not grows in dense mats with stems less than 3 inches (8 cm) tall. Leaves are basal, fleshy, silvery-green, and hairy towards the tips. The fragrant flowers are blue, occasionally white, with a bright yellow throat. Terminal, 5-lobed, tubular corollas are scarcely taller than the leaves. Flowers are in 2 different sizes. The larger male-dominated flowers have stamens above the stigma; smaller female-dominated flowers have larger stigmas. Since each mat has only one type of flower, the risk of inbreeding is reduced. The scientific name *Eritrichium* means "woolly hairs" and *nanum* means "small" or "dwarf," referring to the pubescent leaves and size of the plant.

Range: throughout the Rockies, excluding Alberta and British Columbia.

Manyflower Stickseed
Hackelia floribunda
[Lappula floribunda]

BORAGE FAMILY
Boraginaceae

A hairy biennial or short-lived perennial, Manyflower Stickseed has stiffly erect stems up to 3 feet (1 m) tall. Near the top they support several loose clusters of yellow-centered, blue flowers on curving stalks. Each corolla has a short tubular section that abruptly spreads into 5 lobes. The pistil later produces 4 small nutlets with rows of hooked prickles, which readily adhere to clothing, fur, or hair, thereby giving rise to the common name. Moist meadows, moist woodlands, thickets, and stream banks are likely habitats in which to search for this plant.

Range: throughout the Rockies.

One of the early spring wildflowers, Oblongleaf Bluebells is a perennial generally with a dense cluster of stems. The specific name, *oblongifolia*, reflects the plant's wide, almost ovate leaves. Bell-shaped flowers dangle from leafy stems, rarely more than 16 inches (40 cm) tall. Although the buds are pink, the flowers open a bright blue to purplish. The 5 sepals enclose the 5 petals forming a tubular flower that flares on the open end. The usual habitats for Oblongleaf Bluebells are sagebrush communities in the foothills and montane.

Range: throughout the Rockies, excluding Alberta and British Columbia.

Oblongleaf Bluebells
Mertensia oblongifolia

BORAGE FAMILY
Boraginaceae

These plants bring in summer with their nodding clusters of small, bright blue (sometimes pink or white) flowers. The funnel-shaped flowers, with 4 stamens and a pistil extending beyond the mouth, can be few to many in branched clusters at stem tips or suspended from upper leaf axils. Tall Bluebells is an erect perennial, growing 8–40 inches (20–100 cm) tall, with weak stems. Its lower leaves are long petioled, 6 inches (15 cm) in length, and egg- to heart-shaped; the upper ones are shorter and sessile. The long-pointed leaves have prominent lateral veins and are hairy. This attractive plant is at home along streams, wet meadows, open forests, and clearings primarily in the subalpine zone. A few other species of *Mertensia* occur in the Rockies also.

Range: Alberta, British Columbia, Washington, Oregon, Idaho, and Montana.

Tall Bluebells;
Tall Lungwort
Mertensia paniculata

BORAGE FAMILY
Boraginaceae

Asian Forget-me-not
Myosotis asiatica
[M. alpestris]

BORAGE FAMILY
Boraginaceae

The fortunate wayfarer who sees the exquisite beauty of this glorious little flower in moist subalpine and alpine meadows does not soon forget the sight. The very fragrant flowers tend to be clumped together when they first bloom, and then lengthen into one-sided racemes with maturity. Each wheel-shaped, azure corolla has a prominent yellow eye. In some areas the corolla may be pink in color. The 5 stamens are hidden within the corolla tube. This perennial has lance-shaped to linear leaves, the lower leaves having stems but the upper ones attaching directly to the flowering stem. They are covered with long soft hairs. The word *Myosotis* comes from the Greek and means "mouse-ears" (*mus + otis*), a name probably referring to the short, hairy appearance of the leaves of some members of the genus. Asian Forget-me-not is a tiny plant, seldom more than 8 inches (20 cm) tall. It is the official state flower of Alaska.

Range: throughout the Rockies, excluding Utah and New Mexico.

Lyall's Rockcress
Arabis lyallii

MUSTARD FAMILY
Brassicaceae

The taproots of this small alpine gem may have a variable number of stems. The basal leaves have petioles of about the same length as their lance-shaped blades while smaller leaves clasp the stem. A few cross-shaped flowers, with 4 purplish or rose-colored petals, are borne at the tip of short stems. After flowering, the upper stem continues to grow as the stiffly erect and sharply pointed seedpods mature. Alpine Rockcress may be found on exposed rocky ridges and herbmats above the timberline.

Range: throughout the Rockies, excluding Colorado and New Mexico.

The arresting beauty and heavenly fragrance of Pallas' Wallflower are more than ample reward for a climb to its rocky habitat high above the tree line. Each plant boasts numerous flowers, all a rich purple and cross-shaped. The flowers are on such short stems that they huddle just above the rosette of long, prominently veined, and deeply notched leaves. After fertilization the flowering stems elongate to between 6-12 inches (15-30 cm) and carry long, curved, purple seedpods well above the leaves.

Range: Alberta and British Columbia.

Pallas' Wallflower
Erysimum pallasii

MUSTARD FAMILY
Brassicaceae

To find Mountain Harebell in full bloom on a stony slope or scree high above the timberline is sufficient reward for even the most arduous hike. Recognizable at once by a single bright bloom of a very rich lilac-blue, the bell-shaped flower, as much as 1¼ inch (3 cm) long looks incredibly large compared to its short, slender stem and small leaves. The stem is seldom more than 4 inches (10 cm) tall. The small basal leaves are almost egg-shaped and the stem leaves are narrower; both are sharply toothed. The seeds are contained in an oval-shaped, papery capsule that is covered with hairs. Arctic Bellflower (*C. uniflora*), seen less often because of its short blooming period, is smaller with dark blue, trumpet-shaped flowers.

Range: Alberta, British Columbia, and Washington.

Mountain Harebell
Campanula lasiocarpa

BELLFLOWER FAMILY
Campanulaceae

Parry's Bellflower
Campanula parryi

BELLFLOWER FAMILY
Campanulaceae

This slender-stalked plant is rarely more than 4 inches (10 cm) tall. Basal leaves are entire to minutely toothed and 1¼–2 inches (3–5 cm) long. Stem leaves are alternate, smaller, and the lower ones are often fringed with white hairs. The light to bright purple flowers at the end of the stem are either upright or slightly nodding. The open, bell-shaped flowers, usually only 1 per stem, have 5 pointed petals, 5 stamens, and a 3-lobed stigma. Parry's Bellflower is relatively uncommon in meadows from the montane to the subalpine zones.

Range: throughout the Rockies, excluding Alberta, British Columbia, and Oregon.

Bluebell Bellflower; Common Harebell
Campanula rotundifolia

BELLFLOWER FAMILY
Campanulaceae

As implied by the common name, this plant has bell-shaped flowers, several of which are borne on each slender, wiry stem. Though the buds are erect, the lovely blue bells usually point outward or hang downward; this protects their nectar and pollen from the rain. Like the clapper of a bell, the style ends in a conspicuous 3-lobed stigma. The stem, 6–16 inches (15–40 cm) tall, has long, narrow, alternate leaves, but the basal leaves, which wither early, are roundish to heart-shaped. The hair-thin stems swing in the lightest breeze and yield to violent gales, but bob up fresh as ever after a storm. An oval-shaped, papery capsule contains the many seeds. Bluebell Bellflower is found in a wide variety of habitats from low elevations to the alpine region.

Range: throughout the Rockies.

Once found in its mountain top habitat, Apetalous Catchfly is an unmistakable and unforgettable jewel. Single flowers (rarely 2 or 3), resembling miniature Japanese lanterns, hang daintily from the ends of 2–8 inch (5–20 cm) tall stems, turning erect at maturity. Narrowing at the mouth, the inflated and fused calyx is hairy, translucent, and has 10 prominent purple ribs. Lilac-colored petals protrude slightly beyond the calyx tube, which acts as a miniature greenhouse and speeds up seed development. Linear leaves surround the unbranched flowering stems. According to reports, a green- or cream-colored dye may be made from this plant. Apetalous Catchfly is found in meadows and scree slopes from the subalpine to alpine zones.

Range: throughout the Rockies, excluding Washington, Oregon, and New Mexico.

Apetalous Catchfly; Alpine Lanterns
Silene uralensis

PINK FAMILY
Caryophyllaceae

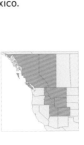

Prairie Spiderwort is a subsucculent perennial monocot growing to 20 inches (50 cm) tall. The stem bends slightly where the leaves are attached. The grass-like leaves are narrow, linear, 4–12 inches (10–30 cm) long, folded into a V-shape, and clasp the stem. Up to 25 flowers, each borne on a thin pedicel, form on the ends of the main stem or branches. Each flower has 3 rounded petals with pointed tips, 3 nearly hairless sepals, and 6 hairy stamens with golden pollen at their tips. Rose to lavender flowers open only for a few hours then wither into a soft, inky mass. Only a single flower within a cluster opens at a time. The unusual name comes from a mucilaginous slime that is exuded when the stems are broken. That material hardens into a thread that somewhat resembles a spider's web. Often used as a horticultural plant, Prairie Spiderwort favors sandy soils from the plains to foothills.

Range: Montana, Wyoming, Utah, Colorado, and New Mexico.

Prairie Spiderwort
Tradescantia occidentalis

SPIDERWORT FAMILY
Commelinaceae

Photo by Katherine Darrow

Ledge Stonecrop; Roseroot
Rhodiola integrifolia
[Sedum rosea]

STONECROP FAMILY
Crassulaceae

Ledge Stonecrop is an alpine plant growing in moist rocky or gravelly sites. It is a perennial with a branching rootstock, each branch producing a leafy stem from 2–6 inches (5–15 cm) tall. The leaves are succulent, egg-shaped to oblong, and may have smooth or toothed margins. Flowers are in flat-topped clusters with the central flower of each cluster blooming first. The male and female flowers may be on different parts of the flower cluster. Male flowers are yellow or purple, while the female flowers are always purple. Petals of the flowers are nearly twice as long as the sepals. The seedpods are plump, erect, and reddish-purple. When young, the succulent stems and leaves are edible as salad or potherb.

Range: throughout the Rockies.

Timber Milkvetch
Astragalus miser

PEA FAMILY
Fabaceae

Beautiful but deadly, Timber Milkvetch is a perennial with numerous prostrate to erect stems, 4–16 inches (10–40 cm) tall, growing from a taproot. Leaves are pinnately compound with 6 to 21 needle-like leaflets that are hairy on both sides. From 2 to 20 pea-like flowers are arranged in a loose, elongated cluster. The keel is mostly white and usually purple tipped; the wings and standard are bluish-purple with some white markings. The calyx is pubescent with a mix of black and white hairs. Long, linear seedpods droop from the flower stalks. Timber Milkvetch contains miserotoxin, which causes acute to chronic toxicity in cattle and sheep. Honeybees foraging on the flowers may also be poisoned. Timber Milkvetch is widespread in grasslands, disturbed soils, and in open Ponderosa Pine and Douglas-fir forests.

Range: throughout the Rockies, excluding Oregon and New Mexico.

Growing from a thick taproot, Bentflower Milkvetch is a profusely branching plant that is mat-like and seldom more than 8 inches (20 cm) tall. Each leaf has 7 to 13 leaflets, which are sharply tipped and lance-shaped. All green parts of the plant are thinly haired. From 2 to 10 flowers cluster along the stems on short stalks. The petals are deep lavender-purple (rarely white). Although most common on dry alpine slopes, this plant is also found at lower elevations on eroded and otherwise disturbed areas.

Range: Alberta, British Columbia, Idaho, Montana, and Wyoming.

Bentflower Milkvetch
Astragalus vexilliflexus

PEA FAMILY
Fabaceae

Utah Sweetvetch is a low, bushy perennial, up to 20 inches (50 cm) tall, whose unusual seedpods look like short strings of flat beads rigidly joined to each other. The constrictions between each seed in the pod are a useful characteristic to distinguish hedysarums from milkvetches and locoweeds, which have similar flowers, but pods shaped more like those of garden peas. Short gray hairs cover the 9 to 13 leaflets, which are elliptical to almost egg-shaped. Each leafy stem ends in a crowded cluster of large, rose-purple, pea-shaped flowers, which are sweet-scented. The lower petal, or keel, has a distinctive shape like the forepart of a boat. Grizzly bears eat the roots and often make large excavations in their quest for these delicacies. When Utah Sweetvetch forms large colonies on grassy slopes or on well-watered gravel flats, the rousing color of the blossoms is a delight to the eye.

Range: throughout the Rockies.

Utah Sweetvetch; Northern Sweetvetch
Hedysarum boreale

PEA FAMILY
Fabaceae

Silvery Lupine
Lupinus argenteus

PEA FAMILY
Fabaceae

Silvery Lupine is a perennial forb growing 12–35 inches (30–90 cm) tall from a taproot. The long petioled leaves are about 2 inches (5 cm) long with the tips divided into 6 to 8 narrow leaflets radiating like fingers from a hand. Both the stems and undersides of the leaves are covered with dense, flat-lying hairs that give the plant a silvery appearance, as reflected in the specific epithet *argenteus,* meaning "silvery" in Latin. Blue-purple to partially white flowers form in narrow terminal clusters above the leaves. These pea-like flowers are 3-parted: a broad upper petal (banner) bent backwards on both sides, 2 lateral petals (wings), and 2 lower petals that fuse together (keel) and contain the stamens and style. Lupines hybridize readily and can be difficult to identify, but that should not distract from the enjoyment of the numerous species that flower from spring to fall within the Rockies. Both the leaves and seeds contain alkaloids and are reported to be toxic in some places. Silvery Lupine has a wide distribution from open to shaded sites in the plains to the subalpine zone.

Range: throughout the Rockies.

Silky Lupine
Lupinus sericeus

PEA FAMILY
Fabaceae

Highly variable, Silky Lupine is a common plant within the Rocky Mountains. Meadows and forest openings may be blued with its flowers during the spring and summer. It is a perennial herb, 16–32 inches (40–80 cm) tall, often growing in dense clumps or bunches. The leaves consist of 5 to 9 very narrow leaflets with densely silky hairs on both sides. Blue to bluish-purple flowers cluster along the top third of the stem. The standard is densely hairy on the back. The pods are ¾–1¼ inch (2 or 3 cm) long and contain 4 to 6 seeds. Alkaloids in the seeds may be poisonous, particularly to sheep. Nodules on the roots of this legume contain nitrogen-fixing bacteria that enrich the soil.

Range: throughout the Rockies, excluding New Mexico.

This pretty little alpine plant usually grows from a rosette of leaves that lies flat on the ground, spreading out from a stout taproot. The leaves are ¾–2 inches (2–5 cm) long and consist of between 9 and 25 tiny, linear leaflets that are covered with silky hairs. The leafless stalks, barely overtopping the leaves, terminate with up to 3 flowers (most commonly with 2) about ¾ inch (2 cm) long. Each pale purple, pea-like flower has a dark purple, hairy calyx. The characteristic beak of the keel, formed from the 2 lowermost fused petals, is distinctive and will distinguish an *Oxytropis* from an *Astragalus* (Milkvetch). More spectacular than the flowers are the inflated pods, ¾–1¼ inch (2–3 cm) long, which turn bright red to purple in autumn; these pods are egg-shaped, with a style that remains attached. Various insects and small mammals eat the seeds within the fat pods. Stalkpod Locoweed is a plant of windblown, gravelly slopes and ridges high above the timberline.

Range: Alberta, British Columbia, Montana, Wyoming, and Colorado.

Stalkpod Locoweed; Inflated Oxytrope
Oxytropis podocarpa

PEA FAMILY
Fabaceae

An attractive legume, Showy Locoweed has silvery, silky leaves growing from a branched woody base. Each leaf is comprised of numerous leaflets. The flower stalks generally elongate to hold dense clusters of 10 to 35 flowers above the silvery foliage. The flowers are blue to reddish-purple, drying to violet. Individual flowers are ⅜–¾ inch (1–2 cm) long, with a densely hairy calyx about half that length. This boldly handsome plant is widely distributed throughout low-elevation grasslands.

Range: Alberta, British Columbia, Montana, Wyoming, Colorado, and New Mexico.

Showy Locoweed
Oxytropis splendens

PEA FAMILY
Fabaceae

Alpine Clover
Trifolium dasyphyllum

PEA FAMILY
Fabaceae

Alpine Clover is a mat-forming perennial, ¾–4 inches (2–10 cm) tall with slender, leafless, arching stems. Basal leaves are long-stalked and divided into 3 narrow, pointed leaflets that are hairy beneath. The 2-lipped, pea-like flowers have white petals and are usually bicolored with pink or purple tips. Sepals are white, slender, and hairy. Spine-like bracts that are green and white subtend the ball-like flower clusters. Two other clovers are found in similar habitats. Dwarf Clover (*T. nanum*) is a hairless species with only 1 to 3 rose-colored flowers per cluster on ⅜–1¼ inch (1–3 cm) tall stalks; Parry's Clover (*T. parryi*) is hairless with 4 to 30 fragrant, reddish-purple flowers in each head on 4 inch (10 cm) tall stalks. Alpine Clover is common in subalpine and alpine habitats on rocky or gravelly slopes.

Range: Montana, Wyoming, Utah, Colorado, and New Mexico.

American Vetch
Vicia americana

PEA FAMILY
Fabaceae

A creeping or climbing vine, American Vetch is a square-stemmed perennial forb up to 3 feet (1 m) tall. From 8 to 14 narrow leaflets connect to a midrib forming leaves about 2 inches (5 cm) long. Small, curly tendrils growing from the leaf tips wrap around other plants for support. Rich hues of bluish to reddish-purple flowers form in loose clusters at the stem tips. The 3 to 9 flowers widely spaced along each branch of the upper stem produce ¾–1½ inch (2–4 cm) long flat pods later in the season. Mule deer, black bears, grizzly bears, small mammals, and birds enjoy the leaves, flowers, or seeds of this plant. Often forming tangled masses, American Vetch is found in meadows, grassy slopes, thickets, and openings in forests from the plains to the montane zone.

Range: throughout the Rockies.

Perhaps the most elegant of all gentians in the Rocky Mountains, the huge blue flowers of this plant never fail to arouse admiration. Although they are generally solitary, there may be up to 3 flowers at the tip of a stem 4–12 inches (10–30 cm) high, with 1 or 2 more in axils of the upper leaves. The long, funnel-shaped corolla is divided into 5 lobes, each separated by a shredded pleat or fold. Each stem is crowded with bright green opposite leaves. These 3-veined leaves are ovate in shape. Rainier Pleated Gentian grows in clumps at high elevations in the subalpine and alpine zone.

Range: throughout the Rockies, excluding Colorado and New Mexico.

Rainier Pleated Gentian; Big Mountain Gentian
Gentiana calycosa

GENTIAN FAMILY
Gentianaceae

Pale Gentian is a small perennial of alpine and subalpine meadows. The stems rise 1¼–4 inches (3–10 cm) from basal rosettes of glossy, yellowish-green leaves. There are also 2 or 3 pairs of leaves along the upright stem. The long, dark blue to greenish-blue blossoms, in a few-flowered terminal cluster, appear unusually large in relation to the size of the plant. The calyx lobes are pointed and unequal in size. This charming little plant prefers to grow in damp, stony places at high altitudes.

Range: Alberta, British Columbia, Washington, and Montana.

Pale Gentian
Gentiana glauca

GENTIAN FAMILY
Gentianaceae

Pygmy Gentian
Gentiana prostrata

GENTIAN FAMILY
Gentianaceae

The most inconspicuous gentian in the Rockies, this very small plant, ⅜–4 inches (1–10 cm) tall, is an annual or biennial with creeping stems. Its tiny, pale green leaves have white margins. The flowers sit alone at the tip of each branch and are usually sky-blue in color with 4 or 5 pointed petals. These blossoms open only in bright sunshine, closing even when a cloud obscures the sun, or when they are touched. Gentians have been used as medicinal tonics and cleansers since the 1st century. Alpine tundra and rocky ledges are good places to look for this mite of a plant.

Range: throughout the Rockies, excluding Washington and New Mexico.

Autumn Dwarf Gentian
Gentianella amarella

GENTIAN FAMILY
Gentianaceae

Easily overlooked except when in flower, Autumn Dwarf Gentian is a highly variable, circumboreal plant. Growing from 2–16 inches (5–40 cm) tall, this plant may be an annual or biennial. Basal leaves are mostly oblanceolate and ¼–1½ inch (0.5 to 4 cm) long; stem leaves are opposite, from lance-shaped to oblong or ovate, clasping the stem or not, and up to 2½ inches (6 cm) long. Flowers may be single or in clusters at the top of the plant. The calyx is cleft nearly to the base and the petals, usually pale purple but occasionally purple or even white, taper abruptly to a point. The corolla tube is fringed at the throat. As suggested by the common name, this is a late flowering plant. The gentian family and the genus *Gentianella* derive their names from Gentius, King of Illyria who discovered the medical virtues of these plants. The specific name *amarella* means "bitter" in Latin. Roots of this and other gentians were used as a herbal bitter in the treatment of digestive disorders and as a tonic. Autumn Dwarf Gentian is widely distributed in meadows from the foothills to the alpine zone.

Range: throughout the Rockies.

This annual is quite variable in size and structure. At lower elevations it may branch from the base and have 10 to 12 flowers on pedicels from the upper leaf axils, whereas flowering stems in exposed alpine situations are short and unbranched. The stems are often purplish, and the leaves are lance-shaped and entire. The flower at the end of the stem, always the largest, is about ¾ inch (2 cm) long with a blue to pale violet corolla, which fades with age. Corolla tubes, which open only slightly at the top, are divided into 4 lobes, a characteristic that gives rise to one of the popular names, Fourpart Dwarf Gentian.

Range: Alberta, British Columbia, Oregon, Idaho, Montana, and Wyoming.

Fourpart Dwarf Gentian; Felwort
Gentianella propinqua

GENTIAN FAMILY
Gentianaceae

Macoun's Fringed Gentian is an annual with a single to few-branched stems from 4–16 inches (10–40 cm) tall. Basal leaves are ¾–1¼ inch (2–3 cm) long, lance-shaped and blunt tipped; 2 to 4 pairs of opposite stem leaves are narrower with pointed tips. Deep blue flowers bloom at the stem ends or in upper leaf axils. The tubular corolla is ¾–2 inches (2–5 cm) long with 4 broad spreading fringed lobes. Small white bumps at the base of the calyx are best examined with the aid of a hand lens. The presence of those bumps helps to distinguish Macoun's Fringed Gentian from Windmill Fringed Gentian (*G. detonsa*), which lacks that characteristic. *Gentianopsis* is a highly variable, wide-ranging genus. Three other members are found in the Rockies: Perennial Fringed Gentian (*G. barbellata*), Oneflower Fringed Gentian (*G. simplex*), and Rocky Mountain Fringed Gentian (*G. thermalis*). The latter is the official flower of Yellowstone National Park, named *thermalis* after the hot spring basins where it often grows. Macoun's Fringed Gentian grows in boggy soils of wet meadows and fens in the foothills and the montane zone.

Range: Alberta, British Columbia, and Montana.

Macoun's Fringed Gentian
Gentianopsis macounii

GENTIAN FAMILY
Gentianaceae

Ballhead Waterleaf
Hydrophyllum capitatum

WATERLEAF FAMILY
Hydrophyllaceae

After a long winter, Ballhead Waterleaf is among the first harbingers of spring. The purplish-blue to white flowers grow in a dense head or ball-like cluster. The individual flowers are cup-shaped, with both anthers and 2-lobed stigmas extended well beyond the corolla. The whole plant is loosely hairy and the sepals are bristly. Each flower cluster is generally overtopped, and sometimes hidden, by a small leaf. Most of the leaves have long petioles and form a basal cluster. Each of the 5 to 11 segmented leaflets ends in a sharply pointed tip. This unusual and very attractive plant is found in moist woods and on shaded grassy slopes.

Range: throughout the Rockies, excluding New Mexico.

Threadleaf Phacelia
Phacelia linearis

WATERLEAF FAMILY
Hydrophyllaceae

This widespread and showy annual rises 4–16 inches (10–40 cm) tall from a branched or unbranched stem, which is often reddish in color. Leaves are alternate and generally linear but some leaves near the base have side-lobes. The widely bell-shaped flowers, ranging from pale lavender to bluish-violet with a white throat, are crowded into the axils of the upper leaves. Threadleaf Phacelia is able to grow in dry areas because its densely hairy stems, leaves, and calyxes conserve moisture. The genus name *Phacelia* means "bundle," referring to the clustered flowers, while the species name *linearis* refers to the narrow leaf shape. This plant grows in dry, open areas at low elevations on the foothills and plains.

Range: throughout the Rockies, excluding Colorado and New Mexico.

The flowers of Silky Phacelia, a plant up to 20 inches (50 cm) high, are densely clustered on a spike. Their intense violet-blue petals are accented by the long violet filaments of the stamens and the brilliant orange anthers. All this contrasts sharply with the silvery leaves, which are divided into many narrow sections. Both the stems and leaves are covered with silky hairs, which make the setting of the long-stemmed flower spike all the more striking. This perennial graces open slopes, screes, and rock crevices at high altitudes.

Range: throughout the Rockies.

Silky Phacelia
Phacelia sericea

WATERLEAF FAMILY
Hydrophyllaceae

Most people are familiar with the beautiful arching flowers of the domesticated iris that flourish in gardens. Rocky Mountain Iris resembles those plants. Growing from a thick, knotted rhizome, this plant stands 8–20 inches (20–50 cm) tall with glaucous, blue-green leaves generally 4–16 inches (10–40 cm) long and less than ⅜ inch (1 cm) wide. The flowers usually occur 2 (occasionally 3 to 4) to a stem. Each pale blue or blue-violet (rarely white) flower has 9 petal-like segments: 3 sepals, 3 petals, and 3 enlarged styles. The outer segments, which are spreading, recurved, bearded, and up to 2½ inches (6 cm) long, have purple veins radiating from a yellow spot. Although the plant is considered poisonous, it has been used for medical purposes. Pale Yellow Iris (*I. pseudacorus*) has escaped cultivation and may be found at low elevation within the Rockies. Rocky Mountain Iris often grows in extensive patches in seasonally moist environments such as meadows, seeps, ditches, and edges of lakes from the foothills to the subalpine zone.

Range: throughout the Rockies.

Rocky Mountain Iris
Iris missouriensis

IRIS FAMILY
Iridaceae

Photo by Bill Hitz

Strict Blue-eyed Grass
Sisyrinchium montanum

IRIS FAMILY
Iridaceae

These charming flowers, like gems of azure, are scattered among the grasses of moist meadows from low to moderate elevations. The distinctly flattened stems are 8-12 inches (20-30 cm) in height, about twice as tall as the grass-like basal leaves. Borne in inflorescences carrying up to 5 blooms, each star-shaped flower has 3 virtually identical sepals and petals, each tipped with a minute point, and with a bright yellow eye in the center. The blossoms wither and droop within a day, to be replaced by fresh ones on the succeeding day. Small black seeds are contained in the globular, 3-parted capsules.

Range: throughout the Rockies, excluding Washington and Oregon.

Blue Giant Hyssop
Agastache foeniculum

MINT FAMILY
Lamiaceae

A bushy upright plant, Blue Giant Hyssop grows up to 3 feet (1 m) on square stems. The opposite leaves are medium green above with a paler underside covered with white, felt-like hairs. They are 1¼-3 inches (3-8 cm) long, egg-shaped, and sharply pointed with serrated edges. The leaves have a scent similar to anise, a combination of licorice with a touch of mint. They are used in making herbal teas and jellies or included in salads. Violet-blue flowers are borne in a dense spike from 2¾-4 inches (7-10 cm) in length. A spike is often without flowers for a short space. The corolla is tubular and 2-lipped with 2 long and 2 short stamens that protrude noticeably beyond the corolla tube. Bees and butterflies are attracted to the nectar-filled flowers. Blue Giant Hyssop is a plant of grasslands, thickets, and Quaking Aspen groves in the plains and foothills.

Range: Alberta, British Columbia, Washington, Montana, Wyoming, and Colorado.

As in other members of the mint family, this plant has irregular flowers, square stems, and opposite leaves. The leaves are egg- or lance-shaped with glandular dots on both surfaces. They are pointed at the tips and have teeth on the margins. The simple or sparsely branched stems are covered with hair. Crowded whorls of light pink or purple flowers stud several of the upper leaf axils. The upper flower lobe is notched and is usually broader than the 3 others. Four stamens and 2-lobed pistils project well beyond the mouth of the flower tube. Bruise a few leaves and note the very aromatic menthol fragrance. Native Americans used the leaves for flavoring meat and pemmican and as a refreshing tea. Typical habitats for Wild Mint include wet woods, stream banks, and lakeshores.

Range: throughout the Rockies.

Wild Mint; Field Mint
Mentha arvensis

MINT FAMILY
Lamiaceae

Bright patches of Wild Bergamot flaunt their showy flowers in grasslands and open woods during the summer. This perennial, with stiffly erect, square stems 12–27 inches (30–70 cm) tall, has a strong and distinctive minty odor. A dense cluster of pink to lilac flowers tops each stem. The petals, about 1¼ inch (3 cm) long, are deeply cleft into narrow upper and lower lips that open wide at the mouth. Two stamens and a pistil extend beyond the lips. The sepals are fused into a narrow tube, which is crowded with dense white hairs. Both petals and sepals are marked with glandular dots. The opposite, strongly toothed, gray-green leaves are triangular-ovate in shape and pointed at the tip. Wild Bergamot was used by Native Americans to relieve acne, bronchial complaints, and stomach pains.

Range: throughout the Rockies.

Wild Bergamot; Horsemint
Monarda fistulosa

MINT FAMILY
Lamiaceae

Common Selfheal; Healall

Prunella vulgaris

MINT FAMILY
Lamiaceae

Common Selfheal has all the typical characteristics of the mint family: square stem, opposite leaves, and 2-lipped flowers. The upper lip is arched or hooded; the lower is 3-parted, with the middle part much larger, and attractively fringed with white hairs. The flowers are generally purplish-blue, rarely pink or white. The calyx, usually purplish-green, is covered with long hairs. Small brownish-green, bractlike leaves are interspersed among the flowers in the thick terminal spike. As suggested by the common names, the plant was once esteemed for healing wounds. A refreshing beverage can be made by chopping and boiling the leaves. This attractive plant is fairly common in damp fields and woods in the montane zone.

Range: throughout the Rockies.

Hairy Hedgenettle

Stachys pilosa

MINT FAMILY
Lamiaceae

This rather handsome plant reproduces by seed and underground rhizomes. Hairy Hedgenettle is distinguished by its hairy leaves, 1½–3 inches (4–8 cm) long, and hairy stems from 8–35 inches (20–90 cm) tall. Leaves are opposite, lanceolate to narrowly ovate, pointed at the tips, toothed, and short-stalked to stalkless. Like other members of the mint family, the stems are square in cross section. *Stachys* means "spike" in Greek, in reference to the spike-like form of the flower whorls on the upper part of the stems. The united 2-lipped flowers are rose-purple to white, mottled with darker spots; with the upper lip shorter than the 3-lobed lower one. Hairy Hedgenettle occurs on wet ground beside ponds and streams, wet meadows, and roadside verges.

Range: throughout the Rockies.

The beautiful violet-purple, irregularly shaped flowers of Common Butterwort are on leafless stalks up to 4 inches (10 cm) high. The calyx is notched into 3 upper and 2 lower lobes, forming a funnel-like structure. The spur is whitish to dark in color with short hairs. Pale green leaves press close to the ground and overlap one another in a basal rosette. Common Butterwort is one of the few carnivorous plants in the Rockies. Its yellowish-green, thickened leaves, with rolled-in edges, exude a sticky substance that attracts, ensnares, and digests tiny insects, enabling the plant to obtain nitrogen and other nutrients. The insect-catching and digestive powers of this plant help compensate for the lack of nutrients in the ecological niche in which it grows. This intriguing plant may be found in bogs, on wet rocky banks, and on mossy streamsides, mainly in valleys at low elevation.

Range: Alberta, British Columbia, and Montana.

Common Butterwort
Pinguicula vulgaris

BLADDERWORT FAMILY
Lentibulariaceae

The genus *Allium* includes so many beautiful species that it should not be condemned for a smell that is never offensive unless the plants are roughly handled. Wild Chives has a densely clustered head of showy blossoms at the end of each stem. They are rose to purplish-pink, with darker veins. Both the straight, stout flowering stems and hollow cylindrical leaves spring from a pink to purple bulb with a white membranous coat. The edible bulb has a strong, hot flavor. Our garden chives were derived from this wild species. These handsome bright-flowered chives may be found in damp open habitats from low elevations to the timberline.

**Range: throughout the Rockies,
excluding New Mexico.**

Wild Chives
Allium schoenoprasum

LILY FAMILY
Liliaceae

Sagebrush Mariposa Lily
Calochortus macrocarpus

LILY FAMILY
Liliaceae

Drop dead gorgeous may be an apt way of describing Sagebrush Mariposa Lily. Growing from oval-shaped bulbs, this perennial ranges from 8–20 inches (20–50 cm) in height. Grass-like leaves are 2–4 inches (5–10 cm) long, decreasing in size upward along the stem. Both the leaves and stem are an unusual bluish-green. Generally 1 to 3 (occasionally up to 6) flowers project upward on each stem. Both the sepals and petals are pale to dark lavender. Petals are marked with a green stripe on the outside and are purple-banded and bearded above the nectary on the inside. Flowers with white petals and a red-purple band occur in small areas of Washington and Idaho. The thin, lanceolate-shaped capsules that follow are upright and 3-parted lengthwise. Upon drying, both the capsules and strongly flattened seeds are straw-colored. Sagebrush Mariposa Lily bulbs can remain dormant for a period of up to 4 years, a strategy by the plant to avoid unfavorable conditions. It is highly palatable to livestock and considerably less common than in the past because of grazing and habitat loss. Dry grasslands and open Ponderosa Pine forests at low elevations are the favored habitats for this lily.

Range: British Columbia, Washington, Oregon, Idaho, and Montana.

Small Camas
Camassia quamash

LILY FAMILY
Liliaceae

The onion-like bulbs of Small Camas were a very important food plant for Native Americans, trappers, and early settlers. They were baked, boiled, roasted, or eaten raw; they were made into a molasses and into "Camas" pie, or ground into flour for bread. So important were the bulbs that some Native Americans fought battles over the rights to certain large meadows containing the plant. Arising from the bulbs are rather stout stems 12–24 inches (30–60 cm) tall, with long, narrow, grass-like leaves about two-thirds as long as the naked stem. The startling blue to purplish-blue flower has 6 separate, but similar, petals and sepals, which are spreading and somewhat unevenly spaced. These segments contrast vividly with the 6 golden stamens. Flowering in the spring, Small Camas grows in seasonally wet meadows and along stream banks.

Range: throughout the Rockies, excluding Colorado and New Mexico.

Checker Lily is a highly variable species growing from a bulb to a height of 12–20 inches (30–50 cm). Leaves are long and narrow and in whorls of 3 to 5 around the lower two-thirds of the stem. The bell-shaped, nodding flowers may be solitary to a few in a loose raceme on curved stalks. Tepals are alike, but the color can range from yellowish or chocolate brown with lots of yellow mottling to purplish-black with little mottling, or yellow-green mottled with purple. The flowers are gland-bearing near the base; stamens, with yellow anthers, are shorter than the tepals. As the broad, 6-winged seed capsules mature the flower stem straightens to an erect position. Checker Lily is sometimes referred to as "rice-roots" because many tiny rice-like bulblets cluster around the roots and bulbs. Traditionally the bulbs were cooked and eaten, or dried for future use by Native Americans and early explorers. Grasslands, meadows, and open forests to the lower subalpine provide suitable habitat for this striking plant.

Range: British Columbia, Washington, Oregon, Idaho, and Montana.

Checker Lily; Chocolate Lily
Fritillaria affinis

LILY FAMILY
Liliaceae

Inset photo by Barry Gordichuk

The lovely blue-lavender, tube-shaped flowers of Largeflower Triteleia are arranged in rather open umbels on the end of smooth stems from 8–27 inches (20–70 cm) tall. Five to 20 flowers are present in each umbrella-shaped cluster. Each flower has 6 petals that flare at the open end and have darker midveins; the 3 inner petals have ruffled edges at the point of flare. Generally only 1 to 2 linear leaves grow from the bulbous stem base. The flat leaves are ridged and usually shorter than the stem. Because the bulbs are up to 8 inches (20 cm) below the ground, the plants can survive even in extreme drought conditions. The bulbs, reported to be the tastiest in North America, have a sweet nut-like flavor and can be used like potatoes. Largeflower Triteleia is distributed in dry grasslands, sagebrush deserts, and open Ponderosa Pine forests.

Range: throughout the Rockies, excluding Alberta and New Mexico.

Largeflower Triteleia; Wild Hyacinth
Triteleia grandiflora
[Brodiaea douglasii]

LILY FAMILY
Liliaceae

Prairie Flax;
Wild Blue Flax
Linum lewisii var. lewisii

FLAX FAMILY
Linaceae

Prairie Flax is a perennial, 8–24 inches (20–60 cm) tall, that grows in coarse soils. Borne at the summit of slender stems that bend to the slightest breeze, the sky-blue flowers in loose clusters flicker and ripple in nearly ceaseless motion. The sepals, petals, stamens, and styles of the flower are each in 5 parts. The delicate petals, which are marked with radiating lines of blue, soon fall. Shining brown capsules containing 10 seeds that are rich in oil replace the flowers. The numerous linear leaves are small, sharply pointed, and gray-green in color. This plant provided cordage and fishing tackle for Native American people and was also used as a healing oil, laxative, and food. This is the genus from which linen fabric and linseed oil are produced. Prairie Flax is wide ranging from prairies to the alpine zone.

Range: throughout the Rockies.

Oneflowered Broomrape;
Naked Broomrape
Orobanche uniflora

BROOMRAPE FAMILY
Orobanchaceae

Growing almost entirely underground, the stem is visible only ⅜–1¼ inches (1–3 cm) above the ground. Each stem bears a single, curved flower, pinkish-white to purple in color, and about ¾ inch (2 cm) long. Both the stem and flower are covered with dense glandular hairs. Stem leaves are alternate and often reduced to scales that are a whitish-tan. The tubular corolla with 2 yellow bearded strips is screaming an invitation to a passing bee or wasp. Lacking chlorophyll to manufacture its own food, Oneflowered Broomrape is parasitic on the roots of alumroots, stonecrops, and several other vascular plants. Clustered Broomrape (*O. fasciculata*) has a similar range, but as the name suggests it grows in clusters. Oneflowered Broomrape, although not abundant, occurs in the foothills and montane.

Range: throughout the Rockies.

Pulcherrimum means "very handsome" and that is indeed an apt description for this beautiful perennial. It is a tufted plant, 2–10 inches (5–25 cm) tall, with sparingly branched stems. The fern-like leaves are mostly basal, each with 11 to 23 leaflets; there are a few reduced leaves on the stem. These leaflets are so evenly spaced that the leaves look like miniature ladders, thereby giving rise to the popular name. Pale to dark cobalt-blue, cup-shaped flowers, with a vivid orangish-yellow ring at the base, are borne in an open cluster. The brilliant cascade of blossoms entices bees to settle and collect nectar while leaving pollen from another flower. Jacob's-ladder grows in open, well-drained sites from the montane zone to just above the timberline. The plant is best enjoyed out-of-doors because of its unpleasant odor.

Range: throughout the Rockies.

Jacob's-ladder
Polemonium pulcherrimum

PHLOX FAMILY
Polemoniaceae

Sticky Polemonium is a strikingly handsome alpine plant of exposed scree slopes. Its closely packed leaves are short and consist of numerous roundish, 3- to 5-parted leaflets, which are unpleasantly sticky to handle and have a heavy odor suggestive of skunk. The flower clusters are dense and rounded. Their funnel-shaped corollas have 5 expanded lobes, a circle of 5 stamens, and a long thread-like style. The brilliantly blue petals contrast with the orange pollen on the stamens. Despite the offensive odor of the leaves, the flowers are sweet-scented.

Range: throughout the Rockies.

Sticky Polemonium; Sky Pilot; Skunkweed
Polemonium viscosum

PHLOX FAMILY
Polemoniaceae

Darkthroat Shootingstar
Dodecatheon pulchellum

PRIMROSE FAMILY
Primulaceae

Pulchellum means "beautiful" and the name is certainly appropriate as the varied pink to lilac-purple colors of the flowers are unusually lovely. Clusters of nodding flowers grow from the tip of the stem, which varies from 4–8 inches (10–20 cm) in height. The petals bend back and are often more intensely colored near the base, which is ringed with deep yellow and trimmed with a zigzag of rose-purple. The dark green basal leaves are erect and lance-shaped, with the broadest part toward the tip. As the brown seed capsules ripen, they assume an upright position, thus aiding in the dispersal of the seeds. Darkthroat Shootingstar can be very abundant in moist meadows, the flowers producing waves of color from spring to early summer depending on the elevation.

Range: throughout the Rockies.

Parry's Primrose
Primula parryi

PRIMROSE FAMILY
Primulaceae

A stunning plant of high elevations, Parry's Primrose grows to 12 inches (30 cm) tall on a stout, smooth, leafless, and curving stem. Basal leaves are nearly as tall as the flower stems, and are thick, fleshy, toothed at the edges, and prominently mid-veined. The stems support an elongated cluster of 3 to 12 tubular flowers with 5 notched, flaring petals. The vivid magenta to purplish-red flowers have yellow throats to alert insects to the nectar source. Such beauties can have their limitations; with even the slightest touch the plants emit an unpleasant fetid odor, likely to attract pollinators. Parry's Primrose likes to grow in wet habitats such as waterfall ledges, snowbank areas, streamsides, and pond margins in the subalpine and alpine zones.

Range: Idaho, Montana, Wyoming, Utah, Colorado, and New Mexico.

Photo by Katherine Darrow

An attractive and unusual plant, this tuberous perennial has stems that are usually stout, erect, and 20-60 inches (50-150 cm) tall, but occasionally weak and reclining. The large leaves are palmately divided into 3 to 5 parts and further divided or toothed, becoming smaller upward. Columbian Monkshood has a unique flower. Each has 5 deep bluish-purple sepals, but the ones higher on the stems may be tinged with lighter blue or white. The largest upper sepal fits over the rest of the flower like a helmet. There are numerous stamens but only 2 petals that are much reduced in size and hidden by the sepals. Flowering starts at the bottom of the showy raceme and progresses upward. Alkaloids (aconitine) in the plant, especially in the roots, are highly toxic to animals. Columbian Monkshood is shade tolerant and prefers moist habitats along stream banks, seepage areas, and wet meadows in the montane to alpine zones.

Range: throughout the Rockies, excluding Alberta.

Columbian Monkshood
Aconitum columbianum

BUTTERCUP FAMILY
Ranunculaceae

A northern species, Larkspurleaf Monkshood has light blue to navy blue flowers scattered along a smooth, erect stem. The upper sepal is curiously hood-shaped and thus the plant is aptly named Monkshood. The 1¼-2 inch (3-5 cm) hoods are wider than high. Stems may be up to 3 feet (1 m), but much smaller in alpine habitats. The leaves have 5 deeply divided, narrow lobes that are often divided again into 3 linear leaflets. The whole plant is highly toxic, especially the seeds and roots. Even skin contact has caused numbness in some people. Larkspurleaf Monkshood is at home in meadows, stream margins, thickets, woods, and rocky slopes in the subalpine and alpine zones.

Range: Alberta and British Columbia.

Larkspurleaf Monkshood
Aconitum delphiniifolium

BUTTERCUP FAMILY
Ranunculaceae

Smallflower Columbine
Aquilegia brevistyla

BUTTERCUP FAMILY
Ranunculaceae

Most of the Rocky Mountain columbines closely resemble the cultivated varieties found in gardens. Each species is distinctive and easy to identify. Smallflower Columbine has tall stems, 10–20 inches (25–50 cm) high, skirted at the base by long-stalked, pale green compound leaves, which are divided into several segments. Drooping bicolored, cream-white and blue flowers hang gracefully at the top of the curving stems. The flower is composed of 5 blue, wing-shaped sepals and 5 creamy white, tube-shaped petals, flaring at the open end with a brush-like tuft of stamens and styles, and tapering to a hooked, bluish spur at the other end. These spurs bear a fanciful resemblance to doves perched and facing inward around a drinking dish, their wings being represented by the sepals. Numerous seeds are borne in 5 pods, which are erect at maturity. Smallflower Columbine is found in meadows, open woods, and rock crevices.

Range: Alberta, British Columbia, Montana, and Wyoming.

Colorado Blue Columbine
Aquilegia caerulea

BUTTERCUP FAMILY
Ranunculaceae

Colorado Blue Columbine, an herbaceous perennial growing 8–24 inches (20–60 cm) tall, is one of the most beautiful of the wild columbines and is the state flower of Colorado. Leaves are mostly basal on long slender stalks with blades that are deeply dissected into rounded lobes. Stem leaves are much smaller and often reduced to bracts. Leaves are green above and bluish-green underneath. A few to several upward-tipped flowers, 2–2¾ inches (5–7 cm) across, are borne on elongated racemes. Flowers are variable in color ranging from pale blue to white, pale yellow, or pinkish; bicolored flowers with the sepals a different shade than the petals are common. The 5 scoop-shaped petals trail behind straight, exceptionally long spurs. The spurs help to distinguish it from other columbines. Numerous yellow stamens and 5 long pistils protrude at the center of the flower. The nectar-laden spurs are generally available only to hummingbirds, butterflies, and moths with long tongues, but short-tongued bees and others nip off the spurs to obtain their rich reward. Colorado Blue Columbine prefers moist, open to shaded sites from the foothills to the subalpine zone.

Range: Idaho, Montana, Wyoming, Utah, Colorado, and New Mexico.

A dwarf alpine plant, Jones' Columbine stands 2–4 inches (5–10 cm) high on rocky limestone screes. Those who find the plant in full flower will not soon forget its arresting beauty. Each stem produces a single flower that is much larger than other parts of the plant. Both the sepals and petals are generally deep blue or purplish, but white-flowered specimens may be found. Some populations have deep blue sepals ringing cream-colored petals, resulting in a particularly gorgeous flower. The 5 petals extend backward into a somewhat incurved spur, which may be filled with nectar. Each flower has many stamens and 5 pistils. The lightly hairy, bluish-green leaves, divided into small lobes, are in dense tufts near ground level. This elegant plant is limited in distribution to calcareous soils in the subalpine and alpine zones and is endemic to a small area of southwestern Alberta, western Montana, and northern Wyoming.

Range: Alberta, Montana, and Wyoming.

Jones' Columbine
Aquilegia jonesii

BUTTERCUP FAMILY
Ranunculaceae

Western Blue Virginsbower, a climbing or trailing vine, drapes itself over shrubs and herbs and around the trunks of trees. The strong, slender stems produce opposite leaves, each divided into 3 leaflets, between 1¼–2¾ inches (3–7 cm) long. Flowers occur singly in the axils of the leaves. These flowers lack true petals, but they attract attention because of the large petal-like sepals, which are blue or lavender, accented by darker veining, and sharply pointed. Later in the season a mop of long, grayish-white, fuzzy styles that prolong the beauty of this vine replaces the flowers. Open woods and thickets are favored habitats for this showy plant.

Range: throughout the Rockies, excluding New Mexico.

Western Blue Virginsbower
Clematis occidentalis

BUTTERCUP FAMILY
Ranunculaceae

Subalpine Larkspur
Delphinium barbeyi

BUTTERCUP FAMILY
Ranunculaceae

Subalpine Larkspur is a tall plant, up to 5 feet (1.5 m), with coarse, sticky hairs, and hollow stems arising from a woody rootstock. The large attractive leaves, much like those of Columbian Monkshood, are palmately clefted into 5 to 7 lobes and further divided into coarsely toothed segments. The fragrant flowers, which occur in terminal spike-like clusters, are distinctive with 5 inky-blue to deep purple sepals, the upper one extending backward to form a spur with a bent tip and the two lower ones gradually tapering to a point. There are also small purple petals with white margins and numerous stamens in the center of the flower. These plants contain potent alkaloids that are responsible for the majority of cattle deaths on some mountain ranges. Subalpine Larkspur is an eye-catching plant often growing in masses in wet meadows and in spruce-fir and Quaking Aspen forest openings in the subalpine zone.

Range: Wyoming, Utah, Colorado, and New Mexico.

Little Larkspur
Delphinium bicolor

BUTTERCUP FAMILY
Ranunculaceae

Growing from prairie meadows to alpine ridges, this strikingly handsome plant blooms from May to July, depending on the elevation. It arises from somewhat fleshy roots, its stems 6–14 inches (15–35 cm) tall with deeply cut leaflets that are chiefly basal. From 3 to 12 flowers are borne in a loose spike. Each of the 4 lower sepals is an intense blue-purple color, widely flared, and appreciably larger than the upper sepal, which extends backward into a prominent hollow spur. Smaller than the sepals, the 4 petals are of two kinds: the lower 2 petals are dark blue and hairy and the upper 2, even smaller, are creamy white with purple veins when fresh. The mature fruit is an erect cluster of pods about ¾ inch (2 cm) long, containing many seeds. Little Larkspur is poisonous to cattle, particularly in the early spring; the leaves contain several toxic alkaloids, including delphinine. Curiously, sheep are unaffected by the alkaloids and they have been used to eradicate the plant in some pastures. While not common, Little Larkspur may be locally abundant.

Range: Alberta, British Columbia, Idaho, Montana, and Wyoming.

As harbingers of early spring, the blooms of the Cutleaf Anemone emerge from the ground before its leaves have developed, often before the snow has melted. The cup-shaped flowers, in varying colors from royal purple to bluish-lavender and occasionally white, often paint entire hillsides in the grasslands and open woods. These 6-parted flowers are often a paler color inside than outside, and they enclose a cluster of bright yellow stamens. The deeply cleft leaves and the stems, cloaked in an army of silky white hairs, develop after the flowers appear. In time, a wad of achenes, each with a long, feathery tail, replaces the flowers. This conspicuous and lovely plant is the floral emblem of Manitoba and the state flower of South Dakota.

Range: throughout the Rockies, excluding Oregon.

Cutleaf Anemone; Prairie Crocus

Pulsatilla patens ssp. multifida
[Anemone multifida]

BUTTERCUP FAMILY
Ranunculaceae

While other saxifrages may dress in flowers of white or yellow, Purple Mountain Saxifrage is garbed with flowers of the richest rose-purple to royal purple. Each stem produces a solitary, star-shaped flower on a short stalk at the end of the stem. However, the mat of tightly packed leafy stems, each with its own flower, may result in such a mass of bloom that the tiny leaves are nearly concealed. The crimped petals, accented by brownish-orange anthers, are narrowed to a blunt tip. Overlapping, scale-like leaves, ranked in fours and with hairy margins, distinguish this saxifrage from Moss Campion, which is found in similar habitats. Look for carpets of these charming flowers above the timberline, on meadows, and on scree slopes soon after snowmelt.

Range: throughout the Rockies, excluding Utah and New Mexico.

Purple Mountain Saxifrage

Saxifraga oppositifolia

SAXIFRAGE FAMILY
Saxifragaceae

Wyoming Besseya; Kittentails

Besseya wyomingensis

FIGWORT FAMILY
Scrophulariaceae

Wyoming Besseya, a small perennial 6–12 inches (15–30 cm) tall, is covered with fine white hairs on all green parts. The lance-shaped basal leaves have long petioles and toothed margins, whereas the stem leaves are much smaller and lack petioles, clasping the stem directly. The flowers consist of 2 or 3 green sepals, no petals, 2 deep purple stamens, and a purple style with a button-like stigma. The flowers are in a dense spike, with numerous small green bracts. The other common name, Kittentails, is derived from the halo-like cluster of long purple stamens. These showy flowers add a splash of color to grasslands and alpine slopes in the early summer.

Range: throughout the Rockies, excluding Washington, Oregon, and New Mexico.

Purple Monkeyflower

Mimulus lewisii

FIGWORT FAMILY
Scrophulariaceae

Favorite habitats of Purple Monkeyflower are near ice-cold mountain streams or other open wet places at moderate elevations. In such habitats the plant, with its luxuriant dark green foliage and showers of glowing rose-red to purple flowers, may grow in solid masses. The clasping leaves are conspicuously veined with widely spaced teeth along the margins. Showy flowers grow on long stalks from the axils of the upper leaves. A round, 2-lipped, funnel-shaped corolla is formed by the 5 lobes. The lower 3-lobed lip has a hairy throat, handsomely marked with deep yellow. Short sticky hairs cover the whole plant. Bees and hummingbirds are frequently attracted to these flowers.

Range: throughout the Rockies, excluding New Mexico.

Bracted Louseworts are unmistakable plants because of their stiffly erect, purplish stems that are naked near the bottom, dense spikes of arching tubular flowers, and fern-like leaves. The stem, 16–40 inches (40–100 cm) tall, arises from a thick, perennial rootstock and is devoid of leaves on the lower third. Much-dissected leaves grow from the upper portion of the stem until they merge into bracts, which are interspersed with flowers in a dense terminal spike. Both the upper stem and leaves are bronze- or wine-tinged. Individual flowers are yellow, often tinged with red or purple, and curve downward at the tip. The corolla is distinctly 2-lipped. The upper lip is long and flattened at the sides and arched at the apex, cupping over the stamens; the lower lip is shorter, 3-parted, toothed, and it curves in so much that it nearly closes the throat. The flowers almost resemble small parrots' bills peeping out from among the bracts. Look for Bracted Lousewort in moist soils in open woods and alpine meadows.

Range: throughout the Rockies.

Bracted Lousewort; Wood Betony
Pedicularis bracteosa

FIGWORT FAMILY
Scrophulariaceae

The flower of this plant bears an amazing likeness to an elephant's head with a high forehead, big ears, long upraised trunk, and small tusks. The upper lip of the corolla resembles the head and upturned trunk, 2 petals of the lower lip form the ears, and the central lobe is the mouth. These purple-pink flowers are arranged at the top of a rather compact spike, which may be up to 20 inches (50 cm) tall. The leaves are deeply divided and fern-like. Both the leaves and stems are often tinged with purple. The carrot-like roots may be eaten raw or cooked in soup. Elephanthead Lousewort is conspicuous in wet meadows and marshes.

Range: throughout the Rockies.

Elephanthead Lousewort
Pedicularis groenlandica

FIGWORT FAMILY
Scrophulariaceae

Alberta Beardtongue
Penstemon albertinus

FIGWORT FAMILY
Scrophulariaceae

Alberta Beardtongue grows in tufts 4–12 inches (10–30 cm) tall. Arranged in an open cluster around the upper part of the stem, the bright blue to purplish flowers are tubular in shape and 2-lipped. Each petal tube is sparsely hairy outside with long white and yellow hairs inside the lower throat. One of the 5 stamens is sterile and densely bearded. The petioled basal leaves are egg- to lance-shaped with inconspicuous teeth on the margins; the alternate stem leaves lack petioles and are lance-shaped with shallowly toothed margins. This attractive plant with its spires of azure flowers is fairly common in dry, open habitats at low to middle elevations.

Range: Alberta, British Columbia, Idaho, and Montana.

Sulphur Penstemon; Taper-leaved Beardtongue
Penstemon attenuatus

FIGWORT FAMILY
Scrophulariaceae

Sulphur Penstemon, a seemingly inappropriate common name, is a variable tufted perennial with stems 12–27 inches (30–70 cm) tall arising from a woody rootstock. Basal leaves are lanceolate to ovate, short-petioled, mostly entire-margined, and smooth or with fine hairs. The opposite stem leaves are reduced in size, bright green, and without a petiole. The terminal inflorescence is glandular-hairy with 3 to 7 whorls consisting of several to many flowers. Although highly variable, the most common flower color is some shade of blue, but pink, yellow, and white can occur. There are 4 fertile stamens and 1 sterile stamen, called the staminode. The anthers of the fertile stamens are hairless, but the end of the sterile stamen, located near the mouth of the petal tube, is covered with yellow hairs. Sulphur Penstemon is found in dry meadows, sagebrush slopes, and open woods from the foothills to the subalpine.

Range: Washington, Oregon, Idaho, Montana, and Wyoming.

There are more than 250 species of *Penstemon* in North America, most of which occur in the West. Of those, Rocky Ledge Penstemon is one of the most handsome and conspicuous. Its large trumpet-shaped flowers, pink to lilac-purple and mostly less than 1¼ inch (3 cm) long, may be so numerous that they form a mass of brilliant color, which obscures the leaves and prostrate stems. The corolla tube is 2-lipped; the lower lip is ornamented with 2 folds and long white hairs. Of the 5 stamens, 1 is sterile with a long yellow beard that protrudes at the widened throat. After the corolla falls, the egg-shaped brown capsule begins to mature. These plants are dwarf shrubs from 4–8 inches (10–20 cm) tall, with trailing leafy stems. They are semi-evergreen, some of the leaves turning red and dropping in the autumn. The leaves are opposite, ovate, and up to 1¼ inch (3 cm) long. Cushions of this flower-bedecked shrub may be found on dry rocky slopes in the subalpine and alpine zones.

Rocky Ledge Penstemon; Creeping Beardtongue
Penstemon ellipticus

FIGWORT FAMILY
Scrophulariaceae

Range: Alberta, British Columbia, Washington, Idaho, Montana, and Wyoming.

Once seen, it is hard to forget the gorgeous bright blue flowers of Waxleaf Penstemon. It is a perennial growing from a woody stem and taproot. Stems 6–12 inches (15–30 cm) tall, can occur singly but there are often several in a clump. The lower leaves are lance-shaped and 4 inches (10 cm) long; upper ones are broader but shorter, 1¼–2 inch (3–5 cm) long, and clasp the stem. Both the stem and bluish-green leaves are smooth and covered with a waxy film on the surface. Each stem bears 10 to 20 tube-shaped flowers about 6–8 inches (15–20 cm) long. The corolla is distinctly 2-lipped, the lower one bearded with fine hairs. One of the 5 stamens is sterile and bears a tuft of hairs. This thread-like male organ protrudes from the flower like a "tongue." In botanical Latin the specific name *nitidus* means "shining," because of the waxy luster of the plant. Look for this handsome plant in dry grassland and foothills.

Waxleaf Penstemon
Penstemon nitidus

FIGWORT FAMILY
Scrophulariaceae

Range: Alberta, British Columbia, Idaho, Montana, Wyoming, and Colorado.

Littleflower Penstemon
Penstemon procerus

FIGWORT FAMILY
Scrophulariaceae

Littleflower Penstemon is nearly identical in appearance and size to Yellow Beardtongue except for its deep purplish-blue (rarely pinkish to white) flowers. It can be distinguished from Alberta Beardtongue by its rather crowded cluster of small flowers in contrast to the open arrangement of slightly larger flowers for the latter. The flowers may be in a dense cluster, as illustrated, or in several crowded whorls (see Yellow Penstemon). Sharply ovate blades on long petioles form a basal rosette of leaves; there are a few stem leaves without petioles. Usually rather common, this plant may be found in open forests to the timberline.

Range: throughout the Rockies, excluding New Mexico.

Sidebells Penstemon
Penstemon secundiflorus

FIGWORT FAMILY
Scrophulariaceae

Sidebells Penstemon has clasping opposite leaves on an unbranched, erect, smooth stem to 24 inches (60 cm) tall. Ovate leaves are up to 4 inches (10 cm) long, fleshy, and a pale bluish-green. Flowers, arranged on one side of the stem as implied by the common name, vary in color from rose-pink, to magenta, to lavender, or dark purple. Like other penstemons, the flowers are 2-lipped, the upper with 2 lobes and the lower with 3 lobes. The sterile stamen or staminode has a yellow beard. Oneside Penstemon (*P. unilateralis*) is similar but lacks hair on the sterile stamen and the flowers are blue on the outside and pinkish on the inside. Sidebells Penstemon is frequently encountered on grassy hillsides, pastures, roadsides, and wooded sites from the foothills to the montane zone.

Range: Wyoming, Colorado, and New Mexico.

Another of the many penstemons found in the Rockies, Whipple's Penstemon is a perennial on tufted stems 8–24 inches (20–60 cm) tall arising from shallow root crowns. The petioled basal leaves have smooth edges and elliptic blades up to 2½ inches (6 cm) long; opposite stem leaves are small and sessile or nearly so. From 2 to 7 whorls of short-stalked flowers bloom in the axils of the upper leaves. The 2-lipped nodding flowers come in two colors: deep wine or cream with purple veins. The 3-lobed bottom lip is longer than the upper one. Four of the stamens have anthers but the sterile stamen is without an anther and has a cluster of hairs at the tip. The outside of the tubular corolla is covered with glandular hairs, as is the upper foliage. Whipple's Penstemon grows on exposed areas such as talus slopes, moraines, meadows, and forest clearings from the montane to the alpine.

Range: Idaho, Montana, Wyoming, Utah, Colorado, and New Mexico.

Whipple's Penstemon
Penstemon whippleanus

FIGWORT FAMILY
Scrophulariaceae

This perennial alpine beauty is easily recognized. It has a flattened, usually 4-petalled corolla, with only 2 stamens and a pistil. The corolla is less than ⅜ inch (1 cm) wide and is a brilliant, dark purplish-blue with even darker veins. Of the 4 petals, the uppermost lobe is considerably wider than the others. The stems rise 3–8 inches (8–20 cm) high from a slender rootstock. Pairs of leaves, elliptical to egg-like in shape and with nearly smooth margins, are well spaced along the stem. Both the stems and leaves of American Alpine Speedwell are covered with fine hairs, and stalks of the flowers are sticky. When the blossom has faded, a heart-shaped seedpod with 2 chambers, not unlike a little locket, remains. Look for this attractive plant in herbmats of the subalpine and alpine zones.

Range: throughout the Rockies.

American Alpine Speedwell
Veronica wormskjoldii
[V. alpina]

FIGWORT FAMILY
Scrophulariaceae

Swamp Verbena
Verbena hastata

VERBENA FAMILY
Verbenaceae

Swamp Verbena is a rather rough, finely haired herb with an erect, 4-sided stem, which typically reaches 3 feet (1 m). It is a clump-forming perennial with an upright habit. Leaves are broadly lance-shaped, sharply toothed, and up to 6 inches (15 cm) long. Tiny, tubular, usually purplish-blue flowers are densely clustered in numerous slender, pencil-like spikes 2–6 inches (5–15 cm) long. Flowers on each spike in the candelabra-like inflorescence bloom from bottom to top, but only a few appear at one time. As the common name suggests, Swamp Verbena inhabits riparian areas such as wet meadows, stream banks, ditches, and springs at low elevations.

Range: throughout the Rockies, excluding Alberta.

Hookedspur Violet; Early Blue Violet
Viola adunca

VIOLET FAMILY
Violaceae

Hookedspur Violet is one of the earliest and loveliest of the spring flowers. It is also highly variable in several characteristics. Although most frequently heart- to kidney-like, the leaf shape is variable. Plants may be smooth to densely hairy. The handsome, long-petioled leaves set off a wealth of blue to deep violet flowers, each with a long hooked spur. The 3 lower petals have purple lines and often a white base, while the lowermost is spurred; the 2 lateral petals have white beards. The head of the style is also bearded. These flowers have an exquisite fragrance. This plant is fairly common from dry to shady places at low elevations.

Range: throughout the Rockies.

Glossary

Achene
A dry, one-seeded fruit that does not open when ripe.

Alternate leaves
A single leaf at each node, alternating on the stem.

Annual
A plant that completes its lifecycle of germinating, flowering, and ripening seed within one year.

Anther
That part of a stamen that bears pollen.

Appressed
Lying close or flat against a surface.

Areola
A small specialized, cushion-like area on a cactus from which hairs, glochids, spines, branches, or flowers may arise.

Axil
The angle between two organs, especially the upper angle between a leaf and the stem.

Basal
Located at the base of a plant or an organ of a plant.

Biennial
A plant that completes its life span within two years.

Bract
A leaflike plant part located either below a flower or on the stalk of a flower cluster. Bracts are usually small but may sometimes be showy and brightly colored.

Bulbil
A small, usually bulb-like body produced in a leaf axil that will germinate to produce a new plant.

Calyx
The outer floral ring, or sepals, usually green, but sometimes brightly colored.

Carpel
A seed-bearing chamber at the base of the pistil of a flower; the pod of a garden pea is an example.

Corm
A solid bulb; an enlarged base of a stem.

Corolla
The petals or inner floral ring.

Corymb
A flat-topped or convex, open flower cluster, the outer flowers opening first.

Cyme
A flat-topped or convex flower cluster, the central flowers of which bloom first.

Deciduous
Falling off at the end of the growing season; not persistent.

Disk floret
The flowers in the central portion of the head in the Aster Family, as distinguished from the ray flowers.

Dissected
Deeply and finely cut or lobed into many divisions.

Drupe
A pulpy or fleshy fruit containing a single seed enclosed in a hard shell or stone.

Entire
A leaf or leaflet having the margins not at all toothed, lobed, or divided.

Filament
The stalk of a stamen below the anther.

Floret
An individual small flower, usually one of several in a cluster.

Follicle
A fruit with a single chamber that opens along one side, as in milkweeds.

Forb
A flowering plant with a non-woody stem that is not a grass.

Galea
A helmet-shaped part, such as the upper petal of certain plants like monkshood.

Glabrous
Smooth, without hairs.

Glandular
Bearing secreting organs or glands.

Globose
Spherical or nearly so.

Glochid
One of the minute barbed hairs or bristles on certain plants, such as prickly pear cacti.

Herb
A plant dying back to the ground at the end of the growing season.

Inflorescence
Arrangement of flowers in a cluster.

Involucre
A whorl or set of bracts surrounding or just below a flower or flower cluster.

Keel
The two lowermost and united petals of members of the Pea Family.

Lanceolate
A leaf much longer than wide, broadest near the base and tapering toward the tip.

Legume
A name for plants of the Pea Family; also a dry pod-like fruit of the Pea Family, splitting down one or both sides at maturity.

Linear
Narrow and nearly uniform in width.

Lobed
Cut so as to leave prominent projections.

Nectary
That part of a blossom that secretes nectar, usually the base of the corolla or petals.

Node
The place on the stem where a leaf is, or was, attached.

Oblanceolate
A leaf much longer than wide, broadest part above the middle.

Oblong
Longer than broad, having the sides nearly parallel for most of their length.

Obovate
Egg-shaped, broadest at top, and with the narrow end attached to the stem.

Offset
A short, prostrate or ascending shoot, usually propagative in function, arising near the base of the plant.

Opposite leaves
Growing in pairs on either side of a stem.

Ovary
The part of the pistil of a flower containing the cells that become seeds.

Ovate
Egg-shaped but broadest near the base.

Palmate
A leaf having the shape of a hand with the fingers spread.

Panicle
A branched cluster of flowers, each stalked, the lower branches longest and opening first. Often applied to any complex cluster.

Pappus
The tufts of hairs on the achene of many species of the Aster and other families.

Pedicel
The stalk of an individual flower.

Perennial
A plant that persists for more than two seasons.

Persistent
Remaining attached.

Petal
One of a whorl of floral organs placed between sepals and stamens, usually brightly colored.

Petiole
The stalk by which a leaf is attached to a stem.

Pinnate leaf
A leaf that is divided into many small leaflets, arranged in rows along either side of a midrib.

Pistil
The female organ of a flower that contains the seeds at maturity.

GLOSSARY

Procumbent
Trailing along the ground without rooting at the nodes.

Pubescence
The various types of hairs that cover the surface of a plant.

Raceme
An elongated flower cluster, the main stem branching only once, the lowermost flowers opening first.

Ray flower
A marginal flower with a strap-shaped corolla in the Aster Family, as distinguished from the disk florets.

Reduced
Smaller in size.

Reflexed
Abruptly turned or bent backward.

Rhizome or Rootstock
An underground, creeping root-like stem.

Saprophyte
A plant that derives its food from non-living organic matter.

Scree
Slanting mass of stone fragments at the foot of cliffs or other steep inclines.

Sepal
One of the separate parts of a calyx, usually green and leaf-like.

Sessile
Without a stalk.

Shrub
A woody plant that remains low and usually produces several stems from the base.

Spatulate
Spoon-shaped; gradually narrowed from a rounded summit.

Spur
A hollow, sac-like extension, usually at the base of certain flowers.

Stamen
The pollen-bearing, male organ of a flower consisting of an anther and a filament.

Staminode
A sterile stamen.

Standard
The uppermost petal of a flower in the Pea Family.

Stigma
That part of the pistil that receives the pollen.

Stolon
A horizontally spreading branch or runner that is inclined to root at the nodes.

Stomata
Minute pores in the epidermis of a leaf or stem through which gases and water vapor pass.

Style
The attenuated part of a pistil between the ovary and the stigma.

Succulent
Fleshy and juicy.

Taproot
A straight tapering root that grows vertically down, often to considerable depth.

Tepal
A plant where the petals and sepals are undifferentiated as to color or shape, such as in lilies and tulips.

Trancate
With the base or apex transversely straight, or nearly so, as if cut off.

Tubercle
A small rounded projecting part or outgrowth that covers the stem of most barrel or ball-shaped cacti.

Umbel
A flower cluster in which all flower stalks arise from one point.

Viscid
Sticky, glutinous.

Whorl
An arrangement of three or more leaves, petals, or other organs radiating from a single node.

WILDFLOWERS OF THE ROCKY MOUNTAINS

FIGURE 4. Parts of a typical flower.

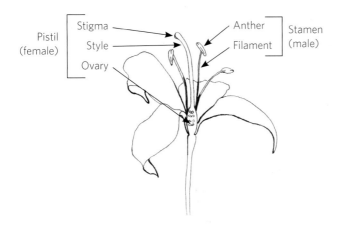

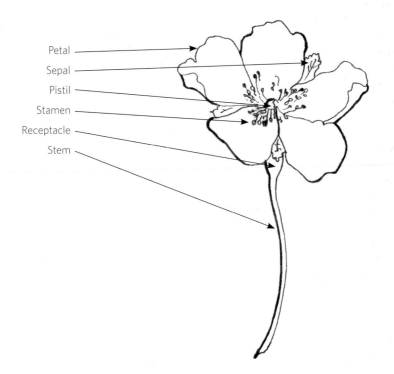

FIGURE 5. Flower parts in Orchid, Mint, Pea and Aster families.

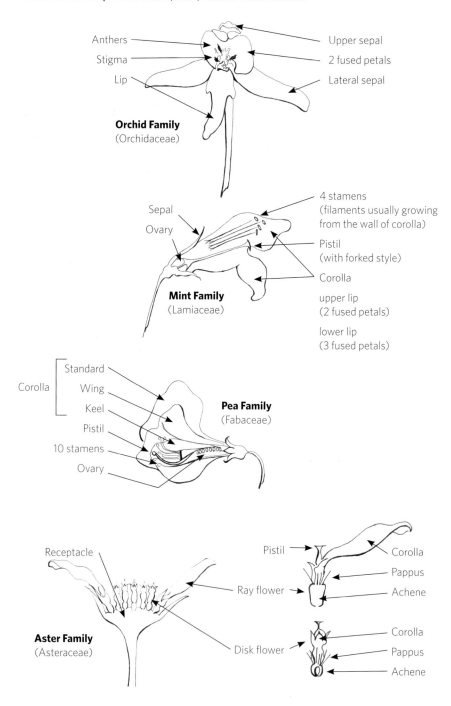

FIGURE 6. Flower arrangements.

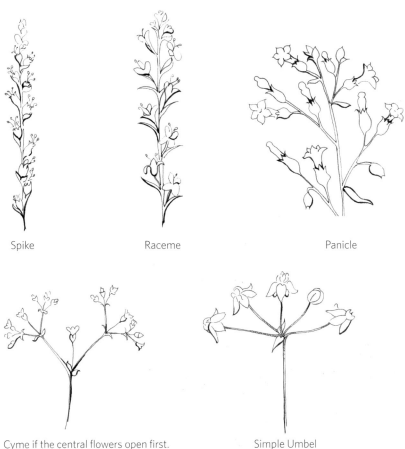

Spike   Raceme   Panicle

Cyme if the central flowers open first.   Simple Umbel
Corymb is the outer flowers open first.

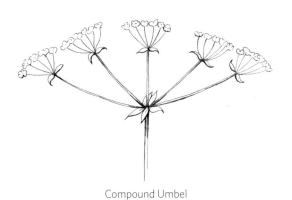

Compound Umbel

FIGURE 7. Leaf arrangements, margins and shapes.

Arrangements

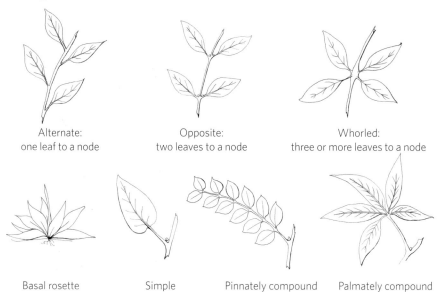

Alternate:
one leaf to a node

Opposite:
two leaves to a node

Whorled:
three or more leaves to a node

Basal rosette   Simple   Pinnately compound   Palmately compound

Margins

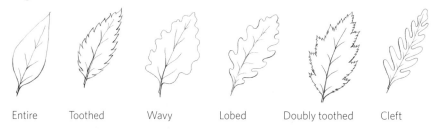

Entire   Toothed   Wavy   Lobed   Doubly toothed   Cleft

Shapes

Linear

Lance

Inverse lance

Oblong

Elliptical

Egg-shaped

Round

Heart-shaped

Spatulate

Triangular

Wedge

Needlelike

Selected References

Bailey, R. G. 1995. Description of the ecoregions of the United States. 2nd ed. United States Department of Agriculture, Forest Service Misc. Publ. No. 1391, Washington, D.C.

Barbour, M. G. and W. D. Billings (eds). 2000. North American terrestrial vegetation. Cambridge University Press, United Kingdom.

Billings, W. D. 2000. Alpine vegetation. In: Barbour, M. G. and W. D. Billings (eds.), North American terrestrial vegetation. Cambridge University Press, United Kingdom.

Boivin, B. 1967-1981. Flora of the prairie provinces. Memoirs de l'Herbier LouisMarie. In 5 parts. Universite Laval, Laval, Quebec.

Cannings, R. 2005. The Rockies: a natural history. Greystone Books, Vancouver, British Columbia. The three maps have been modified from the maps in the Cannings' book.

Cronquist, A., A. H. Holmgren, N. H. Holmgren, P. K. Holmgren, and R. Barneby. 1986-1997. Intermountain flora. In 6 parts. New York Botanical Garden, Bronx, NY.

Cullen, J. 2006. Practical plant identification: including a key to native and cultivated flowering plants in north temperate regions. Cambridge University Press, Cambridge, England.

Davis, R. J. 1952. Flora of Idaho. Wm. C. Brown Co., Dubuque, IA.

Dorn, R. D. 1984. Vascular plants of Montana. Mountain West Publishing, Cheyenne, WY.

Dorn, R. D. 1992. Vascular plants of Wyoming. Mountain West Publishing, Cheyenne, WY.

Douglas, G. W., G. B. Straley, D. V. Meidinger, and J. Pojar (eds.). 1998. Illustrated flora of British Columbia. Volumes 1 and 2, co-published by British Columbia Ministry of Forests and British Columbia Ministry of Environment, Lands and Parks, Victoria, British Columbia.

Douglas, G. W., D. V. Meidinger, and J. Pojar (eds.). 1999-2002. Illustrated flora of British Columbia. Volumes 3-8, co-published by British Columbia Ministry of Forests and British Columbia Ministry of Environment, Lands and Parks, Victoria, British Columbia.

Gadd, B. 1995. Handbook of the Canadian Rockies. Corax Press, Jasper, Alberta.

Harrington, H. D. 1967. Edible native plants of the Rocky Mountains. University of New Mexico Press, Albuquerque, NM.

Harrington, H. D. and L. W. Durrell. 1993. How to identify plants. Swallow Press, Athens, OH.

Harris, J. G. and M. W. Harris. 2001 Plant identification terminology: an illustrated glossary. Spring Lake Publishing, Payson, UT.

Hitchcock, C. L. and A. Cronquist. 1974. Flora of the Pacific Northwest. University of Washington Press, Seattle, WA.

Hitchcock, C. L., A. Cronquist, M. Ownbey, and J. W. Thompson. 1955-1969. In 5 parts. University of Washington Press, Seattle, WA.

Hulten, E. 1968. Flora of Alaska and neighboring territories. Stanford University Press, Stanford, CA.

Hunt, C. B. 1973. Natural regions of the United States and Canada. W. H. Freeman and Co., San Francisco, CA.

Johnston, A. 1970. Blackfoot Indian utilization of the flora of the northwestern Great Plains. Economic Botany 24: 24: 301-324.

Johnston, A. 1982. Plants and the Blackfoot. Natural History Occasional Paper No. 4, Provincial Museum of Alberta, Edmonton, Alberta.

Kershaw, L., J. Gould, D. Johnson, and J. Lancaster. 2001. Rare vascular plants of Alberta. University of Alberta Press, Edmonton, Alberta.

Kindscher, K. 1992. Medicinal wild plants of the prairies. University Press of Kansas, Lawrence, KS.

Kingsburg, J. M. 1964. Poisonous plants of the United States and Canada. Prentice Hall, Inc., Englewood Cliffs, NJ.

Lesica, P. 2002. A flora of Glacier National Park, Montana. Oregon State University Press, Corvallis, OR.

Looman, J. and K. F. Best. 1979. Budd's flora of the Canadian prairie provinces. Publication 1662, Research Branch, Agriculture Canada, Ottawa.

Martin, W. C. and C. R. Hutchins. 1980. Flora of New Mexico. In 2 parts, A. R. Gantner Verlag KG Press, Berlin, Germany.

Moerman, D. E. 1998. Native American ethnobotany. Timber Press, Portland, OR.

Moore, M. 1979. Medicinal plants of the mountain west. Museum of New Mexico Press, Santa Fe, NM.

Moss, E. H. 1983. Flora of Alberta. 2nd edition revised by J. G. Packer, University of Toronto Press, Toronto, Ontario.

Peet, R. K. 2000. Forests and meadows of the Rocky Mountains. In: Barbour, M. G. and W. D. Billings (eds.), North American terrestrial vegetation. Cambridge University Press, United Kingdom.

Ricketts, T. H., E. Dinerstein, D. M. Olson, C. J. Loucks, W. Eichbaum, D. DellaSala, K. Kavanagh, P. Hedao, P. T. Hurley, K. M. Carney, R. Abell, and S. Walters. 1999. Terrestrial ecoregions of North America, a conservation assessment. Island Press, Washington, DC.

Scoggan, H. J. 1978. The flora of Canada. In 4 parts. Publications in Botany No. 7, National Museum of Sciences, Ottawa.

Scotter, George W. and Hälle Flygare. 1986. *Wildflowers of the Canadian Rockies.* Hurtig Publishers Ltd., Edmonton, Alberta.

Smith, J. P. Jr. 1977. Vascular plant families. Mad River Press, Eureka, CA.

Walters, D. R. and D. J. Keil. 1996. Vascular plant taxonomy. 4th ed., Kendall Hunt Publishing Co., Dubuque, IA.

Weber, W. A. and R. C. Wittmann. 1996. Colorado flora: eastern slope. Revised edition, University Press of Colorado, Niwot, CO.

Weber, W. A. and R. C. Wittmann. 1996. Colorado flora: western slope. Revised edition, University Press of Colorado, Niwot, CO.

Welsh, S. L., N. D. Atwood, S. Goodrich, S. Goodrich, and L. C. Higgins (eds.). 1987. A Utah flora. Great Basin Naturalist Memoir No. 9, Brigham Young University Press, Provo, UT.

West, N. E., and J. A. Young. 2000. Intermountain valleys and lower mountain slopes. In: Barbour, M. G. and W. D. Billings (eds.), North American terrestrial vegetation. Cambridge University Press, United Kingdom.

Willard. B. E., and M. T. Smithson. 1988. Alpine wildflowers of the Rocky Mountains. Rocky Mountain Nature Association, Estes Park, CO.

Williams, K. 1984. Eating wild plants. Mountain Press Publishing Co., Missoula, MT.

Zwinger, A. H. and B. E. Willard. 1996. Land above the trees: a guide to American alpine tundra. Revised edition, Johnson Books, Boulder, CO.

INDEX OF COMMON NAMES

INDEX OF COMMON NAMES

Index of Scientific Names

Photo of author George W. Scotter (left) and photographer Hälle Flygare (right).

George W. Scotter

Born and raised in the shadows of the Rockies, George Scotter credits frequent family visits to the mountains with his early interest in nature that developed into a lifelong vocation. He has lived and worked in or near the Rockies throughout his life. With formal training in botany, ecology, taxonomy, and wildlife management, Dr. Scotter has worked in many capacities for the Canadian Wildlife Service of Environment Canada for more than 30 years, serving as a wildlife biologist, research scientist, and research director. He also worked for the Bureau of Land Management in Idaho and as a professor of range science at Utah State University, where he directed research on big game ranges for the Utah Division of Wildlife Resources. In addition, he was an adjunct professor in Forest Science at the University of Alberta and the Natural Resources Institute, University of Manitoba. He has taught courses on wildflowers in the Rocky Mountains for more than 30 years.

Dr. George Scotter has written four books and contributed more than 170 articles, mainly on aspects of natural history in western Canada and the United States. Vice-president and later president of the Canadian Nature Federation, he is an active member of several other conservation groups, and the 1985 winner of the prestigious J.B. Harkin medal, awarded for outstanding contributions towards conservation.

Now retired, George and his wife Etta live in Kelowna, British Columbia.

Hälle Flygare

Hälle Flygare is a professional wildlife and nature photographer who has been photographing the flora and fauna of Alaska, Yukon, the Arctic and the Rockies for over 30 years. Hälle was born in Sweden, where his interest in photography began at a very early age. He came to Canada as a forestry professional and for many years worked as a Forest Technician for the British Columbia and Alberta Forest Services as well as a Park Warden in Banff National Park. After leaving the Park Service Hälle traveled through over 30 countries photographing nature in wild places. He is also an elected member of the Swedish Nature Photographers.

His photographic work has been published in innumerable nature magazines and books. Among his writing credits are two books published in Sweden and two in Canada, including *In the Steps of Alexander Mackenzie* and *Sir Alexander Mackenzie Historic Waterways in Alberta.*

Hälle was the original instigator for the preservation of the 350-km long Nuxalk-Carrier Grease trail in British Columbia. While guiding there in 1972 he discovered trail sections of Mackenzie's 1793 overland trek from the Fraser River to the Pacific, the first recorded crossing of continental North America. In 1989 Hälle received the British Columbia Heritage Award for his outstanding contribution toward the recognition and preservation of the trail.

Hälle and his wife Linda live in Canmore, Alberta, just outside Banff National Park.